Scott, Foresman

Discover SCIENCE

Authors

Dr. Michael R. Cohen
Professor of Science and Environmental Education
School of Education
Indiana University
Indianapolis, Indiana

Dr. Timothy M. Cooney
Chairperson K-12 Science Program
Malcolm Price Laboratory School
University of Northern Iowa
Cedar Falls, Iowa

Cheryl M. Hawthorne
Science Curriculum Specialist
Mathematics, Engineering, Science Achievement Program (MESA)
Stanford University
Stanford, California

Dr. Alan J. McCormack
Professor of Science Education
San Diego State University
San Diego, California

Dr. Jay M. Pasachoff
Director, Hopkins Observatory
Williams College
Williamstown, Massachusetts

Dr. Naomi Pasachoff
Research Associate
Williams College
Williamstown, Massachusetts

Karin L. Rhines
Science/Educational Consultant
Valhalla, New York

Dr. Irwin L. Slesnick
Professor of Biology
Western Washington University
Bellingham, Washington

Scott, Foresman and Company
Editorial Offices: Glenview, Illinois

Regional Offices: Sunnyvale, California • Tucker, Georgia •
Glenview, Illinois • Oakland, New Jersey • Dallas, Texas

i

Consultants

Special Content Consultant

Dr. Abraham S. Flexer
Science Education Consultant
Boulder, Colorado

Health Consultant

Dr. Julius B. Richmond
John D. MacArthur Professor of
   Health Policy
Director, Division of Health Policy
   Research and Education
Harvard University
Advisor on Child Health Policy
Children's Hospital of Boston
Boston, Massachusetts

Safety Consultant

Dr. Jack A. Gerlovich
Science Education Safety
   Consultant/Author
Des Moines, Iowa

Process Skills Consultant

Dr. Alfred DeVito
Professor Emeritus Science
   Education
Purdue University
West Lafayette, Indiana

Activity Consultants

Edward Al Pankow
Teacher
Petaluma City Schools
Petaluma, California

Valerie Pankow
Teacher and Writer
Petaluma City Schools
Petaluma, California

Science and Technology Consultant

Dr. David E. Newton
Adjunct Professor—Science and
   Social Issues
University of San Francisco
College of Professional Studies
San Francisco, California

Cooperative Learning Consultant

Dr. Robert E. Slavin
Director, Elementary School Program
Center for Research on Elementary
   and Middle Schools
Johns Hopkins University
Baltimore, Maryland

Gifted Education Consultants

Hilda P. Hobson
Teacher of the Gifted
W.B. Wicker School
Sanford, North Carolina

Christine Kuehn
Assistant Professor of Education
University of South Carolina
Columbia, South Carolina

Nancy Linkel York
Teacher of the Gifted
W.B. Wicker School
Sanford, North Carolina

Special Education Consultants

Susan E. Affleck
Classroom Teacher
Salt Creek Elementary School
Elk Grove Village, Illinois

Dr. Dale R. Jordan
Director
Jordan Diagnostic Center
Oklahoma City, Oklahoma

Dr. Shirley T. King
Learning Disabilities Teacher
Helfrich Park Middle School
Evansville, Indiana

Jeannie Rae McCoun
Learning Disabilities Teacher
Mary M. McClelland Elementary
   School
Indianapolis, Indiana

Thinking Skills Consultant

Dr. Joseph P. Riley II
Professor of Science Education
University of Georgia
Athens, Georgia

Reading Consultants

Patricia T. Hinske
Reading Specialist
Cardinal Stritch College
Milwaukee, Wisconsin

Dr. Robert A. Pavlik
Professor and Chairperson of
   Reading/Language Arts
   Department
Cardinal Stritch College

Dr. Alfredo Schifini
Reading Consultant
Downey, California

Cover painting commissioned by Scott, Foresman
Artist: Alex Gnidziejko

ISBN: 0-673-42064-7
Copyright © 1989,
Scott, Foresman and Company, Glenview, Illinois
All Rights Reserved. Printed in the United States of America.

8910WAK97969594939291

Reviewers and Content Specialists

Dr. Ramona J. Anshutz
Science Specialist
Kansas State Department of Education
Topeka, Kansas

Teresa M. Auldridge
Science Education Consultant
Amelia, Virginia

Annette M. Barzal
Classroom Teacher
Willetts Middle School
Brunswick, Ohio

James Haggard Brannon
Classroom Teacher
Ames Community Schools
Ames, Iowa

Priscilla L. Callison
Science Teacher
Topeka Adventure Center
Topeka, Kansas

Rochelle F. Cohen
Education Coordinator
Indianapolis Head Start
Indianapolis, Indiana

Linda Lewis Cundiff
Classroom Teacher
R. F. Bayless Elementary School
Lubbock, Texas

Dr. Patricia Dahl
Classroom Teacher
Bloomington Oak Grove Intermediate
    School
Bloomington, Minnesota

Audrey J. Dick
Supervisor, Elementary Education
Cincinnati Public Schools
Cincinnati, Ohio

Nancy B. Drabik
Reading Specialist
George Washington School
Wyckoff, New Jersey

Bennie Y. Fleming
Science Supervisor
Providence School District
Providence, Rhode Island

Mike Graf
Classroom Teacher
Branch Elementary School
Arroyo Grande, California

Thelma Robinson Graham
Classroom Teacher
Pearl Spann Elementary School
Jackson, Mississippi

Robert G. Guy
Classroom Teacher
Big Lake Elementary School
Sedro-Woolley, Washington

Dr. Claude A. Hanson
Science Supervisor
Boise Public Schools
Boise, Idaho

Dr. Jean D. Harlan
Psychologist, Early Childhood Consultant
Lighthouse Counseling Associates
Racine, Wisconsin

Dr. Rebecca P. Harlin
Assistant Professor of Reading
State University of New York—Geneseo
Geneseo, New York

Richard L. Ingraham
Professor of Biology
San José State University
San José, California

Ron Jones
Science Coordinator
Salem Keizer Public Schools
Salem, Oregon

Sara A. Jones
Classroom Teacher
Burroughs-Molette Elementary School
Brunswick, Georgia

Dr. Judy LaCavera
Director of Curriculum and Instruction
Learning Alternatives
Vienna, Ohio

Jack Laubisch
K-12 Science, Health, and Outdoor
    Education Coordinator
West Clermont Local School District
Amelia, Ohio

Douglas M. McPhee
Classroom Teacher/Consultant
Del Mar Hills Elementary School
Del Mar, California

Larry Miller
Classroom Teacher
Caldwell Elementary School
Caldwell, Kansas

Dr. Robert J. Miller
Professor of Science Education
Eastern Kentucky University
Richmond, Kentucky

Sam Murr
Teacher—Elementary Gifted Science
Academic Center for Enrichment—Mid Del
    Schools
Midwest City—Del City, Oklahoma

Janet Nakai
Classroom Teacher
Community Consolidated School District
    #65
Evanston, Illinois

Patricia Osborne
Classroom Teacher
Valley Heights Elementary School
Waterville, Kansas

Elisa Pinzón-Umaña
Classroom Teacher
Coronado Academy
Albuquerque, New Mexico

Dr. Jeanne Phillips
Director of Curriculum and Instruction
Meridian Municipal School District
Meridian, Mississippi

Maria Guadalupe Ramos
Classroom Teacher
Metz Elementary School
Austin, Texas

Elissa Richards
Math/Science Teacher Leader
Granite School District
Salt Lake City, Utah

Mary Jane Roscoe
Teacher and Team Coordinator
Fairwood Alternative Elementary School of
    Individually Guided Education
Columbus, Ohio

**Sister Mary Christelle Sawicki,
    C. S. S. F.**
Science Curriculum Coordinator
Department of Catholic Education Diocese
    of Buffalo
Buffalo, New York

Ray E. Smalley
Classroom Teacher/Science Specialist
Cleveland School of Science
Cleveland, Ohio

Anita Snell
Elementary Coordinator for Early
    Childhood Education
Spring Branch Independent School District
Houston, Texas

Norman Sperling
Chabot Observatory
Oakland, California

Sheri L. Thomas
Classroom Teacher
McLouth Unified School District #342
McLouth, Kansas

Lisa D. Torres
Science Coordinator
Lebanon School District
Lebanon, New Hampshire

Alice C. Webb
Early Childhood Resource Teacher
Primary Education Office
Rockledge, Florida

Introducing *Discover Science* xii

Unit **1** **Life Science** 8

Chapter **1** **Flowering Plants** 10
Discover! • Grouping Plants from Your Area   11

Lesson **1**   How Are Plants Classified?   12

Lesson **2**   What Do the Parts of a Flower Do?   16
Activity • Observing the Parts of a Flower   19

Lesson **3**   How Do Seeds and Fruits Develop?   20
Science and Technology • Keeping Fruit from Spoiling   25

Lesson **4**   How Do Seeds Scatter and Grow?   26
Activity • Germinating Seeds   31
Skills for Solving Problems • Using Metric Rulers and Bar Graphs   32

Chapter Review   34   Study Guide   376

Chapter **2** **Animal Behavior** 36
Discover! • Observing Your Partner Learn   37

Lesson **1**   How Do Animals Live in Groups?   38

Lesson **2**   How Do Different Animals Care for Their Young?   46
Activity • Observing Stages in the Life Cycle of a Beetle   51

Lesson **3**   What Behaviors Do Animals Have?   52
Activity • Observing How Mealworms Respond to Food   56
Science and People • Teaching Monkeys to Help People   57
Skills for Solving Problems • Using Flow Diagrams and Bar Graphs   58

Chapter Review   60   Study Guide   378

Chapter 3 **Food Chains and Food Webs** 62
  Discover! • Testing Plant Parts for Starch 63

Lesson **1** Where Do Green Plants Get Energy? 64

Lesson **2** Where Do Animals Get Food? 68
  Activity • Comparing Teeth 71

Lesson **3** What Is a Food Chain? 72
  Activity • Making Models of Food Chains 75

Lesson **4** What Is a Food Web? 76
  Science and People • Saving Wild Birds 81
  Skills for Solving Problems • Using Metric Grids and Bar Graphs 82

  Chapter Review 84   Study Guide 380

Chapter 4 **Animal and Plant Adaptations** 86
  Discover! • Coloring Insects to Protect Them 87

Lesson **1** How Do Adaptations Help Animals and Plants Survive? 88

Lesson **2** How Are Animals Adapted to Their Environment? 92
  Activity • Studying Protective Coloration 98
  Science and People • Living with Chimpanzees in the Wild 99

Lesson **3** How Are Plants Adapted to Their Environment? 100
  Activity • Observing Plant Adaptations 105
  Skills for Solving Problems • Using Thermometers and Bar Graphs 106

  Chapter Review 108   Study Guide 382

  Careers 110   *How It Works* • Tracking Devices 111

  Unit 1 Review 112   **Projects and Books** 113

Unit **2** **Physical Science** 114

Chapter 5 **Measuring Matter** 116
Discover! • Describing Air 117

Lesson **1** What Is Matter? 118
Activity • Observing How Fast Matter Changes States 121

Lesson **2** What Makes Up Matter? 122

Lesson **3** How Are Length and Volume Measured? 128
Activity • Measuring Volume 132
Science and Technology • Measuring in Meters 133

Lesson **4** How Are Mass and Density Measured? 134
Skills for Solving Problems • Using Graduated Cylinders and Bar Graphs 138

Chapter Review 140   Study Guide 384

Chapter 6 **Work and Energy** 142
Discover! • Observing Moving and Still Objects 143

Lesson **1** What Makes Things Move? 144
Activity • Observing Friction 147

Lesson **2** How Are Work and Energy Related? 148
Activity • Measuring Work 152
Science and Technology • Using Robots to Do Work 153

Lesson **3** How Do Machines Use Energy to Do Work? 154
Skills for Solving Problems • Using Diagrams and Line Graphs 160

Chapter Review 162   Study Guide 386

Chapter 7   Electricity and Magnetism   164

Discover! • Observing Electric Charges   165

Lesson **1**   What Is Electricity?   166

Lesson **2**   What Is Magnetism?   172
Activity • Making a Magnetic Compass   175

Lesson **3**   How Are Electricity and Magnetism Related?   176
Activity • Making an Electromagnet   180
Science and Technology • Making and Using Superconductors   181
Skills for Solving Problems • Using Diagrams and Line Graphs   182

Chapter Review   184   Study Guide   388

Chapter 8   Light and Sound   186

Discover! • Making Colors with Light   187

Lesson **1**   What Is Light?   188

Lesson **2**   How Does Light Travel?   190
Activity • Observing Images in Mirrors   196
Science and Technology • Concentrating the Power of Light   197

Lesson **3**   How Are Light and Sound Similar and Different?   198
Activity • Inferring How Sound Waves Travel   201
Skills for Solving Problems • Using Light Meters and Bar Graphs   202

Chapter Review   204   Study Guide   390

Careers   206   *How It Works* • A Camera   207

Unit 2 Review   208   **Projects and Books**   209

Unit **3** **Earth Science** 210

Chapter 9 **Measuring Weather Conditions** 212
Discover! • Observing the Angle of Light 213

Lesson **1** What Causes Different Air Temperatures Outside? 214

Lesson **2** How Does Temperature Affect Air Pressure and Wind? 218
Activity • Measuring Wind Speed 223

Lesson **3** How Does Temperature Cause Clouds and Precipitation? 224

Lesson **4** How Is Weather Predicted? 228
Activity • Making a Barometer 234
Science and Technology • Observing the Weather from Space 235
Skills for Solving Problems • Using Thermometers and Tables 236

Chapter Review 238   Study Guide 392

Chapter 10 **Changes in Landforms** 240
Discover! • Making a Mountain Model 241

Lesson **1** What Makes Up the Earth? 242

Lesson **2** How Do Volcanoes and Earthquakes Change Landforms? 246
Activity • Making Models of Faults 251

Lesson **3** How Does Weathering Change Landforms? 252
Activity • Studying Weathering by Water 257

Lesson **4** How Are Rocks Made? 258
Science and People • Learning the Life Cycle of an Earthquake 263
Skills for Solving Problems • Using Balances and Bar Graphs 264

Chapter Review 266   Study Guide 394

Chapter 11   Oceans 268
    Discover! • Observing How Much of the Earth the Oceans Cover 269

Lesson 1 What Are the Oceans and How Are They Important? 270

Lesson 2 How Does Ocean Water Move? 274
    Activity • Making Waves and Currents 279

Lesson 3 What Is the Ocean Bottom Like? 280
    Activity • Making a Model of Sediment Layers 284
    Science and Technology • Conquering the Ocean Depths 285
    Skills for Solving Problems • Using Hydrometers and Line Graphs 286

    Chapter Review 288   Study Guide 396

Chapter 12   Movement in the Solar System 290
    Discover! • Making a Model of the Sun Rising and Setting 291

Lesson 1 How Does the Earth Move? 292
    Activity • Observing the Earth's Tilt 295

Lesson 2 What Does the Moon's Movement Cause? 296
    Activity • Making Models of the Moon's Phases 299

Lesson 3 How Do the Planets of the Solar System Move? 300

Lesson 4 What Other Objects Move in the Solar System? 308
    Science and People • Flying into the Future 311
    Skills for Solving Problems • Using Diagrams and Line Graphs 312

    Chapter Review 314   Study Guide 398

    Careers 316   *How It Works* • Weather Satellites 317

Unit 3 Review 318   **Projects and Books** 319

Unit **4** **The Human Body** 320

Chapter 13 **Digestion and Circulation** 322
Discover! • Observing Different Sizes of Food Disappear 323

Lesson **1** How Does Your Digestive System Work? 324
Activity • Observing Changes in Milk 329

Lesson **2** How Does Your Circulatory System Work? 330
Activity • Measuring Your Pulse 336
Science and People • Saving Lives with New Ideas 337

Lesson **3** How Can You Help Keep Your Body Systems Healthy? 338
Skills for Solving Problems • Using Clocks and Bar Graphs 342

Chapter Review 344   Study Guide 400

Chapter 14 **Your Brain and Your Sense Organs** 346
Discover! • Observing Warm and Cold 347

Lesson **1** How Does Your Brain Get Information? 348

Lesson **2** How Do Your Eyes Work? 352

Lesson **3** How Do Your Ears Work? 356
Science and People • Helping People Hear 359

Lesson **4** How Do Your Tongue and Nose Work? 360
Activity • Mapping Your Tongue 363

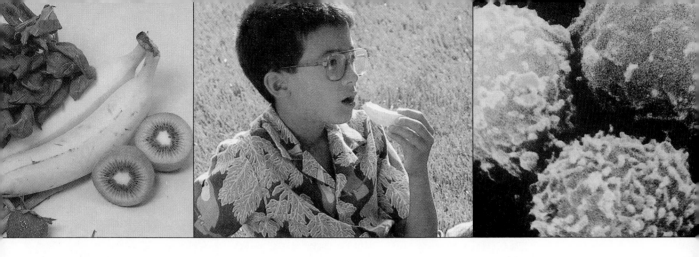

Lesson 5   How Does Your Skin Gather Information?   364
            Activity • Identifying the Closeness of Nerve Endings   367
            Skills for Solving Problems • Using Timers and Line Graphs   368

Chapter Review   370   Study Guide   402

Careers   372   *How It Works* • The Telephone   373

Unit 4 Review   374   **Projects and Books**   375

Science and Society • Disappearing Wetlands   113
                        The Cost of Smashing Atoms   209
                        Offshore Resources   319
                        Truth in Advertising   375

Independent Study Guide   376

Glossary   404

Index   413

Acknowledgments   418

Using Metric   420

Science is learning new things...

Light travels faster than anything else in the universe. Its speed is 300,000 kilometers per second.

A peregrin falcon dives for its prey at 300 kilometers per hour.

The fastest human
ran the 100 meter
dash in 9.83 seconds.

Winds in a tornado
can reach speeds of
480 kilometers
per hour.

The cheetah is the
fastest animal on
Earth. It can run at a
speed of 120
kilometers per hour.

Science is solving problems...

Asking questions

"Why is this room so hot?"

"Maybe the thermostat is set too high."
"Maybe the oven is on."

Collecting Information

"Maybe the heat is coming from the sunny window."

Collecting more information

"The sun was making the room hot."

Finding an answer

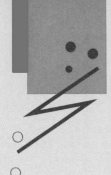

Science is inventing new things...

By 1939, television was out of the laboratory and into people's homes. The first sets had 12.5 centimeter picture tubes. The picture was in black and white.

Scientists began working on the idea of a television before 1900.

In the 1950s, television took a giant leap. The pictures went from black and white to full color.

Today people can buy many kinds of televisions. Some are very small…

…and others are as large as some movie screens.

Satellites send television signals around the world. These satellites let people see live broadcasts from all over the world.

Science is exploring the unknown...

For centuries people have been fascinated with the moon's changes. People used to be able to study the moon with only their eyes.

In the 1600s, Galileo was the first person to study the moon through a telescope. He saw valleys and mountains on the moon.

Space exploration brought new information about the moon. Ranger 7, a lunar probe, flew close to the moon in July, 1964. It took the first close-up pictures of the moon's surface.

Astronauts Neil Armstrong and Edwin E. Aldrin made history on July 20, 1969. They were the first people to step onto the surface of the moon. Armstrong and Aldrin brought moon rocks back to Earth for study. Five more trips have been made to the moon to study the moon and collect rocks and soil.

Life Science

This black-tailed jackrabbit lives in northern Texas. Its large ears help the jackrabbit hear sounds. The jackrabbit has legs that help it run away from danger quickly.

Other animals also have special ways to protect themselves. In this unit, you will discover how animals and plants survive. You will discover how they live and depend on each other.

SCIENCE IN THE NEWS During the next few weeks, look in newspapers or magazines for stories about plants and animals. Make a scrapbook in which you write about each plant or animal in the news. Share your scrapbook with your class.

Chapter 1   Flowering Plants

Chapter 2   Animal Behavior

Chapter 3   Food Chains and Food Webs

Chapter 4   Animal and Plant Adaptations

Flowering Plants

The flower in the picture grows in Mexico and Central America. Notice the yellow pollen grains that stick to the insect's legs. The insect will carry this pollen to the next flower it visits.

Introducing the Chapter

The flower in the picture and the plant that makes it might not grow where you live. Think about the flowers and plants that do grow where you live. The activity below will help you discover some ways these plants are alike and different. In this chapter you will learn how scientists group plants. You will learn how flowers make seeds and fruit. You also will learn how seeds grow into new plants.

Grouping Plants from Your Area

Scientists use the ways plants are alike and different to place plants into large groups. You can group plants by comparing leaves of plants that grow where you live.

Place six different plant leaves on a table. Look at the color, shape, and size of your leaves. How are they alike? How are they different? Choose one way the leaves are different.

Next, use the difference you chose to divide all the leaves into two groups. Label your groups as Group 1 and Group 2.

Talk About It
1. How are the leaves in each of your groups alike?
2. What other ways could you have divided your leaves?

1 How Are Plants Classified?

LESSON GOALS

You will learn
- how plants are classified into two main groups.
- about two groups of plants that make seeds.
- about two kinds of plants that do not make seeds.

reproduce (rē′prə düs′), to make more of the same kind.

classify (klas′ə fī), to sort into groups based on similarities and differences.

Different kinds of plants

How many different kinds of plants can you find in the pictures on these two pages? The vegetables in the garden are plants. The trees are plants. The grass and flowers are plants. What kinds of plants grow where you live?

Classifying Plants into Groups

The number of different kinds of plants is amazingly large. Learning about all of them could be hard. Studying plants is easier when you study groups of plants. All the plants in one group have similarities that make them different from other groups. You made groups when you grouped leaves on page 11.

How plants make new plants—or **reproduce**—is one way plants are similar and different. Scientists use this difference to sort—or **classify**—plants into two large groups. Plants in one group make seeds. Plants in the other group do not make seeds.

12

Plants That Make Seeds

The plants in the pictures on these two pages grew from seeds. You might enjoy eating walnuts, peas, and beans. They are all seeds. Plants that make seeds can be divided into two groups. Plants that have flowers make up one group. Plants that do not have flowers make up the other group.

Flowering plants make up the largest group of plants that make seeds. Notice in the pictures that not all flowers look like you might think they would. The flowers make the seeds. The flowers also make fruit that covers and protects their seeds. You might have eaten such fruits as peaches or apples. Tomatoes and squash also are fruits.

The other group of plants makes seeds but does not have flowers. These plants—called **conifers**—make their seeds inside cones. Most conifers are trees or shrubs and have needlelike leaves. Pine trees and fir trees are conifers. Find the cone and conifer seeds in the picture.

SCIENCE IN YOUR LIFE

Scientists have found ways to grow seedless grapes, oranges, and grapefruit. In nature, these fruits would not exist because the plants that grow them cannot reproduce without seeds.

conifer (kon′ə fər), a plant that makes seeds inside cones.

A conifer, cone, and seeds

Four different flowers

13

Plants That Do Not Make Seeds

Some plants do not make flowers or cones. These plants do not make seeds or fruits. They reproduce by forming tiny cells that can grow into new plants. Each tiny cell is a **spore.**

Mosses are one kind of plant that does not make seeds. Mosses are small plants that do not have leaves, roots, and stems like other plants do. They do have parts that are green and leaflike. Moss spores form in cases on top of short stalks. Find the stalks in the picture on the left. Notice in the enlarged picture that the spores are being released.

Ferns are another kind of plant that does not make seeds. Find the spore cases on the bottom of the fern leaves in the picture on the right. Each case holds many spores. How are these spore cases different from the spore cases made by mosses?

Moss spore cases on stalks   A fern plant and spore cases

14

Study the chart and pictures below to review how to classify plants. How would you classify a rose? What are the two kinds of plants that do not make seeds? How would you classify a pine tree?

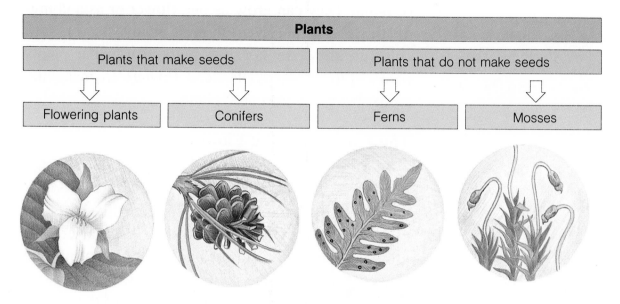

Plants			
Plants that make seeds		Plants that do not make seeds	
Flowering plants	Conifers	Ferns	Mosses

Lesson Review

1. What is one way to classify plants into two groups?
2. How do flowering plants and conifers differ in the way they make seeds?
3. What does a fern make instead of seeds to reproduce?
4. **Challenge!** Which group of plants would be most useful to people moving to a new land? Explain your answer.

Study on your own, pages 376–377.

FIND OUT ON YOUR OWN

Pretend that you have just discovered a new plant. No other person has ever seen this plant. Your job is to classify the new plant into one of the four groups in the chart above. Make a list of questions that you would need to answer before classifying the plant.

2 What Do the Parts of a Flower Do?

LESSON GOALS

You will learn:
- what each of the four parts of a flower does.
- how flowers with fewer than four parts can make seeds.

sepal (sē′pəl), one of the leaflike parts that protect a flower bud and that is usually green.

Flowers can be big or small. They can be colorful or plain. They can grow as one flower or as a clump of tiny flowers. Even though many flowers are colorful, they are not just parts that make plants pretty. Flowering plants need flowers to make the seeds that grow into new plants.

The Four Parts of a Flower

Most flowers have four different parts. Observe the flower buds in the pictures. The parts of the flower buds that you see are **sepals.** These leaflike parts are often green. They cover and protect the flower as it grows inside. These flower buds will bloom into the flowers you see in the pictures with them.

The petals of a flower are the colorful parts of flowers you see in the pictures. The petals are only part of the flower. The petals surround and protect the parts of the flower that make seeds. The petals of many kinds of flowers also attract butterflies, bees, and other living things.

Gladiolus and rose buds and flowers

Thin stemlike parts with knobs at their tips grow inside the ring of petals. These **stamens** make tiny grains of pollen in the knobs. **Pollen** is one of the two materials needed for a flower to make a seed.

One or more **pistils** grow inside the ring of stamens. Each pistil is a stemlike part with a sticky tip and a thick bottom. Pistils contain the eggs that are the other material needed to make a seed. Eggs will grow into seeds when they are combined with material called sperm in pollen.

Find the petals, stamens, pollen, and pistil in the flower below. Most flowers have these flower parts. Look for these parts in flowers that you see.

stamen (stā′mən), part of a flower that makes pollen.

pollen (pol′ən), tiny grains that make seeds when combined with a flower's eggs.

pistil (pis′tl), part of a flower that makes the eggs that grow into seeds.

Parts of a flower

Stamens

Pollen

Petal

Pistil

Flowers with Fewer Parts

Most flowers have sepals, petals, stamens, and at least one pistil. However, some flowers do not have all these parts. Willow trees, for example, have flowers without petals.

Other plants have two kinds of flowers. One kind of flower has one or more pistils but no stamens. The other kind of flower has stamens but no pistils. The sperm in the pollen from the stamens on one flower combine with the eggs in the pistil of the other flower to make seeds.

Some plants have two kinds of flowers on the same plant. Squash plants, maple trees, oak trees, and corn plants have two kinds of flowers on the same plant. The top picture is a corn flower called a tassel. It has stamens. In the bottom picture an ear of corn is growing from the flower that has pistils.

Other plants do not have both kinds of flowers on the same plant. Cottonwood trees have one kind of flower on one tree. The other kind of flower grows on another cottonwood tree.

A corn tassel and a developing ear of corn

Lesson Review

1. If you took apart a flower, what four parts might you find?
2. How can flowers without stamens make seeds?
3. **Challenge!** What parts could a flower be missing and still make seeds? Explain your answer.

Study on your own, pages 376–377.

FIND OUT ON YOUR OWN

Flowering plants reproduce mostly with seeds. Many flowering plants also can grow new plants from roots, stems, or leaves. Read in an encyclopedia or other book to find out how plants can grow from roots, stems, and leaves. Write a paragraph that tells about some plants that can reproduce from these parts.

Observing the Parts of a Flower

Purpose

Observe the parts of a flower by dissecting it.

Gather These Materials

• sheet of white paper • a flower • sharp scissors or tweezers • clear tape • small piece of black paper • small piece of white paper • straight pin • pencil • hand lens

Follow This Procedure

1. Use a chart like the one shown to record your observations.
2. Count the number of petals the flower has. Record this number in your chart. *CAUTION: Be careful when using sharp tools.* Remove the petals from the flower with tweezers or scissors. Tape one of them to a sheet of paper. Label the petal.
3. Locate the stamens. Count the stamens and record the number in your chart. Carefully remove the stamens. Tape one of the stamens to your paper and label it.
4. Use a hand lens to look for powder at the tips of the other stamens. Touch the tip of a stamen and notice if it is sticky. Gently tap a stamen against a small piece of black paper. Gently tap another stamen against a small piece of white paper. Use a hand lens to look at any pollen on the paper.
5. Locate and remove the pistil or pistils. Record the number.

6. Use a straight pin to pick open the base of the pistil. *CAUTION: Be careful with the pin.* Observe what is inside of the pistil. Tape the pistil to your paper and label it.

Record Your Results

Number of petals	
Number of stamens	
Number of pistils	

State Your Conclusion

1. Name the parts you found in your flower and how many of each part you found.
2. In which part of the flower are seeds made?

Use What You Learned

Bees carry pollen from one flower to another flower. What did you observe about pollen that would help bees carry it? Explain your answer.

3 How Do Seeds and Fruits Develop?

LESSON GOALS

You will learn
- three ways pollination occurs.
- how fertilization takes place in flowers.
- the difference between a monocot seed and a dicot seed.
- which part of a flower becomes the fruit.

pollination
(pol/li na/tion), the movement of pollen from a stamen to a pistil.

Imagine bending over on a warm summer day to smell the flowers in the picture. Suddenly, you hear a buzzing sound. You step back to see where the bee is. You also see a beautiful butterfly land on a flower. These insects are gathering nectar from the flowers. The insects use this liquid as food. At the same time, they are helping the flowers.

Pollination

Notice the pollen grains that cover the bee in the picture. When a bee gathers nectar from a flower, pollen grains stick to the bee. As the bee flies to other flowers, it may brush against the sticky top of pistils. Pollen grains on the bee will stick to these pistils.

The movement of pollen from the tips of stamens to the sticky tops of pistils is **pollination.** The pollen can come from the same flower, a different flower on the same plant, or a flower from another plant of the same kind. Pollination must take place before a flower can make seeds.

A field of flowers

20

Besides butterflies and bees, birds and even bats pollinate flowers. The colors and smells of flowers attract the insects and other animals that pollinate them. Brightly colored flowers attract butterflies and birds. Moths and some bats find flowers at night by their smells.

The wind pollinates some flowers. Many trees depend on wind for pollination. Corn plants and grasses also depend on wind. Wind loosens pollen from corn flowers with stamens. The pollen falls or is carried by the wind to the sticky tip of pistils on other corn flowers.

Plants pollinated by wind make huge amounts of tiny, light pollen grains. Many flowers that make wind-carried pollen have no petals and hang under branches. Wind can reach the pollen easily. Notice the flowers hanging from the grass in the picture.

Pollen on a bee and flowers on grass

Fertilization

After pollination, the pollen grains on the sticky tip of the pistil begin to grow. Each pollen grain grows a thin tube from the tip of the pistil to the thick bottom of the pistil. This bottom part of the pistil is the **ovary.** Use your finger to trace the path of the tube.

Find the ovary and ovules in the drawing of the flower. Each **ovule** contains an egg. The sperm from the pollen grain moves through the pollen tube. When the sperm reaches an ovule, it combines with an egg. This combining of the sperm with an egg to make a seed is **fertilization.**

Once fertilization takes place, the flower dries up and loses its petals. Find the pistil and ovary in the second picture. The ovary grows larger as one or more seeds form inside it. Find the seeds growing in the larger ovary that has been cut open. Find the seeds in the dried up ovary on the next page.

ovary (ō′vər ē), bottom part of the pistil in which seeds form.

ovule (ō′vyül), the inner part of an ovary that contains an egg.

fertilization (fėr′tl ə zā′shən), the combination of material from a pollen grain with an egg to form a seed.

Seeds grow from ovules in the ovary.

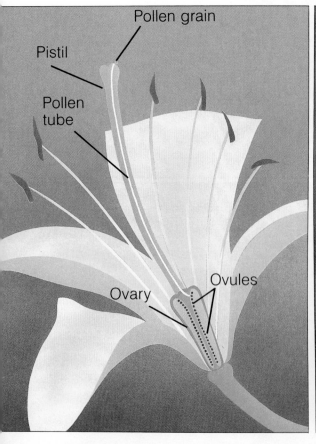

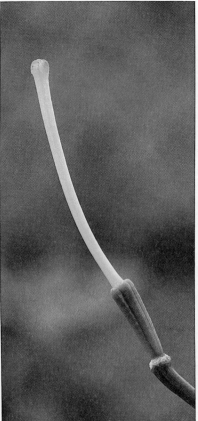

22

Parts of Seeds

Seeds have many different shapes and sizes. You may have eaten popcorn, beans, peanuts, or peas. These foods are all seeds of plants.

All seeds contain a tiny **embryo.** This part of the seed can grow into a new plant. All seeds have at least one seed leaf and stored food. A seed coat covers and protects each seed. Find these parts in the seeds in the picture.

Some flowering plants make monocot seeds. A **monocot seed** has one seed leaf and stored food outside the seed leaf. The corn seed in the picture is a monocot seed.

Other flowering plants make dicot seeds. A **dicot seed** has two seed leaves that contain stored food. You can separate a bean seed into the two seed leaves shown in the picture. Notice that these seed leaves do not look the same as the monocot seed leaf.

embryo (em′brē ō), tiny part of a seed that can grow into a new plant.

monocot (mon′ə kot) **seed,** a seed that has one seed leaf and stored food outside the seed leaf.

dicot (dī′kot) **seed,** a seed that has two seed leaves that contain stored food.

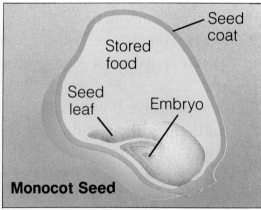

Monocot Seed

Seed coat
Stored food
Seed leaf
Embryo

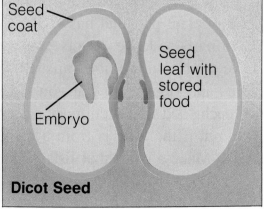

Dicot Seed

Seed coat
Embryo
Seed leaf with stored food

Fruits

As the seeds develop, the ovary swells and forms the fruit that covers and protects the seeds. Find the seeds in the fruits in the picture.

Some fruits have a large amount of water. Apples, tomatoes, peaches, and grapes are examples. Other fruits are dry. Peanuts and peas have fruits that are dry. The peanut shell and the pea pod are the fruits.

Have you ever eaten raspberries or blackberries? The flowers that become these fruits have many ovules. Each berry is a cluster of ripened flower ovaries.

Seeds in fruits

Lesson Review

1. How are plants pollinated?
2. What two things combine during fertilization.
3. How is a monocot seed different from a dicot seed?
4. What part of a flower becomes the fruit?
5. **Challenge!** Imagine that all the living things that carry pollen did not exist. How might the type of plants that live on the earth change?

Study on your own, pages 376–377.

FIND OUT ON YOUR OWN

Any plant part that has seeds is a fruit. Such plant parts as leaves, roots, and stems do not have seeds and are not fruits. Make a list of five fruits and vegetables that you like to eat. Look up each food in a dictionary or encyclopedia to find out if the food is from a fruit, leaf, root, or stem. Make a chart that lists what plant part each food is from.

Keeping Fruit from Spoiling

The Problem Fruit tastes best when it is ripe, but fruit spoils when it gets too ripe. Certain proteins in the fruit make it ripen and spoil. Ripe fruit often gets moldy. Also, bacteria can grow in ripe fruit. From early times, people have tried ways of storing fruit to keep it from spoiling.

The Breakthrough A candy maker in France developed the first modern method of keeping fruits and other foods from spoiling. In the 1790s, he began to put cooked foods in sealed glass bottles. Then he heated the bottles in boiling water. Later, people discovered that heating food to high temperatures destroys the tiny organisms that can spoil food and make people sick. Heating also keeps fruit from getting too ripe.

Freezing was another breakthrough. In 1915, Clarence Birdseye was on a trip to Labrador to trade furs. He noticed that fish that had been frozen tasted very good. He developed ways to freeze foods quickly.

New Technology The technology of drying foods was developed during World War I and World War II. Scientists improved drying methods for space travel. Drying keeps food from spoiling because bacteria and other tiny organisms cannot grow on dry food.

The people in the picture are sorting berries. These berries could be canned or frozen. Automatic can-fillers make it possible to can large amounts of fruit and other foods quickly. Also, airplanes quickly bring fresh fruit from warmer parts of the world before the fruit spoils. Refrigerated trucks keep fruit cool while carrying it across the country.

Food scientists are working on new ways to keep fresh fruit from spoiling. Sometimes scientists add chemicals to fruit. They test the fruit to make sure the chemicals cannot harm people. Scientists have found that exposing fruit to strong types of invisible light keeps it from ripening too fast. They are still testing this method to make sure the light does not change the fruit in ways that will harm people.

What Do You Think?
1. How does canning and drying fruit help keep people from getting sick?
2. What are some ways people can keep fruit from spoiling?

4 How Do Seeds Scatter and Grow?

LESSON GOALS

You will learn
- three ways seeds are scattered.
- what seeds need to grow.
- how corn seeds and bean seeds germinate.

Suppose all the seeds made by a tree fell straight down. How well do you think new trees would grow under the parent tree? Like most plants, the new trees need sunlight to grow well. Since the parent tree makes a lot of shade, the new trees would not get much sunlight. The new trees would not grow very well. The seeds would grow better if they were spread out away from the parent tree.

Scattering Seeds

Many plants make fruits that help get the seeds away from the parent plant. The fruit helps scatter the seeds. However, not all plants need to make fruits that help scatter seeds. Grass, for example, grows well when many grass plants grow close together.

The wind scatters the fruit of many plants. Maple trees make fruit that is carried by the wind. The maple's fruit shown in the picture on the left twirls as it floats away from the tree.

You might have seen tiny parachutes like the milkweed fruit below. Tiny threads help the fruits float on breezes. The wind can carry many fruits with their seeds far away from parent plants.

A maple tree's fruit and seeds

Milkweed fruit and seeds

26

Animals help scatter fruits and their seeds. Notice the burs on the bear in the picture. The burs are fruits that have seeds inside. Hooks on the fruit stick to animals. As an animal moves to new places, some of the burs fall to the ground. Seeds can be moved long distances this way.

Animals also help scatter some fruits and their seeds by eating them. Cherries and berries are food for birds, bats, and bears. The animals eat the fruit, often swallowing the seeds. The seed coats protect the seeds. Later, the seeds pass through the animals' bodies and drop to the ground.

Other fruits are too heavy to float in the air, but they can float on water. Coconuts—fruits of palm trees—can float between islands. When the coconuts get to a beach, they start to grow like the one in the picture on the right.

A coconut growing on a beach

Burs on a bear

Seed coats are important to people. They help preserve grains and other seeds that people use as foods. Because seed coats help keep the seeds alive, the seeds can be stored and will still germinate when planted many years in the future.

dormant (dôr′mənt), a resting state of a seed.

What Seeds Need to Grow

The bean seed on the left is hard and dry. The seed is in a resting state, or is **dormant.** The seed will not begin to grow as long as it is dormant. Seeds can be dormant for a few days, a few weeks, or years.

Seeds remain dormant until they have water, oxygen, and a certain temperature. The dry bean seed in the picture was soaked in water. The bean seed in the middle picture shows what happens. The seed gets larger and the seed coat gets softer. The seed changes because it absorbs or takes in water. If the seed now has enough oxygen and the right temperature, the seed will begin to sprout—or germinate—like the seed in the third picture.

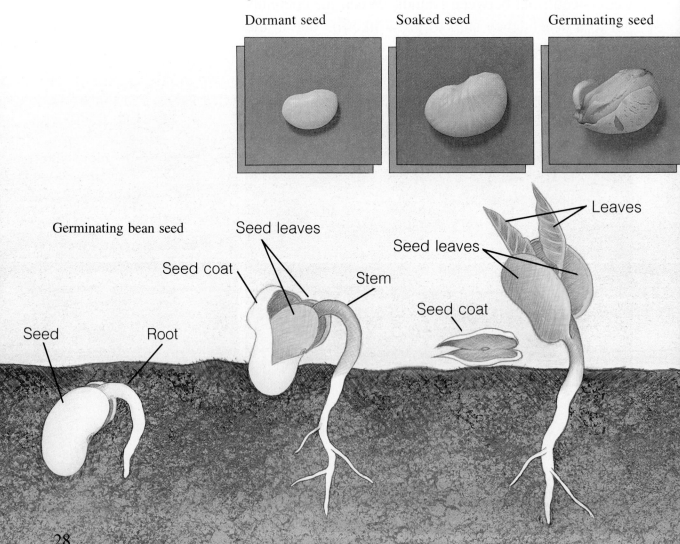

Dormant seed   Soaked seed   Germinating seed

Germinating bean seed

Seed leaves

Seed coat

Stem

Leaves

Seed leaves

Seed coat

Seed   Root

Growing Seeds

In both a corn seed and a bean seed, the seed takes in water. The seed coat gets soft. A root pushes through the seed coat and grows downward. Then the corn seed and bean seed grow differently.

As shown in the pictures on these two pages, the bottom part of the bean root grows downward. The top part of the root grows upward and becomes the stem. This stem carries the seed coat and seed leaves with it. What do you notice happens to the seed coat in the picture? The seed leaves provide food for the growing plant. Two small leaves grow between the seed leaves. Soon, the plant uses up the stored food inside the seed leaves. The seed leaves dry up and drop off. Buds on the stem form more leaves as the bean plant grows taller. The new leaves can trap sunlight to get energy for the plant.

Leaves

Stem

Seed leaves

Seed leaves

Root

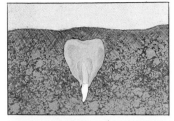

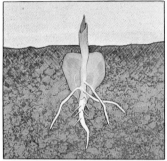

Germinating corn seed

Unlike the bean seed, the corn seed is not pushed up. The seed stays in the soil. Notice in the top picture that a root is starting to grow downward from the seed. The part of the seed that will become leaves grows upward through the seed coat. Find these leaves in the bottom picture. Leaves unroll as they grow. A stem that grows between the leaves forms a cornstalk. The leaves use stored food from the corn seed. Then the green leaves begin trapping energy from sunlight for the new corn plant. Compare the drawings of the growing corn seed with those of the bean seed.

Lesson Review

1. What are three ways seeds are scattered?
2. What conditions do seeds need to germinate?
3. How is what happens to the seed coat of a corn seed that germinates different from what happens to a bean seed coat?
4. **Challenge!** A volcano once erupted on an island in the Pacific Ocean. All plant and animal life on the island was destroyed. Within ten years, many kinds of plants grew on the island. How do you think this could happen?

Study on your own, pages 376–377.

FIND OUT ON YOUR OWN

Use the library or talk to a gardener to find out what different seeds need to germinate and grow. Find out about such plants as lettuce, tomatoes, cucumbers, squash, and green beans. Plan a garden using what you have learned. List each kind of plant you want. Next to each kind of plant, write what it needs to germinate and how much sunlight the plant needs.

Germinating Seeds

Wear cover goggles for this activity.

Purpose
Observe how long different kinds of seeds take to germinate.

Gather These Materials
• 2 clear plastic cups • masking tape • 3 radish seeds • 3 bean seeds • 2 paper towels • small graduated cylinder • water • plastic wrap • 2 rubber bands

Follow This Procedure
1. Use a chart like the one shown to record your observations.
2. Write your name, one kind of seed, and the date on a piece of masking tape. Put the tape on the outside of one cup.
3. Wet one paper towel and squeeze out any extra water.
4. Fold the paper towel in half. Put the paper towel around the inside of the cup. Fold any paper towel that sticks above the cup into the cup. Make sure the paper towel is pressed against the side of the cup.
5. Use your finger to push a seed between the paper towel and the side of the cup. Push the seed about half way down the side of the cup.
6. Repeat step 5 for the other 2 seeds of the same kind. Make sure the paper towel is pushed against the side of the cup to hold the seeds in place.
7. Pour 2 mL of water into the bottom of the cup. Cover the top of the cup with plastic wrap. Use a rubber band to hold the plastic wrap in place.

8. Repeat steps 2–7 for the second kind of seed.
9. Check the seeds every day. When each seed germinates, record the information in your chart.

Record Your Results

Number of Seeds That Have Germinated				
	Day 1	Day 2	Day 3	Day 4
Radish seeds				
Bean seeds				

State Your Conclusion
1. How long did each kind of seed take to germinate?
2. What difference did you find in how long the two different kinds of seeds took to germinate?

Use What You Learned
How would you change this activity to find out if temperature changes how fast seeds germinate?

Skills for Solving Problems

Using Metric Rulers and Bar Graphs

Problem: How does the amount of sunlight plants receive affect the growth of the plants?

Part A. Using Metric Rulers to Collect Information

1. Metric rulers measure the length of objects. Observe the metric rulers shown below. The space between each line on a metric ruler is 1 mm. What does mm mean? Notice that some lines on the rulers are longer than the others. The space between the longer lines is 1 cm. Each cm is made up of 10 mm. What does cm mean?

2. The height of the plant grown in direct sunlight for 5 weeks is 30 cm. How tall is the plant grown in indirect sunlight? How tall is the plant grown in total darkness?

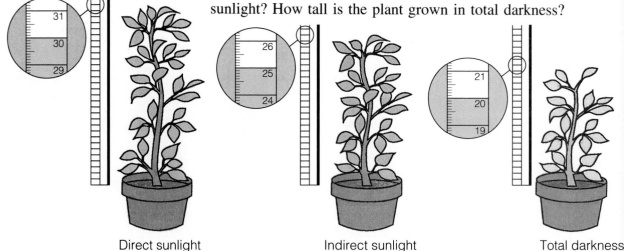

Direct sunlight   Indirect sunlight   Total darkness

Part B. Using a Bar Graph to Organize and Interpret Information

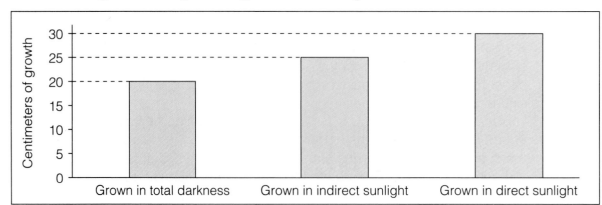

32

3. The graph contains the information you collected in Part A about the height of plants grown in different amounts of sunlight. The plants are placed on the graph from shortest to tallest. What do the lines on the left of the graph represent?

4. Place your finger on the line on the left of the graph that matches the height of the shortest plant. Do the same thing for the other two plants. What is the height of each of the three plants?

5. How does the amount of sunlight plants receive affect the growth of the plants?

Part C. Using Metric Rulers and Bar Graphs to Solve a Problem

Problem: How does the amount of water a plant receives affect the growth of the plant?

6. Use the pictures below to collect the information you need to solve the problem. Make a graph similar to the one in Part B to organize your information.

7. Use your graph to solve the problem. Compare the three plants on your graph. Which plant has grown to the tallest height? How has the amount of water a plant receives affected the growth of the plant?

8. You might want to do this experiment and make a graph to organize your results.

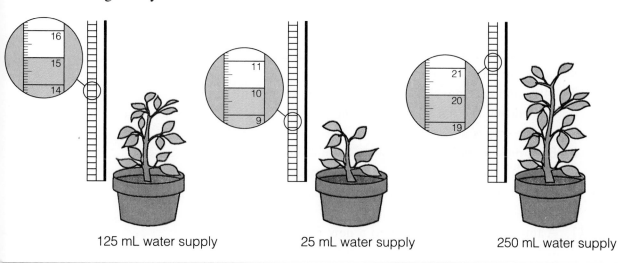

125 mL water supply   25 mL water supply   250 mL water supply

Chapter 1 Review

✔ Chapter Main Ideas

Lesson 1 • Plants are divided into two big groups—plants that make seeds and plants that do not make seeds. • Flowering plants and conifers make seeds. • Ferns and mosses do not make seeds.

Lesson 2 • The four parts of a flower are sepals, petals, stamens, and a pistil. • The stamens and pistil are needed to make seeds. • Some flowers have fewer than four parts.

Lesson 3 • Pollen from a stamen is moved to a pistil during pollination. • Sperm in the pollen must combine with an egg to make a seed. • Plants make monocot seeds or dicot seeds. • The fruit grows from the ovary of the pistil.

Lesson 4 • Seeds are scattered by animals, wind, and water. • Seeds begin to grow when conditions are right. • Monocot and dicot seeds grow in different ways.

✔ Reviewing Science Words

classify	monocot seed	pollination
conifer	ovary	reproduce
dicot seed	ovule	sepal
dormant	pistil	spore
embryo	pollen	stamen
fertilization		

Copy each sentence. Fill in the blank with the correct word or words from the list.

1. Scientist _____ plants into two groups.
2. _____ happens when a bee moves pollen from a stamen to a pistil.
3. _____ happens when sperm combines with an egg.
4. Seeds are one way that plants _____.
5. The wind can move _____ from a stamen to a pistil.
6. A seed that has not started growing is _____.
7. A pine tree is a _____.
8. Bees pick up pollen from the _____ of flowers.
9. The _____ is the part of a flower that makes eggs.
10. The bottom part of the pistil that grows larger when seeds form is the _____.
11. A tiny cell that can grow into a new fern plant is a _____.

12. A ▓ has two seed leaves.
13. The inner part of an ovary that contains an egg is the ▓.
14. A ▓ has one seed leaf.
15. An ▓ is the part of a seed that can grow into a new plant.
16. A leaflike part that protects a flower bud is a ▓.

✓ Reviewing What You Learned

Write the letter of the best answer.
1. Which part of a flower is necessary for that flower to make seeds?
   (a) petals   (b) sepals   (c) pistil   (d) stamen
2. Which part of a flower becomes the fruit?
   (a) ovary   (b) stamen   (c) ovule   (d) sepal
3. Which part of a flower becomes a seed?
   (a) ovary   (b) stamen   (c) ovule   (d) sepal
4. Fruit that has hooks is most likely to be scattered by
   (a) wind.   (b) animals.   (c) water.   (d) germinating.
5. Corn plants make two kinds of
   (a) seeds.   (b) cones.   (c) fruit.   (d) flowers.
6. Plants with tiny, light pollen are most likely to be pollinated by
   (a) animals.   (b) water.   (c) wind.   (d) fertilization.

✓ Interpreting What You Learned

Write a short answer for each statement.
1. Describe the main difference between flowering plants and conifers.
2. Explain why mosses and ferns are not classified in a group with flowering plants and conifers.
3. List the following words in the order that they occur beginning with the word *flower*: germinate, fertilization, pollination, seeds, flower, new plant.

✓ Extending Your Thinking

Write a paragraph to answer each question.
1. You have planted some flower seeds that did not germinate. What are some possible reasons why the seeds did not germinate?
2. Pick one of the reasons that you gave in number 1. What could you do with other seeds of the same kind to find out if this reason is correct?

• For further review, use Study Guide pages 376–377.

Chapter 2

Animal Behavior

The baby moose and its mother below are butting. Although hitting heads together might not seem like fun to you, the baby and its mother are playing. This play helps the baby learn ways of acting it will need as an adult.

Introducing the Chapter

Think about different animals you have seen. Each kind of animal has certain ways of acting. Some of these ways are learned. In the activity below, you will observe learning. In this chapter, you will learn more about how animals act. You will learn how some animals live together and care for their young.

DISCOVER!

Observing Your Partner Learn

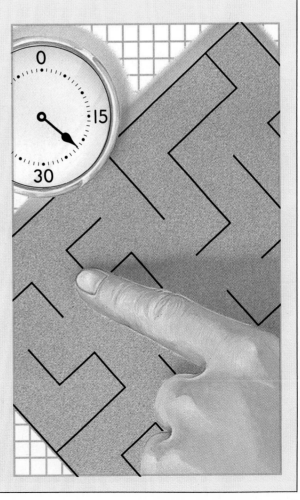

Draw a finger maze on a large piece of paper. Your maze should have a starting place, a finish, paths leading from the start to the finish, and some paths with dead ends. Make your maze as difficult as you can.

Time how long your partner takes to move a finger along the path from the start to the finish. Write the number of minutes and seconds on a piece of paper. Ask your partner to trace this path four more times. Record the number of minutes and seconds your partner takes each time.

Talk About It
1. How long did your partner take to go through the maze each time?
2. How would you explain the differences in the times?

1 How Do Animals Live in Groups?

LESSON GOALS

You will learn
- the different kinds of groups that some animals live in.
- how ants live in colonies.
- how different kinds of animals can live together.

school, a group of one kind of fish that moves together.

pride, a group of lions.

A school of fish and a pride of lions

You may have heard someone speak of a flock of geese or a herd of elephants. *Flock* and *herd* are words that describe groups of animals. Not all animals live in groups. However, many kinds do.

Different Kinds of Groups

Animals form different kinds of groups. The pictures below show a **school** of fish and a **pride** of lions. A school and a pride are kinds of groups. Both fish and lions are helped by living in groups.

The fish move together in a school. They all stay about the same distance from each other in the water. As a group they look larger than they really are. Looking larger helps protect them. Also, they are protected in another way. All the fish will turn if one fish turns away from something in the water. How might this movement be helpful? How might the lions be helped by living in a pride?

Baboons live in groups called **troops.** Look at the troop of baboons in the picture. They live in East Africa. You can see animals of different ages and sizes in the troop. Baboons usually form troops of about fifty members.

The troop moves through the grassland looking for food each day. As they move, the largest animal is in center. The largest animal in the troop is the head male. From the center, this animal can watch the whole troop. Larger troops may have more than one head male. The head male is most often the strongest male in the troop. Other males help the head male defend the troop.

Mother baboons with babies and other young baboons stay close to the head male to be protected. Other adult males and females stay at the edges of the troop and surround the mothers, babies, and young.

When the troop stops moving, the animals stay in the same places. They also sleep in the same places with the head male at the center.

troop (trüp), a kind of group in which animals such as baboons live.

A troop of baboons

When the baboons hunt for food, they do not leave the troop. They stay in their same places in the troop and hunt in smaller family groups. They eat mainly plants and flowers and seeds of plants.

Within the troop, the female baboons take care of the babies. Mothers will fight to protect their babies. The babies take several years to grow into adults. Young baboons play with each other. This time of play for them is a time of learning.

Baboons communicate with each other by the ways they move. A low crouch means the animal is not the strongest. Moving the body back and forth many times means the animal is excited. They also make faces and sounds. A frightened baboon keeps its teeth together and pulls its lips back. The animal below is more frightened. It opens its mouth in a threat yawn and makes a "yakking" sound.

Baboons spend hours every day grooming each other. They use their fingers to pull out dirt and insects that are in each other's hair. Notice the baboon grooming its baby in the picture.

A threat yawn

Baboons grooming

An Insect Colony

Imagine you see an ant hill near a sidewalk. You might just see a pile of sand or dirt. The ant hill might not look interesting, but below that hill is a whole colony of animals. A **colony** is a group of animals in which different animals have different jobs. Ants, honeybees, and termites are some animals that live in colonies.

An ant colony is made up of ants that have different jobs. One ant is the queen ant. She lays all the eggs. The queen ant is the largest ant in the colony. Other ants feed her.

The ants that feed the queen ant are workers. Some workers gather food. Other workers dig tunnels under the ground. Some workers move eggs to and from different rooms. Other workers feed the young ants. Some colonies also have soldier ants which defend the colony.

Another kind of ant in the colony is the drone. The drones are ants with only one job. They mate with the queen ant. Look at the picture of the different kinds of ants. Which kinds of ants have wings?

colony (kol′ə nē), a kind of animal group in which each member has a different job.

An ant colony

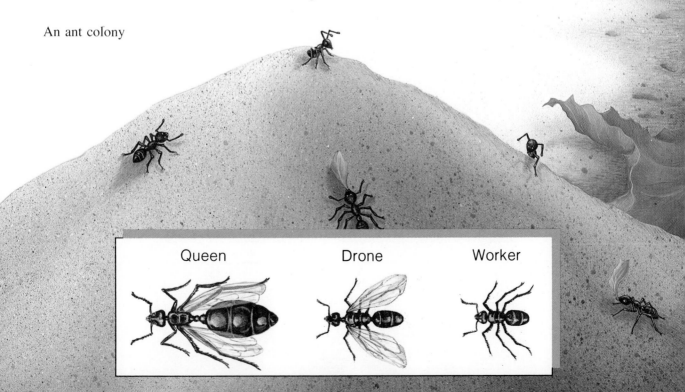

Queen   Drone   Worker

If you look closely at an ant hill, you would see a hole in the top of the dirt. The hole is the opening to halls and rooms under the ground. Look at the many different halls and rooms in the picture. Ants dig out the halls and rooms. Then they store things in the rooms or live in them.

One room is a place for the queen ant to live. Some rooms are places where food is kept. The eggs are kept in other rooms. Some rooms are for larvae and pupae. Larvae and pupae are stages through which the young ants change before they become adults. Some ants spend all their time digging new halls and rooms. Other workers gather food for these ants.

Ants within a colony communicate with each other by touching their antennae, or feelers, together. Ants also leave chemical messages. An ant can mark a path away from the colony by leaving drops of a chemical on the ground. To get home, ants follow the path.

How are the ants communicating in the picture?

Ants communicating

Inside an ant hill

Fresh dirt

Larvae

Food storage

Pupae

Eggs

Queen's room

New room

Sometimes ants keep ant cows in the colony. Ant cows are insects that suck juices from plants. Ant cows are not ants. Ants keep the ant cows so that they can get their juices. Why would such an insect be called an ant cow?

Honeybees form colonies much like those of ants. A honeybee colony is sometimes called a hive. Different bees have different jobs in the hive. A hive has one queen bee and many workers. Drone honeybees' only job is to mate with the queen bee.

Just like ants, honeybees must be able to tell each other where food is. Honeybees do dances to show the way to the food and to tell how far away the food is. The picture below shows two of the dances they do. The dance on the left tells the bees that the food is near. The dance on the right tells the bees that the food is farther away. This dance also shows the bees what direction to fly.

The jobs within a colony are complex. Many things must be done to make sure the members live. With each insect doing its job, the colony survives.

Beekeepers raise honeybees in hives. They collect the wax and honey that the bees make in their colonies.

Honeybee dances that tell where food is

Different Kinds of Animals That Live Together

symbiosis (sim′bē ō′sis), a special way in which two different kinds of animals live together.

Sometimes different kinds of animals have special ways that they live together. A special way that animals live together is called **symbiosis.** There are different kinds of symbiosis.

The white birds in the bottom picture live in a special way with buffalo. These birds stay near the buffalo and eat insects. They are helped because more insects are around the buffalo. The buffalo are helped because the birds remove insects. The bird in the top picture eats insects off the buffalo.

The picture on the right shows a cleaner shrimp and the fish it cleans. The shrimp picks small living things that it eats off the fish. The fish is helped because it is cleaned. How is the shrimp helped?

Oxpecker on cape buffalo

Cattle egrets and buffalo

Cleaner shrimp in fish's mouth

Not all symbiosis helps both kinds of animals. Sometimes one kind of animal is harmed. Perhaps you have a dog or cat that has had fleas. Fleas are insects that live on blood. The fleas are helped by living on the dog or cat. They get food—the blood—from the pet. The fleas are **parasites.** They harm the dog or cat. The fleas take blood, can carry diseases, and make the animal itch. The dog or cat is the **host.**

Sometimes animals live together in a way that helps one kind of animal and does not help or harm the other. Remoras are fish that sometimes live with sharks. Remoras are much smaller than sharks. A remora is helped by staying with the large fish. It gets food that the shark does not eat. It moves around with the shark, too. The shark is not helped or harmed by the small fish.

parasite (par′ə sīt), an animal that is helped by living with another animal that it harms.

host (hōst), an animal that is harmed by a parasite.

Lesson Review

1. How are the different members of a baboon troop arranged when they move through the grassland looking for food?
2. What are some of the jobs that worker ants do in an ant colony?
3. What is an example of two kinds of animals living together in which one kind of animal is harmed?
4. **Challenge!** Insects in colonies have no choice about the job each will have in the groups. How do these animals' jobs compare with humans?

Study on your own, pages 378–379.

Using library books, find out what behaviors baboons use to determine who will be the head male. Write a story about how a baboon becomes the head male.

FIND OUT ON YOUR OWN

2 How Do Different Animals Care for Their Young?

You will learn
- that some young animals can take care of themselves.
- that some young animals need care from an adult.

Think about what you looked like as a baby. You have changed a lot since then. Animals grow and change as they get older. Their young will repeat these changes. Each animal grows old and finally dies. All of these changes make up what is called a life cycle.

Young Animals That Do Not Need Care

When you were born, you could not take care of yourself. You needed much care. Someone had to feed you and keep you warm and clean. Someone had to protect you from harm.

As part of their life cycles, some young animals need adults to take care of them. Other young animals do not need care. They can take care of themselves. The picture on the left shows a mother sea turtle laying eggs. Once she buries the eggs in the sand, the mother swims away.

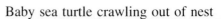

Sea turtle laying eggs   Baby sea turtle crawling out of nest

46

When the eggs hatch, the young take care of themselves. The baby turtle on page 46 has just hatched and is crawling out of its nest. The baby turtle below is crawling toward the ocean where it is more likely to find food. Getting to the ocean also is necessary to keep the sun from drying out the baby turtles.

Not all of the young turtles that hatch will live. Some will be eaten by other animals. Some will dry up in the sun. Even though some will not survive, enough eggs hatch that some young turtles will live.

A frog is another kind of animal that swims away as soon as the eggs are laid. The frog differs from the turtle in that the young of the frog do not look like the parents. A tadpole must develop and go through changes before it becomes an adult frog.

The butterfly, like the one in the picture, also has young that go through changes before they look like adult butterflies. During the changes, the young do not need care from an adult. The mother butterfly lays the eggs and then flies away.

This butterfly's young do not need care.

Baby sea turtle crawling to ocean

Baby black bears are born blind and with little fur. They grow quickly after they are born. Black bears are increasing in North America because fewer are being killed by hunters.

Young kangaroo in pouch

Young Animals That Need Care

Cats, dogs, hamsters, and mice are among the many animals that need care when they are young. The adult animals often find a safe place to have the babies. After the young are born, the babies need much care. The parents give that care.

Parents protect and feed the babies. The young bears below are protected and fed by their mother. Just after the babies are born, the mother feeds them milk. Later she finds food for them and teaches them to find food. When the babies are out learning to find food, they are protected by their mother.

A young kangaroo rides in its mother's pouch. The baby is protected there. Just after the baby is born, it crawls into the mother's pouch and begins to feed. It gets milk from the mother. Find the baby kangaroo in its mother's pouch in the picture.

Brown bear and young

A baby kangaroo is not only protected by staying in the pouch. It is also moved from place to place by the mother. Other animals also are protected and moved around by their parents. Look at the picture of the opossum. The babies cling tightly to the mother as she carries them around and protects them.

Notice how close the young penguin is to its parent. When parents stay near babies, they can protect them and keep them warm. Because babies have small bodies, they lose body heat quickly. Some animals are born without fur or feathers. They will get cold quickly. Notice in the picture that the babies of the flicker are born without feathers. The parent is feeding the babies. Much of the time, the adult birds take turns sitting on the babies to keep them warm and protect them.

Parent birds take care of their young even before they hatch. The birds will move eggs around in a nest and turn them over. Adult birds also sit on the eggs to keep them warm.

Baby flickers getting food

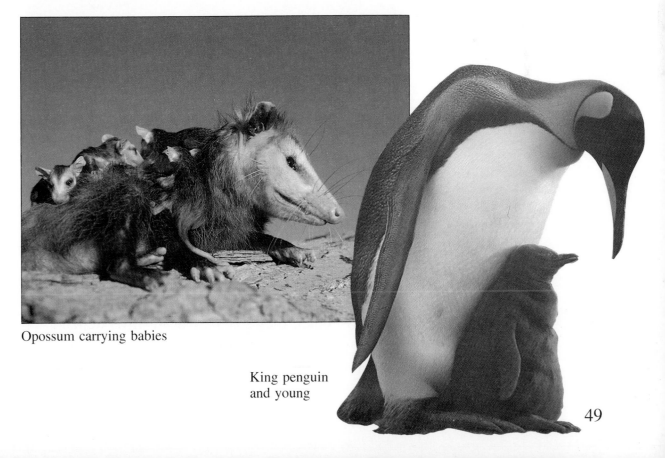

Opossum carrying babies

King penguin
and young

49

When babies look very much alike, it is sometimes hard for parents to tell which ones are their own. Sometimes parents can see differences among babies. Sometimes parents can hear differences. The animals below are marmots. The adult is smelling the young animal to identify it.

Marmots

Lesson Review

1. What care does a baby sea turtle need?
2. What three things do parents who care for their young give to their babies?
3. **Challenge!** A cowbird is a kind of bird that lays its eggs in the nests of other kinds of birds. The parent cowbird then leaves. How are the young cowbirds cared for?

Study on your own, pages 378–379.

FIND OUT ON YOUR OWN

Use library books to find out how different birds look when they hatch. Do all birds depend on their parents in the same ways? Write a report on your findings.

Observing Stages in the Life Cycle of a Beetle

Purpose
Observe stages in the life cycle of a beetle.

Gather These Materials
• small glass jar • mealworms • bran or cereal flakes • paper towel • piece of potato or apple • small piece of cheesecloth • masking tape • hand lens

Follow This Procedure
1. Use a chart like the one shown to record your observations.
2. Mealworms are larvae that grow into adult beetles. Observe the larvae with a hand lens. Record what the larvae look like and how they behave.
3. Put a handful of cereal in the bottom of the jar. Add a few larvae to the jar. *CAUTION: Handle the glass jar carefully.*
4. Cover most of the cereal with a piece of paper towel. Place a piece of apple or potato on the paper towel.
5. Cover the jar with the cheesecloth. Use masking tape to hold the cheesecloth in place.
6. Put the jar in a warm place away from direct sunlight.
7. Observe the larvae once or twice a week for a month. Clean out old pieces of food and put in fresh pieces. Observe any changes in what the larvae look like and how they behave. Look for pupae and adult beetles. Record what the pupae and beetles look like.

Record Your Results
Description

Larva	
Pupa	
Beetle	

State Your Conclusion
1. How did the mealworms change?
2. Why do you think adult beetles do not need to take care of their young?

Use What You Learned
Is the life cycle of the beetle more like that of a butterfly or a bird? Explain your answer.

51

3 What Behaviors Do Animals Have?

LESSON GOALS

You will learn
- about behaviors that animals are born with.
- about behaviors that animals learn.

behavior (bi hā′vyər), the way a living thing acts.

instinct (in′stingkt), a behavior that an animal has at birth and does not need to learn.

Think of all the things you do. You talk with your friends. You can write and do arithmetic. Perhaps you can sing or play a musical instrument. Each of the things you do is a behavior. The way a living thing acts is its **behavior.** All animals have behaviors. A bird will fly away if you come near it. A dog may run toward you. What are some behaviors of other animals?

Inborn Behaviors

Some behaviors are learned. Others are inborn behaviors—ones that animals have without being taught. Some inborn behaviors are **instincts.** When baby sea turtles hatch, they crawl toward the ocean. No parent turtle teaches them which way to go. For baby sea turtles, crawling to the ocean is an instinct. For Canada geese and many monarch butterflies, flying south before winter is an instinct.

Notice in the picture that the baby gull is pecking at the red spot on its mother's bill to get food. The mother does not teach the baby to peck at this spot. This instinct helps the baby get food.

Baby gull pecking at parent's beak

Other inborn behaviors are **reflexes.** A reflex is a simple, automatic behavior controlled by nerves. Reflexes help protect you. If you go out in the wind, you might blink. Your eyes might fill up with tears. You do not stop to think about what your eyes should do. These automatic behaviors are reflexes. When you go into a dark room, at first you cannot see very well. Later you can see better because the pupils in your eyes open wider. They let more light into your eyes. This change in your eyes is another reflex.

A **stimulus** is what brings about a behavior. The wind is a stimulus to your eyes. A dark room is another stimulus. The **response** is how the living thing acts as a result of the stimulus. Your blinking is a response to the wind. The opening of your pupils is a response to the dark room.

Study the eyes of the owl in the pictures. How are they different? What are the stimuli and responses that would cause the owl's eyes to look as they do?

reflex (rē′fleks), a simple, automatic behavior.

stimulus (stim′yə ləs), the cause of a behavior.

response (ri spons′), a behavior caused by a stimulus.

Different responses of an owl's eyes

53

Dogs are being used to help disabled people. You might know of seeing-eye dogs used by the blind. Other dogs are trained to hear for the deaf and to do many jobs for people who cannot move about easily.

Porpoises showing a learned behavior

Learned Behaviors

You learned some of your behaviors. You learned to dress yourself. You learned to comb your hair. A behavior that is learned rather than inborn is called a learned behavior. What are some of your other learned behaviors?

A learned behavior can be a response to a stimulus. Animals can be taught to do tricks by rewarding their responses. Suppose you want to teach your pet dog to shake hands. Putting your hand out to the dog and saying "shake" are the stimuli. At first the dog might not give you its paw, but you might take it. After many tries, the dog might give you its paw. You then reward the dog with praise or food. The dog will learn the response of giving you its paw when you put out your hand and say "shake."

The picture shows porpoises that have learned to do a trick. The trainer gives them fish for the correct response to the stimulus.

Instincts are behaviors that are not easily changed. However, learned behaviors can be changed easily. Suppose you want to make your dog roll over instead of shaking hands when you say "shake." You could give the dog a reward for rolling over, but not for giving you its paw each time you say "shake." In time, the dog will change its response to your "shake" stimulus. Your dog will have learned to roll over when you say "shake."

Animals learn behaviors in many ways. A bluejay is a bird that sometimes eats different kinds of butterflies. Monarch butterflies are poisonous. A bluejay learns not to eat a monarch butterfly after eating one and getting sick. Young coyotes learn about their surroundings by exploring. Monkeys can learn some behaviors by watching other monkeys. The red fox young in the picture are playing. This kind of playing helps them learn skills they will need to hunt for food as adults.

Red foxes playing

Lesson Review

1. How do your eyes change if you go from a sunny room into a dark room? What is the stimulus? What is the response?
2. How do you teach a pet a learned behavior such as a trick?
3. **Challenge!** Suppose you have a dog that barks when you use the telephone. What can you do to change your dog's learned behavior?

Study on your own, pages 378–379.

Using library books, find out what response the planaria worm has to light. How does the planaria worm move when a light is turned on? Make a poster that shows your findings.

**FIND OUT
ON YOUR OWN**

ACTIVITY

Observing How Mealworms Respond to Food

Purpose
Observe how mealworms respond to food.

Gather These Materials
• several mealworms • shoe box • bran or cereal flakes • watch or clock with a second hand

Follow This Procedure
1. Use a chart like the one shown to record your observations.
2. Place the mealworms in the center of the shoe box.
3. Observe the mealworms for 10 minutes. Record how long they stay in the center of the box. Record where the mealworms move to in the box and how long they stay there.
4. Move all the mealworms back to the center of the box.
5. Place a handful of bran or cereal flakes in one corner of the box.
6. Repeat step 3.

Record Your Results

Behavior of mealworms

Before adding cereal	
After adding cereal	

State Your Conclusion
1. Were the movements of your mealworms different in the two parts of the activity? If so, how were they different?
2. What was the stimulus in the activity? What was the mealworms' response?

Use What You Learned
How could you show that the mealworms were responding to food, not just trying to get away from the light in the room?

Teaching Monkeys to Help People

Monkeys, like the capuchin or "organ-grinder" monkey, used to be trained to do tricks. People would enjoy watching these monkeys. Now, Dr. Mary Joan Willard and her staff train these monkeys to help quadriplegics. These people have injured their spines. They cannot move any part of their bodies except their heads.

People who are quadriplegics must depend on others to help them do even simple things. Dr. Willard understands that people like to do things for themselves without asking other people for help. She got the idea for animal helpers. Dr. Willard decided that capuchin monkeys would make good helpers because they are small, clean, friendly, and smart. With monkeys to do many small jobs, quadriplegics could live on their own more easily.

A quadriplegic can tell a monkey what to do by talking or by moving a pointer held in the mouth. Talking or pointing provides a stimulus for the monkey. The monkey responds to each stimulus by doing a certain job. Dr. Willard has trained monkeys to open and shut doors, change books on a reading stand, and bring objects that the owner points to. Also, a helper monkey can bring food and drinks from the refrigerator, help feed its owner, and then clear the table. Dr. Willard is training the monkey in the top picture to open a box. The monkey in the bottom picture is learning to open a magazine and turn pages. Each time the monkey finishes a job correctly, it gets a food reward.

The monkeys learn many new behaviors before they are ready to live and work with a disabled person. Dr. Willard hopes to train many more monkeys in the future. With each monkey she trains, she can give a disabled person not only a helper but a special little friend.

What Do You Think?
1. List three learned behaviors that helper monkeys can be taught.
2. Think of a job you would train a helper monkey to do, and tell what kind of stimulus you would give to the monkey.

Skills for Solving Problems

Using Flow Diagrams and Bar Graphs

Problem: How would the rabbit population increase if all the rabbits born survived?

Part A. Using a Flow Diagram to Collect Information

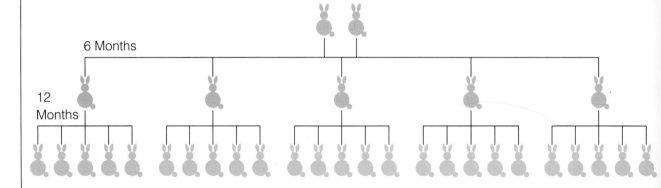

1. The flow diagram shows how many rabbits would be born if every rabbit found a mate and produced five baby rabbits. Start reading the diagram at the top and follow down its branches. How many rabbits does the diagram start with? How many are born after 6 months?
2. After 12 months, each of the young rabbits finds a mate and reproduces. How many rabbits are born? What is the total number of offspring of the original rabbits?

Part B. Using a Bar Graph to Organize and Interpret Information

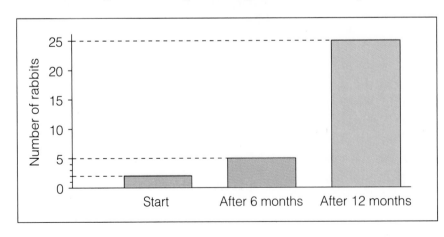

3. The bar graph shows the information you collected about rabbit reproduction. The second bar shows how many offspring were born after 6 months. Move your finger from the top of the bar to the scale at the left of the graph. How many rabbits were born?
4. How many rabbits were born after 12 months?
5. How many rabbits do you predict would be born after 18 months?

Part C. Using Flow Diagrams and Bar Graphs to Solve a Problem

Problem: How many rabbits would result if only two out of every five rabbits born lived to reproduce?

6. Use the flow diagram below to collect the information you need to solve the problem. The gray rabbits are rabbits that were born but died before reproducing. Make a bar graph similar to the one in Part B to organize your information. Record only the rabbits that are born and live to reproduce.
7. Look at your bar graph. How many rabbits would be born and still living after 12 months.
8. What would you predict would be the number of rabbits that would be born and still living after 18 months?

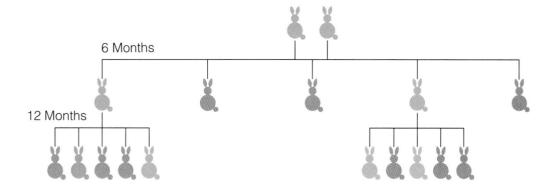

59

Chapter 2 Review

☑ Chapter Main Ideas

Lesson 1 • A school, pride, and troop are three different groups of animals. • Ants in a colony have different jobs. • Two different kinds of animals sometimes live together in a special way that helps one animal but can help or harm the other animal.

Lesson 2 • Young animals, such as young turtles and insects, can take care of themselves. • Young animals, such as baby birds and kittens, need adult animals to take care of them.

Lesson 3 • Animals are born with certain behaviors. • Animals learn other behaviors.

☑ Reviewing Science Words

behavior	reflex
colony	response
host	school
instinct	stimulus
parasite	symbiosis
pride	troop

Copy each sentence. Fill in the blank with the correct word from the list.

1. The way that a living thing acts is its ▨.
2. The action that results from a stimulus is the ▨.
3. Fish move together in a group called a ▨.
4. If you blink due to wind, the wind is the ▨.
5. In a ▨ of ants, the ants have different jobs.
6. A flea is a ▨ because it is helped by living with another animal that it harms.
7. An automatic behavior, such as blinking your eyes, is a ▨.
8. Baboons live together in a group called a ▨.
9. A behavior that an animal is born with is called an inborn behavior or an ▨.
10. A parasite lives on or in a ▨.
11. Two kinds of animals living together in a special way is called ▨.
12. A ▨ is a group of lions living together.

✓ Reviewing What You Learned

Write the letter of the best answer.

1. Fish in a school are protected because they
   (a) are mean. (b) move slowly. (c) look large. (d) swim fast.
2. The mothers with babies are found in a baboon troop near the
   (a) females without babies. (c) edges of the group.
   (b) head male. (d) front of the group.
3. The job of the queen ant is to
   (a) feed ants. (b) feed larvae. (c) gather food. (d) lay eggs.
4. Which of the following is an animal that cares for its young?
   (a) penguin (b) sea turtle (c) frog (d) butterfly
5. If a baboon has its body in a crouch and is making a "yakking" sound, it most likely is
   (a) happy. (b) searching for its young. (c) excited. (d) afraid.
6. Suppose you jump if someone shouts at you. Your jumping is a
   (a) stimulus. (b) symbiosis. (c) response. (d) host behavior.
7. The change of your pupils when you enter a bright room is an example of a
   (a) stimulus. (c) learned behavior.
   (b) reflex. (d) schooling response.
8. Baby sea turtles crawl to the ocean because of
   (a) an instinct. (b) a school. (c) a parasite. (d) a learned behavior.

✓ Interpreting What You Learned

Write a short answer for each question or statement.

1. Compare the job of the queen in an ant colony with the job of the queen in a honeybee colony.
2. What is the relationship between a cleaner shrimp and the fish it cleans?
3. Describe ways in which animals tell which young are their own.
4. What is the difference between a stimulus and a response?

✓ Extending Your Thinking

Write a paragraph to answer each question or statement.

1. Make up an experiment in which you could show how moths respond to light.
2. How is crying both an instinct and a learned behavior for humans?

• For further review, use Study Guide pages 378–379.

Food Chains and Food Webs

Giant pandas live in bamboo forests in China and Tibet. The giant panda in the picture is eating a plant. Pandas eat mostly bamboo plants. By eating plants, pandas get energy to live and grow.

Introducing the Chapter

The plant in the picture also needs energy to live and grow. However, plants do not eat other living things to get energy. In this chapter, you will learn how green plants get energy. You will also learn how green plants are food for almost all animals on the earth. In the activity below, you will find out one way plants store materials that you use as food.

DISCOVER!

Testing Plant Parts for Starch

Some plants store starch. Iodine is a chemical that turns a dark-blue color when it is added to starch. You can test foods to find out if they have starch in them by adding a drop of iodine. *CAUTION: Do not get iodine on your clothes or skin because it stains.*

Get a piece of raw potato, some dry oatmeal, and some cooked rice. Add a drop of iodine to each of the foods.

Talk About It
1. Which of the foods you tested have starch in them?
2. Where did the starch come from?

1 Where Do Green Plants Get Energy?

LESSON GOALS

You will learn
- how green plants get energy and the materials they need.
- why green plants are called producers.

chlorophyll (klôr′ə fil), a green material in plants that traps energy from sunlight and gives plants a green color.

What do you do when you are hungry in the middle of the afternoon? You might have an apple or a glass of milk. This food gives you energy and materials your body needs. Plants do not get hungry. They do not eat food like you do. However, plants do need energy and certain materials.

Getting Energy and Materials

Plants get their energy from the sun. Certain cells in the leaves of green plants change this light energy into a form of energy the plants can use. The picture shows what the inside of a leaf looks like. Find the long, green cells. A material called **chlorophyll** in these cells traps light energy. Chlorophyll gives plants their green color.

The Inside of a Leaf

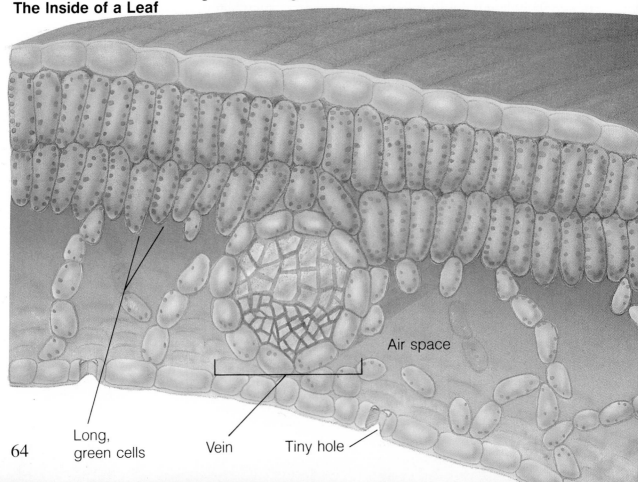

Long, green cells

Vein

Tiny hole

Air space

64

Plants need air before they can use the trapped energy. Find the tiny holes in the bottom of the leaf on page 64. These tiny holes let air move in and out of the leaf. Plants use a certain gas from the air. This gas is **carbon dioxide.**

Plants also need water before they can use the trapped energy. Find the circle of cells in the leaf. These cells form a long pipe called a vein. The plant's roots bring in water and chemicals from the soil. Veins in the roots carry the water and chemicals from the roots up to the leaves.

Green Plants as Producers

Plants use light energy to change carbon dioxide and water into a simple sugar. Find each of the materials plants need in the drawing below. Plants can use light energy to make sugar by carrying on **photosynthesis.** Oxygen and extra water are wastes. They escape through the holes in the leaves.

carbon dioxide (kär′bən dī ok′sīd), a gas in air.

photosynthesis (fō′tō sin′thə sis), the way in which green plants trap the sun's energy and use it to change carbon dioxide and water into sugar.

What Plants Need to Make Sugar

1. Plants get energy from the sun.

2. Plants get carbon dioxide from the air.

3. Plants get water from the soil.

Three chemicals plants need to be healthy are potassium (pə tas′ē əm), nitrogen (nī′trə jən), and phosphorus (fos′fər əs). These chemicals are found in soil. Since plants take them out of the soil, more of these chemicals need to be added. Farmers and gardeners add these chemicals to soil when they add fertilizers. People sometimes call these fertilizers plant "food."

producer (prə dü′sər), a living thing that can use sunlight to make sugars.

Photosynthesis makes plants different from most other living things. Plants can trap light energy and use it to make simple sugars. Plants can combine these sugars with minerals from the soil to make plant parts such as leaves, stems, and roots. Because plants can make or produce sugars, they are called **producers.**

Animals cannot make sugars from sunlight. Plants produce the materials that animals depend on for food and energy. When a rabbit eats part of a plant, it is eating energy and materials that the plant has stored. The rabbit uses this food for energy and to make rabbit tissue. When you eat a strawberry, you are eating energy and materials that a strawberry plant stored. The foods in the picture below are parts of plants. They have energy and materials that plants have stored.

Foods that are parts of plants

Lesson Review

1. How do green plants get energy?
2. Why are green plants called producers?
3. **Challenge!** What would happen to a geranium plant that was left to grow in a dark room for many days?

Study on your own, pages 380–381.

Farmers grow plants for other people to eat. They also grow plants to feed the animals that people will eat. Corn is growing on the farm below. Find out what kind of plants or crops farmers grow in your state.

FIND OUT ON YOUR OWN

2 Where Do Animals Get Food?

LESSON GOALS

You will learn
- why animals are called consumers.
- what herbivores, carnivores, and omnivores eat.

consumer (kən sü′mər), a living thing that depends on producers for food.

All living things need energy and certain materials to live and grow. Where do plants get the energy and materials they need? Other living things get the energy and materials they need from food.

Animals as Consumers

Animals cannot trap light energy. They must eat food. Because animals must eat or consume food, they are called **consumers.** The animals in the pictures are eating food. They are consumers.

Different animals eat different kinds of food. One way scientists group animals is by what they eat. One group of animals eats only plants. Another group of animals eats only other animals. The third group of animals eats plants and other animals.

A moose is a herbivore.

68

Herbivores, Carnivores, and Omnivores

Look at the moose in the picture on page 68. What is the moose eating? Moose are animals that eat only plants. They are **herbivores.** Elephants, sheep, deer, horses, and squirrels are herbivores. Horses eat grass, hay, corn, or oats. Different herbivores might eat fruits, seeds, leaves, stems, or even roots.

The wolves in the picture do not eat fruit or other plant parts. They eat such foods as rabbits and squirrels. An animal that eats only other animals is a **carnivore.** A wolf is a carnivore. Lions, tigers, and most snakes are carnivores. An owl eats mice and other small animals. Is an owl a herbivore or a carnivore? A rabbit eats only plant parts. Is a rabbit a herbivore or a carnivore?

Wolves are carnivores.

SCIENCE IN YOUR LIFE

Most of the foods in your grocery store would not be there if it were not for green plants. Many foods—lettuce, apples, beans—are parts of plants. Chicken and beef come from animals that eat plant parts.

herbivore (hėr′bə vôr), a consumer that eats only producers.

carnivore (kär′nə vôr), a consumer that eats only other consumers.

omnivore (om/nə vôr),
a consumer that eats
producers and other
consumers.

Some consumers, such as the raccoon in the picture, eat both plants and animals. A raccoon might eat insects, toads, and fruits. A consumer that eats both plants and animals is called an **omnivore.** Bears are omnivores. Most people are omnivores. Think about the foods you ate yesterday. Were you a herbivore, a carnivore, or an omnivore?

Lesson Review

1. Why are animals called consumers?
2. What foods do herbivores, carnivores, and omnivores eat?
3. **Challenge!** Some people are vegetarians and do not eat meats. However, some vegetarians do eat eggs and foods made from milk. Are these people herbivores, carnivores, or omnivores? Explain your answer.

Study on your own, pages 380–381.

A raccoon is an omnivore.

**FIND OUT
ON YOUR OWN**

Use encyclopedias or pet care books to find out what different pets eat. You might find out about a dog, cat, parakeet, gerbil, turtle, and fish. Make a list of what each kind of pet eats. Next to each pet's name, write if the pet is a herbivore, a carnivore, or an omnivore.

Comparing Teeth

Purpose
Observe how different teeth work and *infer* which teeth are best for eating different foods.

Gather These Materials
• staple remover • 2 cotton balls • 2 leaves • 2 seeds • 2 stones with flat sides

Follow This Procedure
1. Use a chart like the one shown to record your observations. Do each step with care so that you do not injure your fingers.
2. Imagine that the sharp points on the staple remover are sharp canine teeth. Pretend a cotton ball is a piece of meat. Use the staple remover to grab and tear the cotton ball. Record what happens.
3. Use the staple remover to bite and chew a leaf. Record what happens.
4. Use the staple remover to try to bite and chew a seed. Record what happens.
5. Pretend that the two rocks are two large, flat teeth called molars. Place a cotton ball between the flat sides of the molars and grind the stones back and forth. Record what happens.
6. Place a leaf between the molars and grind the stones back and forth. Record what happens.
7. Place a seed between the molars and grind. Record what happens.

Record Your Results

	Cotton ball (meat)	Leaf	Seed
Staple remover (canine teeth)			
Stones (molars)			

State Your Conclusion
1. Which kind of teeth are better for eating meat, for eating leaves, and for eating seeds?
2. Which kind of teeth does a herbivore not need?

Use What You Learned
You have learned that people are omnivores. Which of these 2 kinds of teeth do you have? How do they help you eat your food?

71

3 What Is a Food Chain?

LESSON GOALS

You will learn
- the way energy and materials pass through a food chain on land.
- the way energy and materials pass through an ocean food chain.

food chain, the path energy and materials take in a community.

All the plants, animals, and other living things that live together in one place make up a community. In all communities, producers make food. Animals eat the producers or other animals. Even animals that only eat other animals depend on producers. The animals they eat use producers for food. Energy and materials are passed from one living thing to another. The path energy and materials take through a community is a **food chain.**

A Food Chain on Land

All living things are parts of food chains. Look at the grasshopper in the food chain in the pictures below and on the next page. By eating the leaves of plants, the grasshopper takes in energy and materials stored in the leaves. After a while, a toad catches and eats the grasshopper. The toad takes in energy and materials stored in the grasshopper.

A food chain

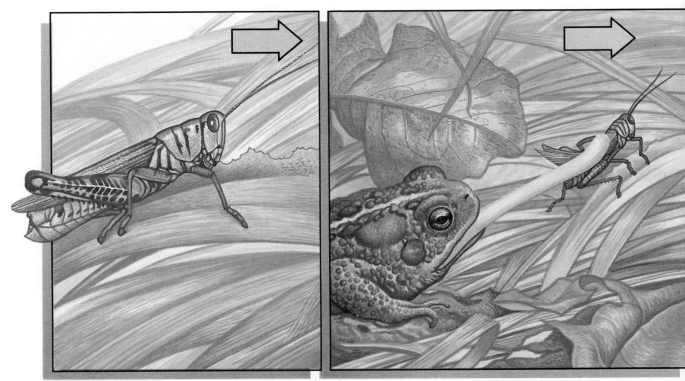

Then a snake takes in energy and materials by eating the toad. A hawk takes in energy and materials when it eats the snake. Energy and materials have passed from the plant to the hawk.

An animal that hunts and kills another animal for food is a **predator.** The snake is a predator. What other animals in the food chain in the picture are predators? Animals that predators hunt are **prey.** The toad is the prey. Notice that an animal can be a predator and prey. The snake is a predator of the toad and prey for the hawk.

In time, the hawk and other living things will die. Another kind of consumer gets energy and materials from the dead hawk. Consumers that get energy and materials from dead plants and animals are **decomposers.** Mushrooms and some bacteria are decomposers. They put the materials stored in the dead plants and animals back into the soil, air, and water. Green plants take in these materials and put them back into a food chain.

predator (pred′ə tər), a consumer that hunts, kills, and eats other animals.

prey (prā), the animal that predators hunt and eat.

decomposer (dē′kəm pō′zər), a consumer that puts materials from dead plants and animals back into soil, air, and water.

An Ocean Food Chain

An ocean food chain is like a land food chain. It begins with producers. Find the tiny living things in the bottom picture. They are so small, you can only see them through a microscope. They are **algae.** Many kinds of algae have only one cell. Other kinds of algae have many cells and look like large plants. Algae are the producers of the ocean. Like land producers, algae can trap light energy from the sun and use it to make sugars.

A herbivore, such as a small fish, eats the producers. The herbivores in the middle picture are tiny fish called anchovies. These fish eat the algae.

Then a carnivore eats the herbivore. The carnivore in the top picture is a sea lion. It eats the fish. The carnivore in an ocean food chain could also be a larger fish. This fish might be eaten by an even larger fish. What do you think decomposers do in an ocean food chain?

algae (al′jē), a group of producers that live in oceans and other water.

Sea lion

Fish

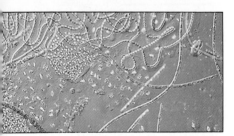
Algae

Lesson Review

1. How does a carnivore get energy?
2. What is the first kind of living thing in an ocean food chain?
3. **Challenge!** Most algae float near the surface of the oceans or grow in shallow water where sunlight is brightest. What might happen if these algae sank to the bottom of the ocean where no sunlight could reach?

Study on your own, pages 380–381.

FIND OUT ON YOUR OWN

Use an encyclopedia to find out what a scavenger is. Find out what a scavenger does in a food chain. Choose one scavenger, such as a crow or vulture, and make a poster of a food chain it belongs to.

Making Models of Food Chains

Purpose
Make models of food chains.

Gather These Materials
• 10 file cards • paper punch • string
• scissors

Follow This Procedure
1. Use a table like the one shown to record your results.
2. Write each of the following plant and animal names on its own file card: grass, garter snake, squirrel, mouse, human, acorn, corn, hawk, fox, cow.
3. Punch a hole in the top and the bottom of each card. Be careful when using the paper punch so that you do not pinch a finger.
4. Put the 3 cards with plants on a desk or table.
5. Above each plant card, place a herbivore that might eat that plant.
6. Above each herbivore, place a carnivore that might eat the herbivore.
7. Put the 1 card you have left above whatever it might eat.
8. Tie each card to the card above it using string. You have made 3 food chains. Record these food chains in your table.

Record Your Results

Food chain 1	Food chain 2	Food chain 3

State Your Conclusion
1. How are the food chains alike?
2. How are the food chains different?

Use What You Learned
How would you change your 3 food chains if you took the grass away but kept all the animals?

4 What Is a Food Web?

LESSON GOALS

You will learn
• how the members of a food web depend on each other.
• some natural changes in a food web.
• how people can change a food web.

food web, the flow of energy and materials through food chains that are connected.

What foods have you eaten during the past two days? You might have eaten many different foods. Most animals also eat different foods. Owls might eat mice, snakes, and moles. Foxes might eat different kinds of birds, rabbits, and snakes. Because most animals eat more than one food, most animals belong to more than one food chain.

A Food Web

All the food chains that are connected in a community make up a **food web.** The pictures on the next page show how some food chains fit together to make a simple food web. Many food webs would have more food chains in them. For example, wolves eat more animals than just raccoons. Hawks eat more than just snakes.

The arrows show the direction that energy and materials are being passed. You can find the food chains that make up this food web by starting with the plants. Then follow an arrow from the plants to an animal. Follow an arrow from that animal to the next animal. When the arrows end, you have reached the end of one food chain.

Use your finger to trace the food chain that has plants, grasshoppers, raccoons, and wolves. Trace the food chain that is made up of plants, grasshoppers, toads, snakes, and hawks. What other consumer might eat the toad? What other food chain has snakes in it?

Notice how each chain in the food web is connected in some way to the other food chains. Each part of the food web depends on the other parts. If one part of the web changes, the rest of the web changes in some way. All parts of the food web depend on decomposers to return materials from dead organisms to the soil, air, and water.

A Food Web

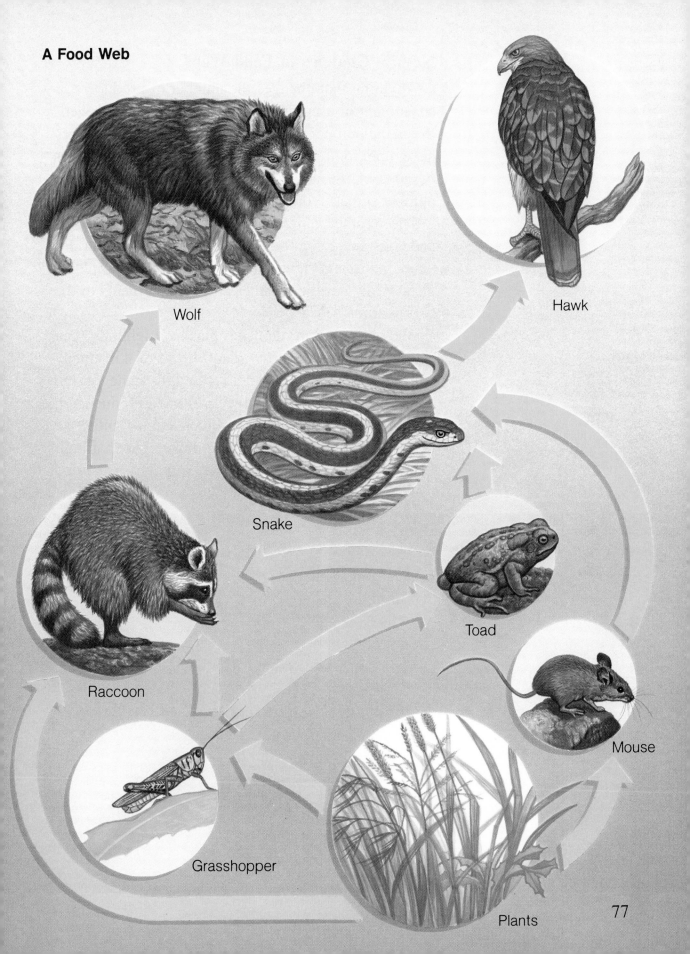

Wolf

Hawk

Snake

Raccoon

Toad

Mouse

Grasshopper

Plants

77

Natural Changes in Food Webs

Anything that changes the number of producers or consumers in a community can change a food web. When the number of producers gets larger, herbivores have more food. The number of herbivores gets larger because of the added food. How do you think the number of carnivores would change?

The weather can change the number of producers and consumers in a food web. Many days of the right temperature and right amount of rain can help plants grow. How has the weather affected the plants in the two pictures below?

Bad storms can damage plants. Lightning can cause fires that destroy plant life and kill many animals. Floods or sickness can kill some of the plants or animals in a food web. If most producers in a community are killed, herbivores must move or they will die. If most herbivores move or are harmed, many carnivores must also move or die. The food web changes greatly.

Zebras

How People Can Change Food Webs

People can change food webs in many ways. Taking trees out of a community is one way people change food webs. Animals that needed the trees for homes or food have to move away. The food web in the community will change.

Sometimes people drain off water and build up the land. The picture shows an area of water and land. Notice that people have built up an area for farmland. If the adding of farmland continues, the plants and animals that live in the water and the land around it can no longer live there. Then the predators that depend on these animals must move or they will die.

People also can change food webs when they add things to a community. **Pollution** happens when people add harmful substances to water, air, or soil. Water pollution can harm animals living in a stream. Animals that eat or drink from the stream are also harmed. Predators that depend on animals from the stream lose their food supply.

SCIENCE IN YOUR LIFE

Many years ago, people took European rabbits to Australia. Many rabbits were kept as pets, but others were turned loose or escaped. The rabbits had no predators, so the number of rabbits grew very large. The rabbits destroyed people's crops. The rabbits that were brought for people to enjoy became a problem.

pollution (pə lü′shən), the addition of harmful substances to a community.

Farmland in a marsh

79

Now people know that they depend on food webs. Scientists study food webs to find ways people can protect them. One way to help is to plant trees to take the place of trees that are cut down. The woman in the picture is taking care of trees growing in a forestry nursery. While the trees below are small, they are protected from animals eating them. Other people work to lower the amount of pollution added to communities.

Trees in a forestry nursery

Lesson Review

1. What is a food web?
2. How can weather change a food web?
3. What are some ways that people can change a food web?
4. **Challenge!** How might adding a large number of carnivores to a community change the food web?

Study on your own, pages 380–381.

FIND OUT ON YOUR OWN

Forest fires can destroy a community's food web. However, forest fires can be helpful to some plants. Look in an encyclopedia or book about nature to find out how. You might look under the words *forestry* and *forest fires*. Write a paragraph about what you find.

Saving Wild Birds

When Dr. George Archibald teaches people about cranes, he tells them how special these water birds are. Cranes are the tallest birds that fly. Their voices can be heard kilometers away. They can fly for long distances. People have even seen cranes flying over Mount Everest, the highest mountain in the world.

Cranes are special for another reason. Not many cranes are left in the world. The wetlands where they nest are being drained to make farms. Many cranes have been killed by hunters. Without help, cranes might become extinct—or no longer exist. No cranes would be seen alive ever again. Of the fifteen kinds of cranes, seven are endangered. They are in danger of becoming extinct.

George Archibald runs a center in Baraboo, Wisconsin, for the protection of cranes. A crane is following Dr. Archibald in the picture. Dr. Archibald travels all over the world to collect cranes. He brings them back to Wisconsin, where the cranes can raise their young safely. Later, the cranes can be returned to the wild. Dr. Archibald also helps people in other countries learn how to protect cranes.

What Do You Think?

1. What other ways can you think of to save and protect cranes?
2. What would happen to other organisms in a crane's food web if that kind of crane became extinct?

Skills for Solving Problems

Using Metric Grids and Bar Graphs

Problem: How much does a caterpillar eat in four days?

Part A. Using a Metric Grid to Collect Information

1. A metric grid has two sets of parallel lines. One set goes from the top of the grid to the bottom. The other set goes from side to side. On the grids below, each line is 1 cm away from the next line. Notice how the lines make squares. Each square measures 1 cm on a side, or 1 square cm. Two squares are 2 square cm. How many square cm would three squares make?

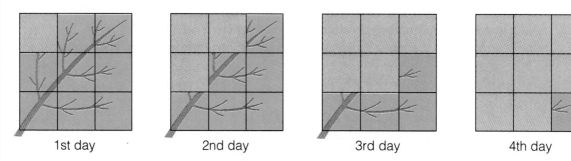

1st day   2nd day   3rd day   4th day

2. The pictures show a leaf that is eaten by a caterpillar for four days. The green squares show how much of the leaf was left each day after the caterpillar finished eating. How many square centimeters did the caterpillar eat by the end of the first day? the second day? the third day? the fourth day?

Part B. Using a Bar Graph to Organize and Interpret Information

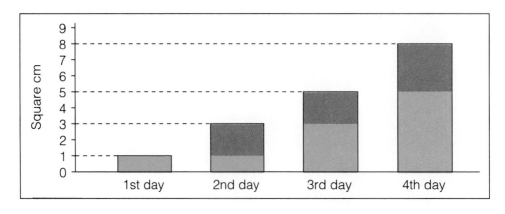

82

3. This bar graph organizes the information about how much a caterpillar eats. What do the numbers on the left of the graph stand for?

4. The first bar tells how much the caterpillar ate the first day. Trace with your finger from the top of the bar to the line at the left of the graph. The first bar stands for 1 square cm. What does the second bar stand for? What do the third and fourth bars stand for?

5. Each bar shows the total that the caterpillar ate that day and the previous days. How much had the caterpillar eaten by the end of the fourth day?

6. On which day did the caterpillar eat the most? To find out, measure the difference in the number of cm between each bar and the bar to its left.

Part C. Using a Metric Grid and a Bar Graph to Solve a Problem

Problem: How much does an inchworm eat in eight days?

7. The pictures show a leaf that is eaten by an inchworm for eight days. Use the pictures to collect the information you need to solve the problem. Make a bar graph like the one in Part B to organize your information.

8. Look at your bar graph. How much did the inchworm eat by the end of the second day?

9. How much did the inchworm eat in eight days? During which days did the inchworm eat the most?

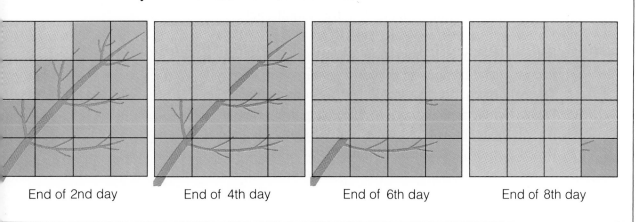

End of 2nd day   End of 4th day   End of 6th day   End of 8th day

Chapter 3 Review

☑ Chapter Main Ideas

Lesson 1 • Green plants trap light energy and use it to change carbon dioxide and water into sugar. • Plants make or produce the food that animals eat.

Lesson 2 • Animals must eat or consume plants and other animals. • Herbivores eat producers. • Carnivores only eat other consumers. • Omnivores eat producers and other consumers.

Lesson 3 • In a food chain, energy passes from the sun to producers. • Energy and materials pass from the producers to consumers. • Decomposers put materials back into the soil, air, and water.

Lesson 4 • Food chains in a community are connected to make a food web. • Anything that changes the number of producers or consumers changes the food web. • People change food webs.

☑ Reviewing Science Words

algae	decomposer	photosynthesis
carbon dioxide	food chain	pollution
carnivore	food web	predator
chlorophyll	herbivore	prey
consumer	omnivore	producer

Copy each sentence. Fill in the blank with the correct word or words from the list.

1. ▦ happens when people add harmful substances to water.
2. Any living thing that depends on a producer for food is a ▦.
3. A gas that plants need to make sugar is ▦.
4. An animal that is hunted and killed for food is the ▦.
5. ▦ is the material in plants that traps light energy.
6. The producers of the oceans are ▦.
7. Because it only eats other animals, a wolf is a ▦.
8. Food chains that are connected in a community make up a ▦.
9. The path of energy and materials in a community is a ▦.
10. Plants can use light energy to make sugars by carrying on ▦.
11. A ▦ is an animal that hunts and kills other animals for food.
12. Because it only eats plants, a horse is a ▦.
13. A consumer that uses dead plants and animals for food is a ▦.

14. Because it eats plants and animals, a bear is an ▒ .
15. A living thing that can use sunlight to make sugars is a ▒ .

☑ Reviewing What You Learned

Write the letter of the best answer.
1. Plants use light energy to make sugar from water and
   (a) oxygen.   (b) sunlight.   (c) carbon dioxide.   (d) chlorophyll.
2. What kind of consumer puts materials stored in dead plants back into the soil?
   (a) decomposer   (b) carnivore   (c) herbivore   (d) producer
3. All living things that use light energy and make sugars are
   (a) plants.   (b) producers.   (c) algae.   (d) consumers.
4. All living things that depend on producers for food are
   (a) herbivores.   (b) consumers.   (c) predators.   (d) prey.
5. What do plants have that traps sunlight?
   (a) vein   (b) hole   (c) chlorophyll   (d) carbon dioxide
6. Toads and raccoons eating grasshoppers are part of
   (a) a land food chain.   (c) pollution.
   (b) an ocean food chain.   (d) a food web.

☑ Interpreting What You Learned

Write a short answer for each question or statement.
1. How do plants get the energy and materials they need?
2. What might happen in a food web if the number of carnivores got larger?
3. List the following in the order that energy flows: herbivore, producer, carnivore.
4. How are herbivores, carnivores, and omnivores alike?
5. How does a food chain depend on decomposers?

☑ Extending Your Thinking

Write a paragraph to answer each question.
1. How might a very cold winter with a large amount of snow change a food web?
2. Pretend that you are going to build a house in a place that has many trees and a pond. What could you do to cause the least amount of change in the food web?

• For further review, use Study Guide pages 380–381.

Animal and Plant Adaptations

Look among the flowers in the picture to find the insect. This ambush bug blends in with the goldenrod. The shape and color of the insect's body make it hard to see. How can looking like the flowers help the ambush bug catch food?

Introducing the Chapter

The insect in the picture on page 86 can catch food better because it is hard to see. In the activity below, you will learn how some insects are protected from their predators. In this chapter, you will learn what animals and plants need to live. You will also learn how animals and plants are suited to life in their surroundings.

Coloring Insects to Protect Them

You are going to make four insects and try to hide them from your partners. Look around the room to find four places you want to hide your insects. You should be able to reach these places easily without standing on anything. The places also should be easy to see—not hidden behind or underneath an object.

Cut an index card into four equal pieces. These four pieces will be your insects. Now color each piece so that it will be hard for your partners to see.

Ask your partners to close their eyes. Then tape your insects in the four places you have chosen. Have your partners open their eyes and look for the insects. Give them thirty seconds to find the insects. Ask your partners what made your insects easy or hard to find.

Talk About It
1. How did you color your insects to try to hide them?
2. How could you change your insects to hide them better?

1 How Do Adaptations Help Animals and Plants Survive?

LESSON GOALS

You will learn
- the needs animals and plants must meet to survive.
- what an adaptation is.
- how different adaptations help living things meet their needs.

The fish in the pictures look very different. The flame angelfish has stripes. The clown triggerfish has large circles. The scorpionfish does not even look like a fish. Try to find its eye and mouth. Each fish's body helps the fish meet its needs.

What Animals and Plants Need

What do animals need to live? You might have thought of food first. Animals also need oxygen and water. They need space to live in and protection from animals that might eat them.

Plants need air and water. They also need to have space to grow. You have learned in Chapter 3 that plants have a special need. They need energy from sunlight to make a simple sugar.

A flame angelfish, scorpionfish, and clown triggerfish

What an Adaptation Is

Living things meet their needs in different ways. Living things in the dry desert must save every bit of water they can get. Fish get plenty of water. Their gills take in oxygen from the water. The picture shows how water moves through a fish's gills.

An animal's body parts and the parts of plants are structures. How a living thing responds to its surroundings is behavior. Any structure or behavior that helps a living thing live in its surroundings is an **adaptation.** Gills are an adaptation to living in water. The colors of fish and the shapes of their bodies are adaptations, too. Notice the different colors and shapes of the fish on these two pages. The structures and behaviors that help living things in the desert save water are also adaptations. Adaptations help living things meet their needs.

adaptation
(ad/ap tā/shən), a structure or behavior that helps a living thing live in its surroundings.

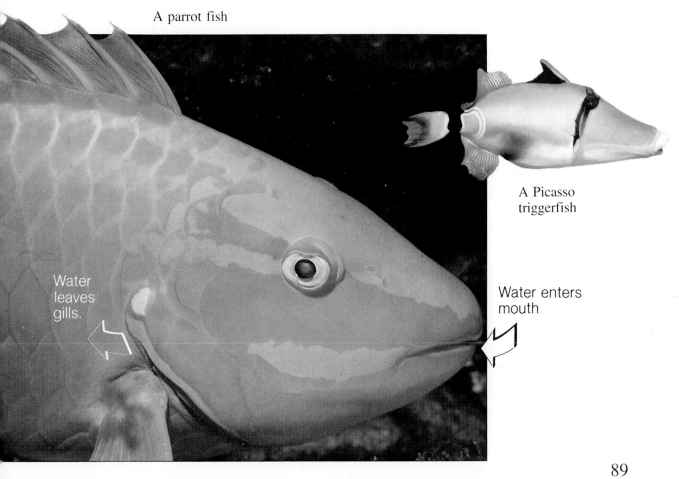

A parrot fish

A Picasso triggerfish

Water leaves gills.

Water enters mouth

How Adaptations Meet Needs

Different kinds of adaptations help fish meet their needs. The shark below has a strong body and tail that help it swim quickly. The shark's short, sharp teeth make it suited to catch and eat other fish.

Many fish with bright colors live near coral reefs. The bright colors of the fish are an adaptation to their surroundings. Some fish's bright colors are a warning to stay away. These fish have sharp spines or teeth to protect themselves. Other fish use their color to say "come near." These fish clean other fish. The cleaner fish removes living things growing on other fish that could make these fish sick.

Many fish have adaptations that protect them from predators. The puffer in the picture on the left behaves in a certain way when it is attacked by another fish. Notice in the picture on the right that the puffer blows itself up into a thorny ball. It becomes too big for another fish to swallow.

A shark

A puffer

Plants have adaptations, too. To make sugar, a plant's leaves need energy from sunlight. Plants also grow toward sunlight. This adaptation helps the leaves get the most energy from sunlight to make the most sugar.

Some plants have adaptations that help protect them from animals. Thorns keep away animals that might eat a plant or its leaves. Some plants make poisons that can make some animals sick or even die. Animals learn to stay away from these plants. People learn to stay away from plants like the poison ivy in the picture. If you touch poison ivy, your skin might break out in a rash.

Some plants produce substances that can be irritating or harmful to animals that try to eat the plants. Some of these substances include peppercorns, quinine, and castor oil. However, people have found these substances useful. For example, quinine is made into a medicine.

Poison ivy

Lesson Review

1. What do animals and plants need to survive?
2. What is an adaptation?
3. How does growing toward sunlight help plants?
4. **Challenge!** What are some adaptations animals have for living on land?

Study on your own, pages 382–383.

A penguin

Penguins, like the one above, have adaptations for living in the cold waters near the South Pole, or Antartica. Use encyclopedias or other books in the library to find out about adaptations of penguins. Draw a poster of a penguin and list some of the penguin's adaptations.

FIND OUT ON YOUR OWN

91

2 How Are Animals Adapted to Their Environment?

LESSON GOALS

You will learn
- some adaptations animals have for getting food and water.
- some adaptations animals have for protecting themselves.
- some animal behaviors that are adaptations.

adapted (ə dapt′ed), made fit to live under certain conditions.

A hawk with food

Many animals spend most of their time searching for food. They also try to escape being eaten by other animals. Different animals have different adaptations that help them get food. Other adaptations help keep animals from being caught and eaten.

Adaptations for Getting Food and Water

Animals that eat meat are **adapted** to find and catch the animals they eat. How is a shark adapted to catch and eat other animals? A hawk is also adapted to catch and eat animals. The hawk's strong wings carry it high into the sky where it can look for food on the ground. The hawk's sharp eyesight allows it to see for long distances. It can see a field mouse from high in the sky. Notice the hawk's sharp claws and strong, hooked beak. They help it catch and eat a field mouse and other animals, such as a rabbit.

Some animals set traps and wait for their food to come to them. Spiders make webs of sticky threads. Find the insect caught in the web. This spider will use the insect for food.

A spider with food

The beaks, or bills, of many birds are adapted to help the birds catch and eat food. Compare the beaks in the pictures. The woodpecker hammers its sharp beak into tree trunks to find insects. The cardinal's short, thick beak helps it break open seeds. The pelican uses its beak to catch fish. A hummingbird has a long, thin beak that reaches deep into flowers to get nectar. A spoonbill takes up mud from pond bottoms in its wide beak.

Different kinds of animals have special adaptations that allow them to get their food. An anteater often tears ant nests apart with its long, sharp claws. Then the anteater uses its long, sticky tongue to draw the ants into its long, tubelike snout. An elephant uses its long trunk to gather clumps of grass and leaves and twigs from trees. The elephant also uses its trunk to gather water. How does the elephant get the food and water to its mouth?

Animals living in hot, dry deserts get most of their water from the food they eat. The desert wood rat gets the water it needs from the juicy stems, leaves, and roots of desert plants. The desert wood rat's body is adapted to keep and use almost all the water it gets.

A woodpecker   A cardinal   A pelican

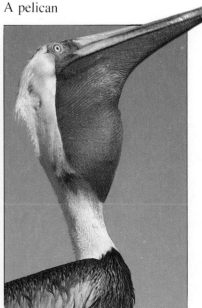

Adaptations for Protection

Many adaptations keep animals from being eaten. Most of these adaptations help the animals run away, hide, or fight.

Many animals that run away have good sight and hearing. A rabbit has large ears. Its ears help the rabbit hear a fox or other predator coming. Then the rabbit can run quickly to a safe place.

Many animals hide from their predators. They are adapted to look like their surroundings. The shape of some animals helps them hide. Notice the insect in the picture on the left. This katydid looks like a leaf. How does looking like a leaf help protect this insect from being eaten?

The colors or patterns of some animals help protect them. This **protective coloration** helps the animals hide from their predators. Find the flounder in the picture. It spends most of its life on the ocean floor. The colors of its upper side change to match the background of its surroundings. What the flounder looks like helps it escape being eaten. The flounder's behavior also is an adaptation. The flounder lies very still and blends into its background.

A katydid

A flounder

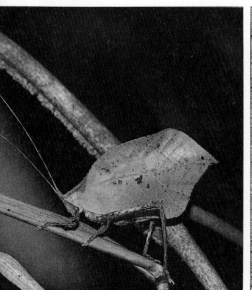

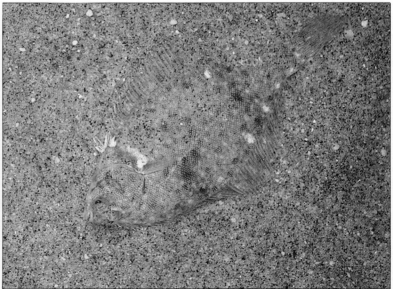

Some animals change color with the seasons. The snowshoe rabbit is brown during summer. It turns white during winter. How does the white winter coat of the snowshoe rabbit in the picture protect it from predators?

Most animals try to fight if an enemy traps them. The leader of a herd of zebras will attack a hyena that is chasing the herd. The zebra will bite with its strong teeth and kick with its powerful hoofs.

The porcupine in the picture protects itself by curling up into a ball. Not many animals would attack a ball of sharp spines. Hard plates cover and protect the body of the armadillo in the picture. Few animals could bite through these hard plates.

Some animals use poisons to defend themselves. Dragonfish have sharp-pointed fins coated with poison. A rattlesnake uses its sharp fangs in hunting food and to protect itself. When the snake strikes another animal, it sends poison through its fangs.

A porcupine

A snowshoe rabbit

An armadillo

Adaptations in Behavior

migration (mī grā′shən), movement from one place to another when the seasons change.

Behaviors that help animals survive are also adaptations. When a toad sees a snake, the toad can fill its lungs with air. It puffs itself up so it looks larger. This behavior sometimes stops the snake from swallowing the toad. Toads that behave this way are more likely to live. Toads behave this way even if they have never seen another toad behave this way.

Some behaviors help animals live through the winter. **Migration** is movement to new places when seasons change. Millions of monarch butterflies fly from parts of the United States and Canada to mountains in Mexico for the winter. The butterflies below have reached their winter home in Mexico. You might have seen Canada geese flying south for the winter. They fly south where ponds do not freeze. Whales and elk also migrate.

Monarch butterflies

96

Some animals **hibernate,** or go into a deep sleep through cold winters. A hibernating animal uses little energy and does not move or eat. It uses stored body fat as food. A woodchuck hibernates during the cold winter.

The toad in the picture lives in a desert in Arizona. During a rainy season, the toad stays buried in mud during the day and comes out at night to eat. At the end of a short rainy season, the toad digs itself deep into the ground. It stays there in a dormant state until the next rainy season.

hibernate (hī′bər nāt), to spend the winter in a state in which the body greatly slows down.

A toad

Lesson Review
1. What are two adaptations animals use to get food?
2. What adaptations help protect animals?
3. What behaviors help animals?
4. **Challenge!** Find the eyes of the flounder in the picture on page 94. How could their location help the flounder survive?

Study on your own, pages 382–383.

Draw an imaginary animal that has adaptations for getting food and for protecting itself from predators and the weather. Tell your classmates about your animal's adaptations.

FIND OUT
ON YOUR OWN

ACTIVITY

Studying Protective Coloration

Purpose

Infer how the color of an animal affects its safety.

Gather These Materials

• meter stick • 4 large nails • piece of string (about 9 meters long) • 25 red wooden toothpicks • 25 green wooden toothpicks • watch or clock with a second hand

Follow This Procedure

1. Use a chart like the one shown to record your observations.
2. Go outside to a grassy area.
3. Measure a square that is 1 meter long on each side. Stick a nail into the ground at each corner of the square.
4. Wrap the string around the nails to make the edges of the square as shown in the picture.
5. Ask your partner to face away from the square. Scatter the red and green toothpicks in the square.
6. Tell your partner to turn around and find as many toothpicks as she or he can. After 30 seconds tell your partner to stop looking for toothpicks.
7. Count the number of red toothpicks and green toothpicks your partner found. Record these numbers in the chart.
8. Switch places with your partner and repeat steps 5–7.

Record Your Results

Number of Toothpicks Picked Up

	Red	Green
Your partner		
You		

State Your Conclusion

1. Did you and your partner find more red toothpicks or more green toothpicks?
2. How can you explain the difference in the numbers of red toothpicks and green toothpicks you and your partner found?

Use What You Learned

Suppose the toothpicks were insects. How could the insects' color help protect them from birds that eat insects? If the insects lived in the grass, which color insect would be least likely to be eaten?

Living With Chimpanzees in the Wild

In 1960, the woman in the picture went to live near a group of chimpanzees in the wild in Africa. Jane Goodall hoped that by living near them, she would be able to study how they behaved. Many months went by before they would let her come near them. She tried to follow them quietly and calmly. Finally, they began to trust her. She was able to watch how chimpanzees, like the ones below, lived and to see things that no one had ever seen before.

One day, Jane Goodall was watching a chimp she had named David Graybeard. She saw him tear the leaves from a long twig. Then he poked the twig into a termite's nest. When he pulled the stem out, it was covered with termites. David Graybeard was making and using a tool to find food! This adaptation surprised Jane Goodall. Until then, scientists thought that only humans made and used tools.

Jane Goodall studied many kinds of adaptations. She observed how the chimps are adapted to move through the forests. With their long, strong arms, they swing from one tree branch to another. She observed that they do not like to get their feet wet, so they swing across streams. When they walk on the ground, they walk on their hands and feet. They lean on their knuckles, not on the palms of their hands. In this way, their hands are protected.

What Jane Goodall learned about chimpanzees helps other people know how to care for chimps in zoos and to protect them in the wild. Her studies also help scientists understand more about animal behavior.

What Do You Think?

1. How are chimps adapted to move through forests?
2. Why do you think it was important to Jane Goodall to study chimps in the wild rather than in a zoo?

3 How Are Plants Adapted to Their Environment?

LESSON GOALS

You will learn
- ways plants get and keep water.
- how some plants adapt to cold.
- adaptations some plants have for getting sunlight.

nitrogen (nī′trə jən), a mineral that plants need to grow.

Plants grow in many types of places. Some places are hot. Some places are cold. Other places are dry or wet. Plants growing in different places have different needs. Their adaptations help them meet their needs.

The pitcher plant in the picture grows in wet places. The soil in these places does not have enough of a certain mineral the pitcher plant needs. This mineral is **nitrogen.** The pitcher plant has adaptations that help it get nitrogen. Hairs on the inside leaves point down. An insect that lands on the leaves cannot move up against the hairs. The insect falls into a pool of liquid at the base of the plant. The insect drowns and is digested by the plant. The insect's body gives the pitcher plant the nitrogen it needs.

Adaptations for Getting and Keeping Water

Some plants grow in places that are cold all year long. These places are often high on a mountain side. Plants growing in these places are called alpine plants. Alpine plants have special adaptations for getting and keeping water. Most of the water high in the mountains is frozen as snow. These plants must gather as much water as they can on a warm day when the snow melts. The plants' shallow, spreading roots gather water from melted snow. The stems and the leaves of alpine plants are covered with a coat of wax and fine hairs. The coat of wax and the fine hairs help keep water from escaping from the plants.

Alpine plants are adapted to live in cold places. These plants grow close to the ground. They also grow close to one another. Growing these ways helps the plants survive the strong, cold mountain winds.

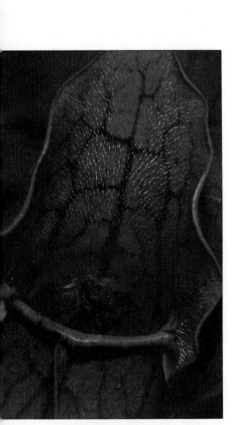

A pitcher plant

Plants growing in deserts have special adaptations for getting and storing water. These plants have shallow, spreading roots to take in large amounts of water when it does rain. These plants store the water in their stems and leaves. The cactus in the picture stores water in its stem. The stem is like a vase that holds water.

Desert plants also have adaptations for keeping the water they take in. Their stems and leaves have a coat of wax that keeps the water from escaping. Some desert plants do not have leaves as you know them. These plants, like the cactus, have spines. A spine is a type of leaf that does not let water escape through it.

A cactus

Spines on a cactus

Adaptations for Winter

annual (an′yü əl), a plant that lives only one year.

evergreen, a plant that stays green all year, including firs, spruces, and pines.

Some plants grow in places that have warm summers and cold winters. These plants have adaptations that help them live through the cold, dry winter. Winter is a dry season for plants because water freezes.

If you live in a place with cold winters, you know that some trees lose their leaves in the fall. The tree below will not lose water from its leaves during winter because it lost its leaves. An **evergreen** like the pine trees in the picture does not shed its leaves in winter. The needlelike leaves have a thick covering that stops loss of water.

An **annual** is a plant that lives only for one year. The plant dies at the end of the warm season. Its seeds stay alive through the winter. Seeds can live through the winter because they have only a little water and do not freeze. The seeds sprout in spring. They grow into new plants. Plants like lettuce, pansies, and daisies are annuals.

Trees in winter

102

A plant that can stay alive for many years is a **perennial.** Trees and bushes are perennials. Their woody trunks stay alive through the cold winter. Underground parts help other plants live through the winter. The soil protects them from the cold. The daffodils below bloom in spring. The parts above the ground die after the plants bloom. The underground bulbs, like the one in the picture, live to grow the following spring. Dandelions have a thick, deep root that lives for many years. The parts above the ground die in winter. A new plant can sprout from the root in the spring.

perennial (pə ren′ē əl), a plant that can live two years or more.

A daffodil bulb and daffodils blooming

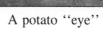

A potato "eye"

The potato in the picture is a stem that grows under the ground. Like most stems, potatoes have buds. These buds are the "eyes" of the potato. They can stay alive under the ground in winter. When the weather gets warmer in the spring, each bud can sprout a new potato plant.

103

Adaptations for Getting Sunlight

Plants growing in thick jungles or forests have adaptations for getting sunlight. Some plants climb to get sunlight. The plant in the picture on the left grows up the side of a tree. You can see the roots of the climber in the middle picture. Some plants climb to the topmost crowns of jungle trees to get sunlight. Climbers are among the longest plants in the world. Other plants, like the ones in the picture on the right, grow on the branches of tall trees to get sunlight. Notice that these plants are blooming.

Plants growing to get sunlight

Lesson Review

1. How is a cactus adapted to get and keep water?
2. How are plants adapted to survive cold winters?
3. How is climbing an important adaptation for some kinds of plants?
4. **Challenge!** Do you think climbing is a behavioral adaptation or a structural adaptation of plants? Explain your answer.

Study on your own, pages 382–383.

FIND OUT ON YOUR OWN

Like orchids, staghorn ferns grow on trees in jungles. Visit a greenhouse that grows house plants, and find a staghorn fern. Ask a greenhouse worker how to care for the staghorn fern. Write a paragraph about what you find out.

Observing Plant Adaptations

Purpose
Observe which plant is best adapted to live in a dry, sunny environment.

Gather These Materials
• 2 large, wide-mouthed jars • centimeter ruler • coarse gravel • sand • small fern • leather gloves • small cactus • plastic spoon • water

Follow This Procedure
1. Use a chart like the one shown to record your observations.
2. Place a layer of gravel, 3 cm deep, on the bottom of each jar. Add a 6-cm layer of sand on top of each layer of gravel. *CAUTION: Handle the jars carefully.*
3. Use the spoon to gently make a hole in the sand in each jar. Plant the fern in one hole and the cactus in the other hole. Wear gloves when touching the cactus. Spoon some sand around each plant to cover the roots.
4. Add two spoonfuls of water to each jar. Set the jars in a sunny spot.
5. Observe how each plant looks every day for five days. Watch for any change in the plants. Record your observations.

Record Your Results

	Fern	Cactus
Day 1		
Day 2		
Day 3		
Day 4		
Day 5		

State Your Conclusion
1. How did each plant look after five days?
2. Which plant is adapted to the environment in the jars? Explain your answer.

Use What You Learned
What might happen to a desert plant if it was planted in a forest?

105

Using Thermometers and Bar Graphs

Problem: How does temperature affect where mealworms will move?

Part A. Using Thermometers to Collect Information

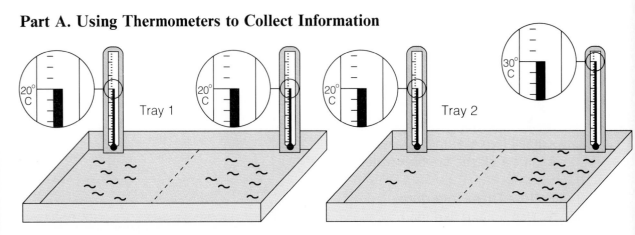

1. The picture on the left shows Tray 1 with mealworms. The thermometers in Tray 1 show the temperature at each end of the tray. Each mark on these thermometers shows one degree C. C stands for Celsius. What is the temperature at each end of Tray 1? How many mealworms are at each end?
2. The picture on the right shows Tray 2 with mealworms. What is the temperature at each end? How many mealworms are at each end?

Part B. Using a Bar Graph to Organize and Interpret Information

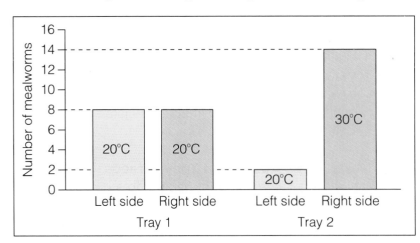

3. The bar graph contains the information you collected in Part A. What do the numbers on the left side of the graph stand for? What do the temperatures in the graph stand for?
4. The first two bars show how many mealworms were at each end of Tray 1. Put your finger at the top of each of these two bars and move it across to the scale on the left. How many mealworms were at each end?
5. Look at the bars for Tray 2. How many mealworms were at each end of Tray 2. How does temperature affect where mealworms will move?

Part C. Using Thermometers and Bar Graphs to Solve a Problem

Problem: How does temperature affect how fast mealworms move?

6. Use the pictures below to collect the information you need to solve the problem. What is the temperature of each tray? How far did the mealworm in each tray move in one minute?
7. Make a bar graph similar to the one in Part B to organize your information. Look at your bar graph. Which mealworm moved the farthest in one minute? How does temperature affect how fast mealworms move?

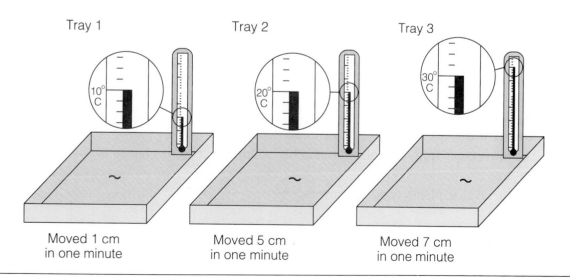

Tray 1   Tray 2   Tray 3

10°C   20°C   30°C

Moved 1 cm in one minute   Moved 5 cm in one minute   Moved 7 cm in one minute

Chapter 4 Review

☑ Chapter Main Ideas

Lesson 1 • Animals and plants have certain needs they must meet to live. • Adaptations are structures or behaviors that help animals meet those needs. • Adaptations help animals find food and protect themselves from predators.

Lesson 2 • Animals have such adaptations as beaks and claws that help them get food. • Most animals have adaptations that help them run away, hide, or fight. • Migration and hibernation are two behaviors that help some animals survive cold winters.

Lesson 3 • Different plants have different adaptations that help them get and keep water. • Different plants have different adaptations that help them live through cold winters. • Plants have adaptations that help them get sunlight.

☑ Reviewing Science Words

adaptation   migration
adapted   nitrogen
annual   perennial
evergreen   protective coloration
hibernate

Copy each sentence. Fill in the blank with the correct word or words from the list.

1. Because a pine tree does not shed its leaves for the winter, it is called an ▓ .
2. Anteaters are ▓ to catching and eating ants.
3. A plant that lives for only one year is an ▓ .
4. Animals that ▓ spend the winter in a deep sleep.
5. An ▓ helps make a living thing suited to its surroundings.
6. Colors and patterns that help an animal blend with its surroundings are an adaptation known as ▓ .
7. A plant that lives for two years or more is a ▓ .
8. The movement from one place to another when the seasons change is ▓ .
9. A mineral that plants need to grow is ▓ .

✔ Reviewing What You Learned

Write the letter of the best answer.

1. The bright colors of some animals help them
   (a) find food. (c) warn other animals.
   (b) hide. (d) live through the winter.
2. Looking like something in the surroundings is a form of
   (a) migration. (c) hibernating.
   (b) protective coloration. (d) adapting for cold.
3. A cactus stores water in its
   (a) shallow roots. (b) root hairs. (c) leaves. (d) stem.
4. Some perennials can live through cold winters because they
   (a) store water. (c) have roots that store food.
   (b) migrate. (d) have underground parts that stay alive.
5. For a plant, climbing is an adaptation for
   (a) getting sunlight. (c) avoiding being eaten.
   (b) keeping water. (d) staying alive in winter.
6. Gills are an adaptation fish have for
   (a) defending themselves. (c) catching food.
   (b) getting oxygen. (d) hibernating.

✔ Interpreting What You Learned

Write a short answer for each question or statement.

1. How are adaptations of desert animals and plants similar?
2. How does migration help animals stay alive?
3. How are desert plants and alpine plants similar?
4. Explain the importance of a plant having its leaves in the sunlight.
5. How does protective coloration help an animal stay alive?
6. How do annuals make new plants in the spring if all the plants die at the end of the warm season?

✔ Extending Your Thinking

Write a paragraph to answer each question.

1. Whales are mammals that must breathe oxygen from the air and must keep warm. They live their whole lives in the water. What adaptations might they have to meet their needs?
2. Some fish have light-colored scales on their stomachs and dark scales on their backs. How might this protective coloration help these fish?

• For further review, use Study Guide pages 382–383.

Careers

If you are like most people, you probably love to go to the zoo. Perhaps you have a favorite zoo that you visit again and again. A zoo can be an exciting place to work as well as to visit.

Zoo designers help plan new zoos and improve older zoos. They must study the natural surroundings of all animals that will live in the zoo. Then, they try to design a setting for each animal that will be like its natural home. A zoo designer must also know about each animal's habits. Some animals jump or fly. Some animals sleep in a cave or swim in a pond. Planning a zoo to fit an animal's habits helps keep the animal happy and healthy.

Zoo veterinarians also help keep the animals healthy. They examine and treat sick or injured animals. Sometimes, a zoo veterinarian must operate on an animal to make it well again.

Zoo veterinarians work closely with **animal nutritionists.** The nutritionist must know what foods each animal needs to stay healthy. He or she plans meals for the animals and orders the huge amounts of food needed.

Zoo keepers, like the woman in the picture on the left, often become trusted friends of the animals. They clean the exhibits and feed the animals. Zoo keepers also keep records of what the animals do each day.

To become a zoo designer, veterinarian, or animal nutritionist, you must graduate from college and then take more special training. Zoo keepers can learn their skills on the job.

Some people who work at zoos do not work with animals at all. A **landscape architect,** like the man in the picture, designs outdoor areas to make them beautiful and useful. He or she might work with the zoo designer. A **park management technician** takes care of the lawn, trees, and other plants. He or she might work in a large zoo or a park.

Landscape architects study in college for four or five years. To become a park management technician, you need to go to college for two years.

Tracking Devices

The Arctic tern holds the record in the animal world for long-distance travel. Each year, these birds fly 16,000 kilometers from their home near the North Pole to the Antarctic. Then, six months later, they fly the same distance back.

Scientists study animal movements like these for many reasons. Some animals are endangered —or dying out. By studying the habits of these animals, people can help keep them alive. Park rangers might want to follow the movements of grizzly bears to see how many live in Yellowstone National Park. Then, the rangers will know better how to protect the bears. Also, scientists hope to learn more about the ways animals live, such as how far they travel, and when they sleep.

Scientists have many ways of keeping track of animals. One way involves the use of radio signals to follow an animal's movement. Here is how the system works.

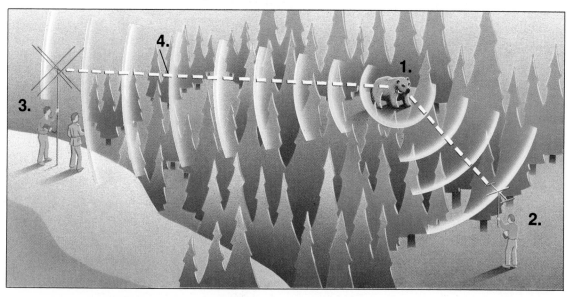

1 A small radio transmitter is attached to the animal. The radio often weighs no more than 25 grams. The radio sends out signals in all directions.

2 Scientists use an antenna to listen for the radio signals. They rotate the antenna until the signals are loudest. Then, the antenna will be pointing at the animal. The louder the signals are, the closer the animal is.

3 Sometimes the antennas are simply stuck in the ground. The higher in the air they are, the farther away they can pick up the radio signals. At other times, one antenna is carried on a car or truck. The scientists can follow the animal while they listen to the radio signals in the truck.

4 Sometimes two antennas are used. Then the scientists draw an imaginary line from each antenna toward the animal. The place where the two lines cross is the place where they can find the animal.

Unit 1 Review

Complete the Sentence

Fill in the blank with the correct word or words from the list.

adapted   ovary
chlorophyll producers
classify   reflexes
evergreens   response
hibernates   stamens
nitrogen   symbiosis
omnivores

1. Pollen is made by the ____ of a flower.
2. Predators are ____ to catch the animals they eat.
3. The cleaner shrimp and the fish it cleans are an example of ____.
4. An animal that ____ uses little energy during its deep sleep.
5. Scientists ____ plants into two large groups.
6. Blinking and other automatic behaviors are ____ that are controlled by nerves.
7. Pine trees are ____ that do not lose their needlelike leaves in the winter.
8. People are ____ because they eat both plants and animals.
9. A ____ is a behavior caused by a stimulus.
10. Plants need the mineral ____ to help them grow.
11. At the bottom of a pistil is the ____ in which seeds form.
12. Plants are ____ because they can use sunlight to make sugars.
13. Plant leaves contain ____, which gives them a green color.

Short Answer

Write a short answer for each question or statement.

1. Describe the major difference between the two types of plants that make seeds.
2. How could a person help fertilize a flowering plant that is grown indoors without insects or wind?
3. Why would you expect baby animals that do not need care from their parents to have many instincts?
4. In what ways do all adults who care for their young act the same?
5. How might an instinct be changed by learning?
6. A living thing grows deep inside a cave. Is it a producer or a consumer? How do you know?
7. Why are decomposers an important part of all food chains?
8. Animals that are poisonous when eaten often are brightly colored. How does this adaptation help them survive?
9. Why would plants that grow in one place have trouble surviving in a different kind of place?

Essay

Write a paragraph for each question or statement.

1. Is the relationship that humans have with their pets an example of symbiosis? Use examples to support your answer.
2. Describe some of the adaptations that people must have to live in places with long, cold winters?

Science Projects

1. Observe a pet's behavior. If you do not have a pet, observe the behavior of a friend's pet. What kinds of things does the pet do? Are the behaviors learned, or are they instincts? How do you know? Write a report of your observations.

2. Use an encyclopedia to find out more about decomposers. Write a paragraph about a decomposer. Tell where the decomposer lives and how it is important to a food chain.

3. An ecosystem is made up of the living and nonliving things in a certain environment. An ecosystem can be as large as the ocean or as small as a flower box. Choose one ecosystem. Then give an example of an animal that lives in the ecosystem. What adaptations does the animal have that makes it suited to live in the ecosystem? Cut out a picture of the animal from an old magazine. If you cannot find a picture, then make a drawing of the animal.

4. Look up the terms *conservation* and *natural resource* in an encyclopedia. Write a definition for each term. Make a list of some ways that people can save natural resources.

Science and Society

Disappearing Wetlands The Barnum Company wants to build a marina on Willow Bay. To do so, it has to drain Van Doorn's Marsh. The Willow Bay Wetlands Group wants to save the marsh. "The marsh has no value," says the president of The Barnum Company. "It may be pretty, but people do not need it." A conservationist disagrees. "The marsh helps control floods," he claims. "It also takes pollutants out of the water." The president replies, "The marina would bring in money and jobs. It has to be built by the water." The conservationist states, "Many plants and animals, including birds from far away, depend on the marsh. They will die if the marsh is filled." What are the arguments for building the marina on the Bay? What are the arguments against building the marina?

Books About Science

From Flower to Flower: Animals and Pollination by Patricia Lauber. Crown, 1987. Learn how different animals pollinate plants.

Ant Cities by Arther Dorros. T. Y. Crowell, 1987. Learn about ants—how they behave and how they live.

Ecosystems and Food Chains by Francene Sabin. Troll Assoc., 1985. Find out about different ecosystems and food chains.

The Seven Sleepers: The Story of Hibernation by Phyllis S. Busch. Macmillan, 1985. Find out how and why animals hibernate and how they survive during their long winter sleep.

Physical Science

The wheels on this train and other trains move people and things from one place to another. You probably depend on wheels often. Bicycles, cars, and even airplanes need wheels.

Wheels are one of the machines that use energy and make people's work easier. In this unit, you will discover different kinds of energy. You also will discover how to measure matter.

SCIENCE IN THE NEWS During the next few weeks, look in newspapers or magazines for stories about how different kinds of machines help people. Also look for news about the kinds of energy that the machines use. Share the news with your class.

Chapter 5   Measuring Matter
Chapter 6   Work and Energy
Chapter 7   Electricity and
            Magnetism
Chapter 8   Light and Sound

Chapter 5

Measuring Matter

A powerful stream of air blows up through the floor in the special flying room in the picture. The stream pushes the people up in the air and holds them there. Although you cannot see air, it is made of matter.

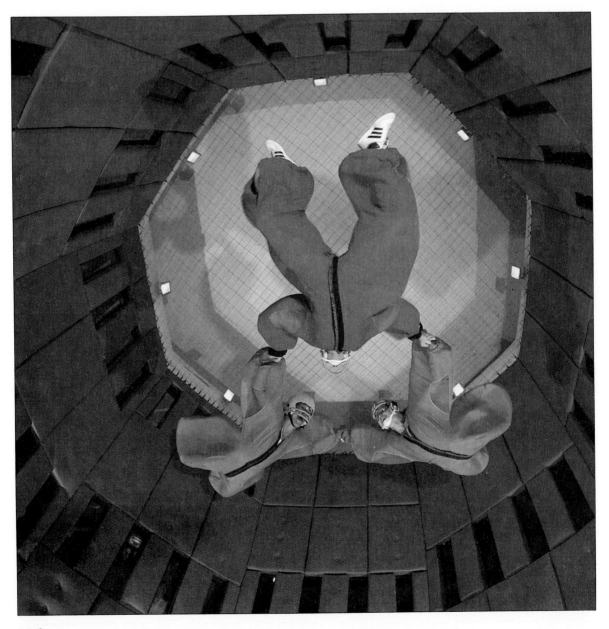

Introducing the Chapter

Matter can be described in many different ways. You might describe some matter by its color or its length. In the activity below, you will learn another way matter can be described. In this chapter, you will learn about the tiny bits that make up matter. You also will learn different ways you can measure matter.

Describing Air

One way you can describe air is that it takes up space. You can show that air takes up space by pouring air from one plastic cup to another.

Fill a large plastic container with enough water so that you can hold a cup completely underwater. Hold one plastic cup under the water to fill it with water. Carefully turn the cup upside-down underwater so that the water stays in the cup.

Hold the second cup upside-down above the water. Keeping the cup upside-down, slowly push it into the water until it is under the water. What is inside the cup?

Move the cups next to each other. Now raise the cup filled with water slightly higher than the cup filled with air. Now pour the air from one cup to the other.

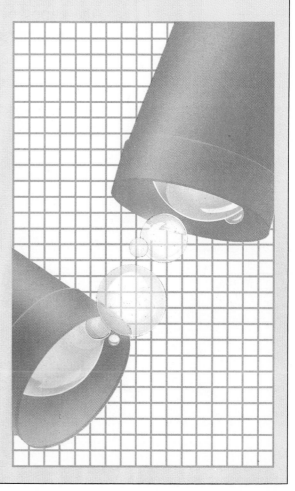

Talk About It
1. What happened to the water in the cup when you poured air into it?
2. What can you tell about air from what you observed?

1 What Is Matter?

LESSON GOALS

You will learn
- two properties of objects made of matter.
- three states of matter.

mass (mas), the amount of material that an object has in it.

volume (vol′yəm), the amount of space that matter takes up.

The puppy has a larger volume and more mass than the kitten does.

Read the title of this lesson. Do you think a word has been left out? Someone might have asked you, "What is *the* matter?" In that question, the word *matter* means "problem." In science, *matter* means something else. This book is made of matter. You are made of matter. Water and food are made of matter. Even the air around you is made of matter.

Mass That Takes Up Space

Anything that takes up space is made of matter. The puppy and kitten in the picture take up space. The glass and the milk on the next page take up space. What takes up space inside the balloons? **Volume** is the amount of space matter takes up. Does the puppy or the kitten have a larger volume?

Anything that has **mass** is made of matter. Mass measures the amount of material an object has in it. The puppy has more mass than the kitten does.

Three States of Matter

You can tell the differences among many kinds of matter. For example, you know if you are drinking milk or tomato juice. They have different colors, for one thing. The color that milk has is a property of milk. A property is something about matter that can be observed and tells you what the matter is like. Another property of milk is that it is a liquid at room temperature. What are some other properties of milk?

The state—or form—that matter has is an important property. Liquid, solid, and gas are three states of matter. You can tell if matter is a solid, liquid, or gas by what its shape and volume are like.

A solid has a certain shape and volume of its own. The glass in the picture is a solid. What are some solids in your classroom?

A liquid has a certain volume but has no shape of its own. A liquid can change shape. How could you change the shape of the milk in the glass in the picture? The plastic bag in the picture holds the milk from the glass. The milk's volume is the same, but its shape changed.

A gas does not have a shape or a volume of its own. Air is made up of different kinds of gases. After you put air in balloons like the ones in the picture, the air takes the shape of the balloon. When you let the air out of a balloon, the gases in the air spread out around you and take up more space.

The air inside the balloons has the same shape and volume as the balloons.

The milk's volume is the same in both containers.

119

When you leave wet clothes on a clothesline in the sun, a change in a state of matter takes place. Heat in the air changes the water in the clothes to water vapor. A liquid changes to a gas. This change in state makes the clothes dry.

Matter changes from one state to another when its temperature changes beyond a certain point. If you freeze a liquid, it becomes a solid. If you boil a liquid, it becomes a gas. The bubbles in the picture of the boiling water are gas escaping from the water. The gas is water vapor. What is water called when it is a solid?

The states of matter are physical properties of matter. A change in the state of matter is a physical change. This kind of change does not change the kind of matter. Ice and water vapor are still water. They are just in different forms.

Lesson Review

1. What is matter?
2. How are the properties of the three states of matter different?
3. **Challenge!** What would happen if you added four large rocks to an aquarium filled with water? Explain your answer.

Study on your own, pages 384–385.

Bubbles of water vapor in boiling water

FIND OUT ON YOUR OWN

Use an encyclopedia or other books in the library to find out about the different states of matter in Halley's Comet. What kind of change takes place as the comet moves toward the sun?

Observing How Fast Matter Changes States

Purpose
Observe, measure, and *compare* how fast water changes states under different conditions.

Gather These Materials
• 2 clear jars • 1 jar lid • large shallow bowl • water • graduated cylinder

Follow This Procedure
1. Use a table like the one shown to record your observations.
2. Add 200 mL of water to each jar and the bowl.
3. Put the lid on 1 of the jars.
4. Put the 2 jars and bowl in a warm place in the room.
5. Wait for 3 or more days. Then use a graduated cylinder to measure the amount of water that is left in each jar and the bowl. Record this information in your table.

Record Your Results

Container	Water after 3 days
Opened jar	
Jar with lid	
Bowl	

State Your Conclusion
1. Which container lost the most water?
2. Which container lost the least water?
3. In this activity, under what conditions does liquid water change to water vapor the fastest?

Use What You Learned
Do you think the same amount of water in a large, shallow puddle or in a small, deep puddle would dry up faster? Explain your answer.

2 What Makes Up Matter?

LESSON GOALS

You will learn
- what atoms and elements are.
- what molecules and compounds are.
- what mixtures and solutions are.

atom (at′əm), the smallest whole bit of an element.

A close-up of the painting

Look at the people in the painting below. Now look at the other painting below. This picture is a close-up of a small part of the first painting. The artist painted tiny dots to make the painting. When you look at the painting from a distance, you see the whole picture. Like the painting, all matter is made up of smaller and smaller bits. However, you cannot see the small bits of matter.

Atoms and Elements

An **atom** is the smallest whole bit of each kind of matter. Atoms are much too small to see. A toy balloon the size of your head would hold many billions of atoms of the gases found in air.

Most of the matter you see around you is made up of many different kinds of atoms. However, some matter is made up of only one kind of atom. You might have used the substance in the picture. This foil is made from aluminum. Aluminum is an **element**—matter that is made of only one kind of atom. Aluminum is made of atoms of aluminum.

Scientists know of 109 different elements. The pipe in the picture is made from the element copper. Gold, mercury, silver, and carbon are other elements in the objects below. Oxygen is an element that you need from the air you breathe. Your body is made of atoms of many different elements. Atoms of the element calcium make bones and teeth strong.

Look at the black tip of your pencil. It is made of a soft material that is a form of the element carbon. Your pencil point is very small, but it contains billions of carbon atoms.

element (el′ə mənt), matter that has only one kind of atom.

Some elements in different objects

Gold

Silver

Copper

Carbon

Mercury

Molecules and Compounds

You could not live without water. Yet water is not one of the 109 elements. Water is made up of two elements—hydrogen and oxygen. Water is a **compound.** A compound is a new substance that forms when atoms of two or more different elements join together. Most kinds of matter on the earth are compounds.

You know that the smallest whole bit of an element is an atom. The smallest bit of the compound water that has the same properties as water is a molecule. A **molecule** is two or more atoms joined together. For example, two atoms of oxygen join together to form an oxygen molecule.

Think about the drops of water in the picture. Imagine dividing a drop of water into smaller and smaller drops. Finally, you could not make any smaller drops that would still be water. The smallest drop of water with the properties of water is a molecule of water.

Every water molecule is the same. Each water molecule is made up of two hydrogen atoms and one oxygen atom. Pretend the two blue circles in the picture are atoms of hydrogen. The gray circle is an atom of oxygen. Two atoms of hydrogen join with one atom of oxygen to form a molecule of water.

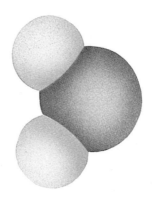

A water molecule

Small drops of water

124

Some kinds of molecules have only two atoms. A molecule of carbon monoxide always has one atom of carbon and one atom of oxygen. Other molecules have thousands of atoms.

The properties of a compound are usually very different from the properties of the elements in it. How would you describe the sugar in the picture? Every molecule of this compound has twelve atoms of carbon, twenty-two atoms of hydrogen, and eleven atoms of oxygen. However, carbon is often a black solid like the form of carbon below. Carbon has no taste. Hydrogen and oxygen are both gases. Neither gas has a color, an odor, or a taste. When atoms of carbon, hydrogen, and oxygen are joined in a certain way, they make a white solid that tastes sweet.

Magnified sugar crystals

Pieces of carbon

Combining Matter into Mixtures and Solutions

Notice the grapes and pieces of orange, banana, and apple in the fruit salad in the picture. The fruits taste good together, but each piece of fruit keeps its own taste. The pieces of fruit can easily be separated. They do not join together to make a new substance.

A **mixture** is two or more substances that are placed—or mixed—together but can be easily separated. Each substance in a mixture keeps its own properties. A mixture can have different amounts of each kind of matter. You can make fruit salad with any kinds of fruit. You also can use any number of pieces of each kind of fruit.

The air you breathe is a mixture of gases. Some of these gases are elements, like oxygen and hydrogen. These elements float freely around each other. Some of the gases in air are compounds, like carbon dioxide and water vapor.

Because air is a mixture, the air in different places has different amounts of these gases. The air over a desert has less water vapor than the air over a warm forest. The air in a city might have more carbon dioxide than the air near a farm.

The soil that covers the earth is a mixture of solids. Some of these solids are sand, clay, and pieces of plant matter. Soil in different places has different amounts of these kinds of matter.

A solid and a liquid can also make a mixture. Stirring sand into water makes a mixture of a solid and liquid. Like all mixtures, sand and water are easy to separate. How would you separate a mixture of sand and water?

Two liquids can make a mixture. For example, vinegar and oil is a mixture that makes salad dressing. This mixture separates so easily that it is sometimes hard to keep the two liquids mixed. People shake salad dressing made with vinegar and oil just before pouring it to mix the two liquids.

A mixture of fruits

The glasses in the picture hold a special kind of mixture. In the glass on the left, sugar and water are mixed together. Notice that you cannot see the sugar. The molecules of sugar dissolve—or spread evenly in the liquid. One substance spreading evenly throughout another substance forms a **solution.** The substances in a solution can be separated easily. If the water evaporates, the sugar is left in the glass.

Many soft drinks are a solution of sugar and water. Soft drinks also have another kind of solution—a gas dissolved in a liquid. You cannot see the gas carbon dioxide until it starts to separate from the water. You can see this gas as bubbles in the glass on the right.

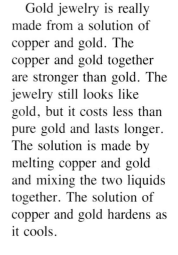

SCIENCE IN YOUR LIFE

Gold jewelry is really made from a solution of copper and gold. The copper and gold together are stronger than gold. The jewelry still looks like gold, but it costs less than pure gold and lasts longer. The solution is made by melting copper and gold and mixing the two liquids together. The solution of copper and gold hardens as it cools.

solution (sə lü′shən), a mixture in which one substance spreads evenly throughout another substance.

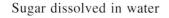

Sugar dissolved in water

A gas dissolved in water

Lesson Review

1. What is an element made of?
2. How is a compound different from an element?
3. How is a solution different from other mixtures?
4. **Challenge!** How are the properties of the compound water different from the properties of the elements in it?

Study on your own, pages 384–385.

Atoms are made of even smaller parts. Look in an encyclopedia to find out what the parts of an atom are. Make a drawing that shows the parts of an atom and name each part.

FIND OUT ON YOUR OWN

3 How Are Length and Volume Measured?

LESSON GOALS

You will learn
• how to measure length.
• how to measure volume.

Measuring height

Imagine that you have a pen pal. You want to describe yourself to this person you have never met. Think about how you would describe yourself. You might say, "I am tall." However, your pen pal could get a better idea of how tall you are if you said, "I am 140 centimeters tall." Scientists describe matter in similar ways by measuring properties of matter.

You can measure some properties. You can measure your height as the boy in the picture is doing. Before your family takes a trip, you might want to know how far you will travel. You need to know the length or distance from one place to the next. Length measures the distance between two points. You can also measure volume. Volume is the amount of space that matter takes up. When people fill their car's gas tank, they pay for the volume of gasoline they take.

Measuring Length

A long way means different things to a baseball player, to an airplane pilot, and to an astronaut. People need measurements in order to be clear. Every measurement includes two things—a number and a unit. "I ran 5 this morning" does not explain how far you ran. "I ran kilometers this morning" also does not explain how far you ran. "I ran 5 kilometers" is a clear measurement.

People used to measure length by comparing what they wanted to measure with the length of familiar objects. Even today you might say that your classroom is about five tables wide. However, tables come in different sizes. To be clear, scientists around the world use the same units.

A unit for measuring length is the **meter.** You would measure your classroom with a meter stick. Your meter stick is the same length as all meter sticks in the world.

In the English language, people often add a prefix to a word to change its meaning. Adding *un-* to the word *happy* changes the word's meaning. When scientists make measurements, they also use prefixes. Find the meaning of the prefixes for *meter* in the chart. How much of a meter is a **centimeter?** How much of a meter is a **millimeter?** How many meters are in a **kilometer?**

The picture shows part of a meter stick. Find the lines that stand for millimeter and centimeter. How many millimeters are in a centimeter? How many millimeters are in 10 centimeters? What is the length of the paper clip in millimeters?

meter (mē′tər), a unit for measuring length.

centimeter (sen′tə mē′tər), 1/100 of a meter.

millimeter (mil′ə mē′tər), 1/1,000 of a meter.

kilometer (kə lom′ə tər), 1,000 meters.

centi-	= 1/100	centimeter (cm)	= 1/100 of a meter
milli-	= 1/1,000	millimeter (mm)	= 1/1,000 of a meter
kilo-	= 1,000	kilometer (km)	= 1,000 meters

Prefixes for *meter*

Part of a meter stick

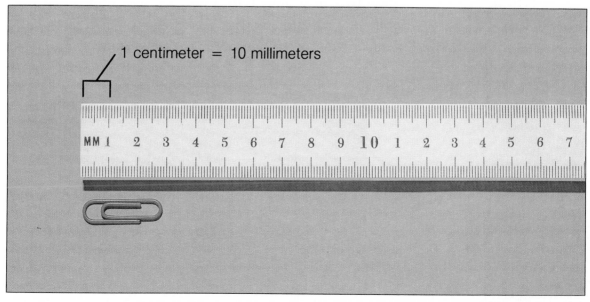

1 centimeter = 10 millimeters

A bottle with a volume of 2 liters

Measuring Volume

The meter stick you use to measure length can also be used to measure volume. How could you find the volume of your room by using a meter stick? First, measure its length, width, and height. What units do you think you should use? Suppose you found that the room is 4 meters long, 3 meters wide, and 3 meters high. To find the volume of the room, multiply length times width times height. Multiply 4 meters × 3 meters × 3 meters. The volume of the room is 36 cubic meters. A **cubic meter** is a unit for measuring volume. One cubic meter is a cube 1 meter long, 1 meter wide, and 1 meter high. Since the room has a volume of 36 cubic meters, it can hold 36 cubes this size.

Some products you have at home were sold by volume. The bottle in the picture has a volume of 2 liters. The **liter** is another unit for measuring volume. One liter is equal to 1,000 **milliliters.** Liters and milliliters are used to measure the volume of liquids.

Scientists use **graduated cylinders** to measure the volumes of liquids. A graduated cylinder is a special kind of measuring cup. Lines mark equal spaces on the graduated cylinder. The graduated cylinder in the picture below has 1 milliliter of water in it. Notice that 1 milliliter is the same as a cube that is 1 centimeter by 1 centimeter by 1 centimeter.

1 milliliter = a cube 1 cm × 1 cm × 1 cm

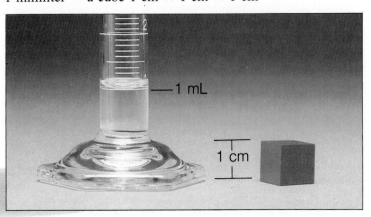

Notice that the surface of the water in a graduated cylinder curves at the edges. The water climbs up the sides of the graduated cylinder a little. Measure the volume by reading the height of the liquid at the flat part. Notice that the flat part of the liquid on page 130 is at the 1 milliliter line. How many milliliters of water are in the picture below? Other liquids curve down instead of up. The flat part is above the curve.

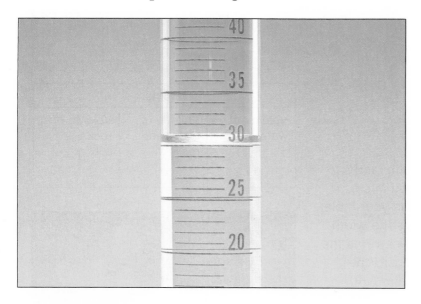

Do you usually have a quart or gallon of milk in the refrigerator at home? In the United States, many people use different units than scientists and people in other countries. Many people use cubic feet, cubic inches, cups, quarts, and gallons to measure volume. People often measure length in inches, feet, yards, or miles.

Each line in this graduated cylinder is 1 milliliter.

Lesson Review

1. What is a unit scientists use for measuring length?
2. What are two different units scientists use for measuring volume?
3. **Challenge!** What is the volume of a box that has a length of 5 centimeters, a width of 2 centimeters, and a height of 2 centimeters?

Study on your own, pages 384–385.

Melting point and boiling point are two properties of matter that can be measured. Find out what melting point and boiling point are and what unit scientists use to measure them. What are the melting point and boiling point for water and for iron?

FIND OUT ON YOUR OWN

ACTIVITY

Measuring Volume

Purpose
Measure the volume of solid objects in two ways.

Gather These Materials
• small wooden block • ruler • water
• 50 mL graduated cylinder • small rock

Follow This Procedure
1. Use tables like the ones shown to record your results.
2. Measure the length, width, and height of a block of wood in cm. Record these numbers in your table.
3. Multiply the length times the width times the height. Your answer is the volume of the block. Record the volume in cubic centimeters in your table.
4. Add 30 mL of water to a graduated cylinder. You have measured the volume of the water. Record this number in your table.
5. Carefully add a small rock to the water in the graduated cylinder. Read the graduated cylinder again and record this number in your table. This number is the volume of the rock added to the volume of the water.
6. Find the volume of the rock by subtracting the original volume of the water from the new volume of the water and the rock. Record this volume in your table.

Record Your Results

Block			
Length	Width	Height	Volume

Rock		
Volume of water	Volume of water and rock	Volume of rock

State Your Conclusion
1. How can you use a ruler to find the volume of a solid object?
2. How can you use a graduated cylinder to find the volume of a solid object?

Use What You Learned
How could you measure the volume of a piece of chalk?

Science and Technology

Measuring in Meters

The Problem Early civilizations came up with ways of measuring objects. However, the units they used were confusing. Many units were based on parts of the human body, such as the length of a person's foot. However, people's feet come in different lengths. A foot might mean one thing to a big person and another thing to a smaller person. Also, people from different places each had their own way of measuring things. When people traveled, measurements became very confusing because they varied. How could you compare the cost of things when they were measured differently? How would you know how much to buy?

The Breakthrough In 1790 France became the first country to set up a standard unit—one that did not depend on something that varied. The unit of length equaled a ten-millionth of the distance from the North Pole to the Equator through Paris. The French named this unit the *metre* from a Greek word meaning "a measure." The French system became known as the metric system. Over the years, more and more countries began to adopt the metric system. In the 1870s seventeen countries, including the United States, agreed to change to the metric system wherever needed. The countries set up the International Bureau of Weights and Measures, with its headquarters near Paris. In 1889, a standard meter was defined. It is the distance between two lines on the metal bar in the picture.

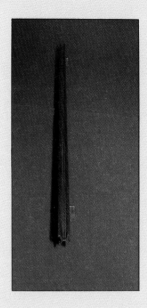

New Technology The meter of 1889 is not accurate enough for today's needs. New developments in technology have led to new ways of defining a meter. Scientists now define a meter in terms of light. Scientists can measure the speed of light very accurately. The speed of light through empty space—a vacuum—has been measured at 299,792.458 kilometers per second. In 1983 scientists used the speed of light to set the official definition of a meter. A meter is "the length of the path traveled by light in a vacuum during a time interval of 1/299,792,458 of a second." Scientists probably will find still more accurate ways of defining the meter.

What Do You Think?
1. How did the early units of measure cause problems for people who traded with other countries?
2. Why is today's definition of a meter more accurate than the definition used in 1790?

4 How Are Mass and Density Measured?

LESSON GOALS

You will learn
- how to measure mass.
- how to measure density.

---

kilogram (kil′ə gram), a unit for measuring mass.

gram (gram), 1/1,000 of a kilogram.

milligram (mil′ə gram), 1/1,000 of a gram.

Have you ever had a bar of soap that sank when you dropped it in water? Have you ever had a bar of soap that floated in water? You can measure the property that causes the soap to float or sink by measuring the soap's mass and volume.

Measuring Mass

A unit for measuring mass is the **kilogram.** The girl in the picture has a mass of 30 kilograms. A smaller unit is the **gram.** The mass of the small paper clip in the picture is about 1 gram. A kilogram has 1,000 grams. Some medicines are measured in even smaller units called **milligrams.** In Lesson 3, you learned that the prefix *milli-* means 1/1,000. A milligram is 1/1,000 of a gram.

A mass of 30 kilograms

A mass of 1 gram

134

You can use a tool called a balance to measure mass. To find the mass of an object, you balance it with objects whose masses you know. The girl in the picture is measuring the mass of an apple. Notice what happens to the top left balance when an object has less mass than the apple. The apple drops lower.

When the object has more mass than the apple, the apple rises. Does the object in the bottom left picture have more or less mass than the apple?

Notice in the bottom right picture that the pans are even when the objects and the apple have the same mass. The pans look balanced, and an arrow on the lines in the middle of the balance points straight down. When the girl adds together the masses of these objects, she will know the mass of the apple.

Measuring the mass of an apple

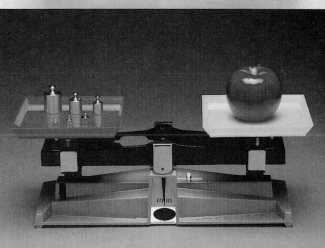

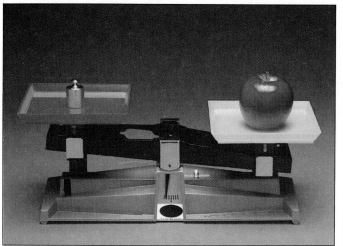

Measuring Density

density (den′sə tē), how much mass is in a certain volume of matter.

Find the three liquids in the picture. The top liquid is rubbing alcohol that has been colored blue. The middle liquid is vegetable oil. The bottom liquid is water that has been colored red. These liquids float or sink because each has a different density.

Density is how much mass is in a certain volume of matter. Each liquid in the picture has the same volume—or takes up the same amount of space. What is the volume of each liquid? However, each liquid has a different mass—or amount of matter—in that space. The water has more matter in it than the same volume of oil does. The water has a greater density than the oil does. The oil has more matter in it than the same volume of alcohol does. Which of the three liquids has the greatest density? Which of the three liquids has the least density?

Density is another property of matter that you can measure. A unit for density uses both a unit used for measuring mass and a unit used for measuring volume. For example, 1 cubic centimeter of water has a mass of 1 gram. Water's density is 1 gram per cubic centimeter.

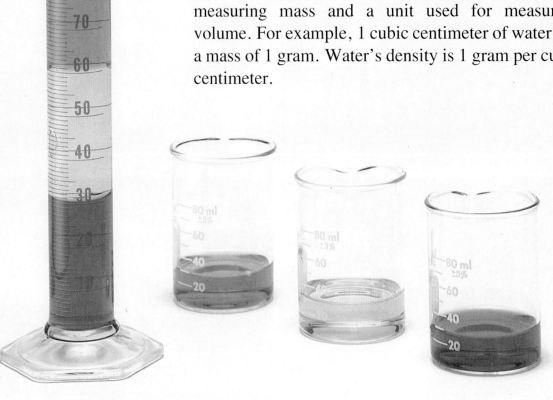

Each liquid has a different density.

136

You can easily compare the density of one kind of matter with another kind of matter if you have the same volume of each object. If you measure the mass of 1 cubic centimeter of wood, you will find that it has a mass of a little less than 1 gram. If you measure the mass of 1 cubic centimeter of salt, you will find that it has a mass of about 2 grams. Does the wood or the salt have a greater density?

You also can easily compare the density of one kind of matter with another kind of matter if you have the same mass of each object. Notice in the picture that the cork and the wood balance. They balance because they both have a mass of 1 gram. Which of the two objects has the greater density? The wood has the greater density because it has the same amount of matter in a much smaller volume.

SCIENCE IN YOUR LIFE

If a solid object has a greater density than water has, it will sink in water. If an object has a lower density than water has, it will float. Most people can float. Their density is slightly less than the density of water.

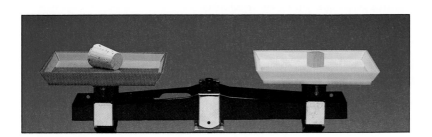

The cork on the left has the same mass as the wood on the right.

Lesson Review

1. What tool can you use to measure mass?
2. What two measurements do you need to measure density?
3. **Challenge!** Imagine you have a kilogram of feathers and a kilogram of lead. Which has more mass? Explain your answer.

Study on your own, pages 384–385.

Look up the Greek inventor Archimedes in an encyclopedia. Find out how and why he measured the density of his king's crown. What did he find out? Write a paragraph telling what you learn.

FIND OUT ON YOUR OWN

Skills for Solving Problems

Using Graduated Cylinders and Bar Graphs

Problem: How does the volume of water change when water freezes?

Part A. Using Graduated Cylinders to Collect Information

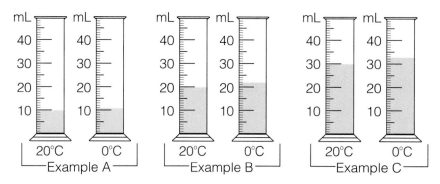

1. Graduated cylinders measure volume. Spaces between the short lines on the cylinders in the pictures measure 1 mL. Spaces between the longer lines measure 10 mL. What is mL an abbreviation for?
2. In Example A, notice that the volume of water at 20°Celsius is 10 mL. Room temperature is about 20°C. This cylinder was then placed in a freezer at 0°C. Water freezes at 0°C. What is the volume in the cylinder in Example A at 0°C?
3. What is the volume of the water in the graduated cylinder in Example B at 20°C? at 0°C?
4. What is the volume of the water in the graduated cylinder in Example C at 20°C? at 0°C?

Part B. Using a Bar Graph to Organize and Interpret Information

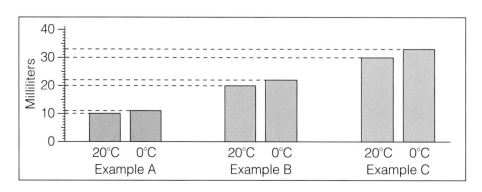

5. The bar graph contains the information you collected about volume in Part A. What does each line on the left side of the graph represent?

6. Look at the first bar on the left. The height of the bar represents the volume of water in Example A at 20°C. Look from the top of this bar across to the marks on the left side of the graph. What is the volume in Example A at 20°? at 0°C?

7. Compare the volumes of the water in the cylinder in each example at each temperature. How do the volumes differ in Example A? in Example B? in Example C?

8. How did the volume of water change when the water froze? If you had 50 mL of water at room temperature, what would the volume be if the water froze?

Part C. Using Graduated Cylinders and a Bar Graph to Solve a Problem

Problem: How does the volume of water change when the water is open to the air for a week?

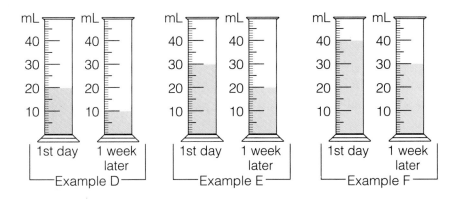

9. Use the pictures to collect the information you need to solve the problem. Make a bar graph similar to the one in Part B to organize your information.

10. Look at your bar graph. How does the volume of water change when the water is open to the air for a week?

11. You might want to do this experiment and use your own results to make a bar graph.

Chapter 5 Review

☑ Chapter Main Ideas

Lesson 1 • Anything that has mass and takes up space is made of matter. • Three states of matter are solid, liquid, and gas.

Lesson 2 • An element is matter that is made up of only one kind of atom. • Most matter is made up of compounds, which have two or more kinds of atoms joined together. • Mixtures and solutions have different kinds of matter that are mixed together and can be easily separated.

Lesson 3 • A meter stick measures length in millimeters, centimeters, and meters. • A graduated cylinder measures volume in milliliters. • Volume can be measured in cubic meters.

Lesson 4 • A balance measures the mass of an object. • Density is the amount of mass in a certain volume of matter.

☑ Reviewing Science Words

atom	element	liter	millimeter
centimeter	graduated cylinder	mass	mixture
compound	gram	meter	molecule
cubic meter	kilogram	milligram	solution
density	kilometer	milliliter	volume

Copy each sentence. Fill in the blank with the correct word or words from the list.

1. The smallest whole bit of an element is an ____ .
2. The unit you would use to measure a room's length is the ____ .
3. Matter that has only one kind of atom is an ____ .
4. Each of the 1,000 smaller units in a gram is a ____ .
5. The amount of material an object has in it is its ____ .
6. ____ is the amount of mass in a certain volume of matter.
7. A ____ is a tool used to measure the volume of a liquid.
8. Each of the 100 smaller units in a meter is a ____ .
9. Each of the 1,000 smaller units in a kilogram is a ____ .
10. Most kinds of matter on earth are ____ .
11. ____ is the amount of space matter fills up.
12. A ____ is a large unit for measuring volume in a graduated cylinder.
13. If you walked 1,000 meters, you walked 1 ____ .
14. A mixture in which one substance spreads evenly throughout another is a ____ .

15. A ___ is a unit of mass larger than a gram.
16. Each of 1,000 smaller units in a meter is a ___.
17. Two hydrogen atoms and one oxygen atom make a water ___.
18. A ___ is a unit you could use to measure the volume of a room.
19. Each of 1,000 smaller units in a liter is a ___.
20. A ___ is two or more substances that can be separated easily.

✓ Reviewing What You Learned

Write the letter of the best answer.
1. Which unit measures mass?
   (a) milliliter   (b) gram   (c) centimeter   (d) atom
2. Which unit measures length?
   (a) milliliter   (b) gram   (c) centimeter   (d) atom
3. Anything that takes up space and has mass is made of
   (a) matter.   (b) density.   (c) length.   (d) volume.
4. One of the states of matter is a
   (a) solution.   (b) mixture.   (c) compound.   (d) liquid.
5. Two atoms that join together make a
   (a) molecule.   (b) atom.   (c) element.   (d) mixture.
6. If you dissolve sugar in water, you have made a
   (a) compound.   (b) solution.   (c) molecule.   (d) balance.

✓ Interpreting What You Learned

Write a short answer for each statement.
1. List the following units from smallest to largest: kilometer, millimeter, meter, centimeter.
2. Describe how a mixture is different from a compound.
3. List two different ways volume can be measured.
4. Describe how density is different from mass.

✓ Extending Your Thinking

Write a paragraph to answer each question.
1. If you put two different objects on opposite sides of a balance and they balance, why might you not know their mass?
2. A balloon filled with the gas helium goes up instead of down. How would you compare the density of helium to the density of air? Explain how you know.

• For further review, use Study Guide pages 384–385.

Chapter 6

Work and Energy

Muscles in the bicycle rider's legs provide the energy to move the bicycle quickly. The simple machines that make up the bicycle let the rider do the most work while using the least energy.

Introducing the Chapter

How would you compare the amount of work you have to do to get a stopped bicycle going and to keep a moving bicycle moving? What happens to you if you are riding along and your bicycle stops suddenly? In the activity below, you will observe moving and still objects. In this chapter, you will learn about motion, energy, and work.

Observing Moving and Still Objects

Place a sheet of paper on a desk or table. Then, place a heavy book, such as a dictionary, on the paper. Pull the book quickly across the table or desk by pulling on the paper. Suddenly stop pulling the paper. Observe what happens to the book.

Keep the same book on the paper. The book should be still—not moving. With a sudden movement of your hands, jerk the paper toward you. Observe what happens to the book.

Talk About It

1. Which of your observations shows that an object that is still tends to stay still?
2. Which of your observations shows that an object in motion tends to stay in motion?

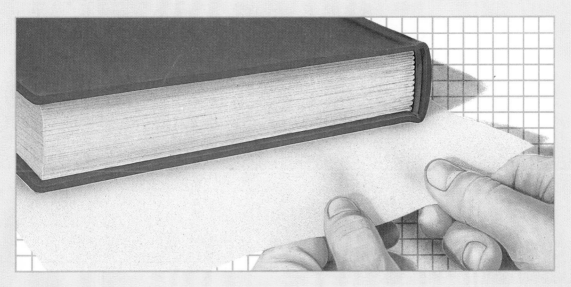

1 What Makes Things Move?

LESSON GOALS

You will learn
- what makes things move.
- how motion is measured.
- how friction changes motion.

gravity (grav′ə tē), a force that pulls any two objects together, such as you and the earth.

The world is filled with moving objects. Cars, buses, trucks, and trains move. People move through the halls of your school. The leaves on trees move as the wind blows. The earth and the other planets move around the sun.

Force

The boys in the picture are raking leaves. As the boys pull the rakes, the leaves are moved into piles. The leaves move because the boys are using a force. A push or a pull is a force.

Only a force can change the motion of an object. A force can move something that is standing still. A force can make a moving object move faster, slow down, or stop. The direction of a moving object changes only when a force acts on it.

When you sit at the top of a slide, you slide down. Gravity pulls you down. **Gravity** is the force that pulls objects toward the center of the earth. Gravity made the leaves in the picture fall to the ground.

Using a force to rake leaves.

144

How Motion Is Measured

Have you ever wondered how fast an airplane flies? If you have, you wondered about the airplane's speed. To know what an object's speed is, you need to know how far the object moves each second, minute, or hour.

The speedometer in a car measures the car's speed. Look closely at the speedometer in the picture. Find the speedometer and the numbers labeled km/hr. Imagine that the car is moving at a speed of 88 kilometers per hour. The car will move 88 kilometers in one hour if its speed does not change. How far will the car move in 30 minutes?

Inertia and Friction

About three hundred years ago, the scientist Isaac Newton realized that a moving object will keep moving unless a force acts on the object. Newton also realized that a still object will remain still unless a force acts on the object. The tendency of an object to stay in motion or to stay still is called **inertia.** You observed inertia if you did the activity on page 143.

inertia (in ėr′shə), the tendency of a moving object to stay in motion or a resting object to stay still.

A speedometer measures speed.

Friction helps you do things every day. The friction between your shoes and the sidewalk helps you walk. Without friction, you would slip and fall. Friction makes cars stop. Friction helps keep tires from slipping on the road.

friction (frik′shən), a force that slows the motion of moving objects.

Look at the girl playing with the checkers. When the girl pushes a checker, it slides across the board. As the checker moves across the board, it slows down. What will happen to the checker when it reaches the carpet?

Friction is a force that slows down or stops moving objects. When an object rubs against another object, friction results. The friction between smooth surfaces is less than the friction between rough surfaces. The friction between the checker and the board was less than the friction between the checker and the carpet.

Friction slows down the checker.

Lesson Review

1. What causes objects to move?
2. What is the speed of an object?
3. How does friction change an object's motion?
4. **Challenge!** How can you reduce the friction between two objects rubbing together?

Study on your own, pages 386–387.

FIND OUT ON YOUR OWN

Use an encyclopedia to find out about different kinds of friction. Make a poster that describes what you learned. Include pictures that illustrate the different types of friction.

Observing Friction

Purpose
Observe how the kind of surface and the weight of an object affect friction.

Gather These Materials
• flat wooden board, abut 25 cm long and 15 cm wide • enough sandpaper to cover half the board • 4 thumbtacks • thin rubber band • masking tape • small paper cup • 20 large metal washers

Follow This Procedure
1. Use tables like the ones shown to record your observations.
2. Tack the sandpaper to half of the board. Use a tack in each corner so the paper lies as flat as possible.
3. Tape the rubber band near the bottom of the paper cup as shown in the picture. Put ten washers in the cup.
4. Drag the cup slowly and steadily across the smooth surface of the board by pulling the rubber band. Friction between the cup and the surface causes the pull. Record whether the rubber band stretches a little or a lot and whether the cup is easy or hard to pull.
5. Pull the same cup slowly and steadily across the sandpaper. Observe how much the rubber band stretches and how much you pull. Compare these observations with your observations of the smooth surface. Record any differences.
6. Repeat step 4 using ten washers and then using twenty washers in the cup. Record any differences.

Record Your Results
How Stretch and Pull Compare

	Smooth surface	Rough surface
Ten washers		

	Ten washers	Twenty washers
Smooth surface		

State Your Conclusion
1. How does the roughness of a surface affect friction?
2. How does the weight of an object affect friction?

Use What You Learned
Why is sand put on icy roads in the winter?

2 How Are Work and Energy Related?

LESSON GOALS

You will learn
- what work is.
- how energy and work are related.
- what the different forms of energy are.

work, the result of a force moving an object.

What does the word *work* mean to you? Does it mean studying? Does it mean doing your chores? Work means both these things to most people. However, work has a special meaning for scientists.

What Work Is

Scientists say that **work** is done only when a force makes something move. Look at the people in the pictures. Both people are using a force. The girl is using a force to push against the wall. The boy is using a force to lift the book to the shelf. Which person is doing work?

Pretend that you and a friend who is exactly your size and weight are climbing up a hill. Both of you are doing work because you are using a force to move something—yourselves.

Now imagine that you carried a heavy box while you climbed the hill. Because you used extra force to carry the box, you did more work than your friend. The more force you use to move something a certain distance, the more work you do.

No work is being done.

Work is being done.

148

You could do more work in another way. Suppose you climbed farther up the hill than your friend while using the same force. You would have done more work because you would have moved yourself a greater distance than your friend.

What Energy Is

What is energy? You may think about energy as what you use to walk, run, play, or think. Just as scientists have a certain meaning for work, they also have a certain meaning for energy. When scientists talk about **energy,** they are talking about the ability to do work.

Anything that does work uses energy. The energy you use to do work comes from the food you eat. A windmill uses energy from the wind to pump water. Cars get energy from gasoline. They use this energy to move people from one place to another. The objects in the pictures get energy from different things. What gives each object the energy to do work?

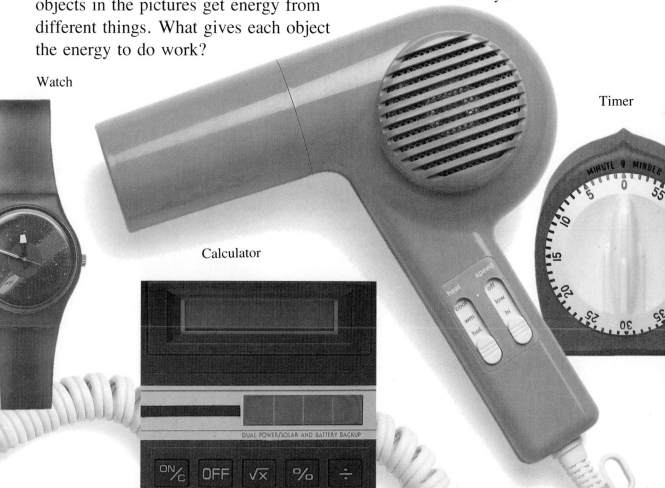

Watch

Calculator

Hair dryer

Timer

You may have seen clocks with swinging pendulums. A pendulum is a weight that hangs from a string and moves from side to side. As a clock's pendulum swings, its potential energy changes into kinetic energy and then back to potential energy.

***

kinetic (ki net′ik) **energy,** energy of motion.

potential (pə ten′shəl) **energy,** stored energy.

A girl on a swing has kinetic and potential energy.

Different Forms of Energy

The girl on the swing below has small lights hooked to her. These lights show her movement. As she is moving forward and upward, she has energy of motion—or **kinetic energy.** The faster the girl moves, the more kinetic energy she has.

At the highest point of her swing, the girl is not moving for an instant. She has no kinetic energy for that instant. Instead, all her energy is **potential energy.** Potential energy is stored energy. The girl's potential energy came from her kinetic energy.

As the girl swings downward, her potential energy changes back into kinetic energy. As she swings up again, her kinetic energy changes back into potential energy. The girl on the swing always has the same total amount of energy. The kind of energy she has depends on whether or not she is moving.

Energy constantly changes from potential energy to kinetic energy and back again. All objects can have kinetic energy and potential energy.

Kinetic and potential energy can take many forms. **Mechanical energy** is the energy an object gets from its motion. When you wind the rubber band on a model airplane, you are storing mechanical energy in the rubber band. As the rubber band unwinds, its mechanical potential energy changes into mechanical kinetic energy. The motion of the rubber band turns the propeller on the plane, causing it to fly.

Chemical energy is energy that results from chemical changes. It is a kind of potential energy. Chemical energy is stored in gasoline and other fuels. Chemical energy also is stored in batteries. Your body uses chemical energy stored in the foods you eat. Other forms of energy include electric energy, light energy, heat energy, and sound energy.

Usually, energy cannot be made or destroyed. However, energy often changes from one form to another. The television in the picture changes electric energy into light, sound, and heat energy. The battery in the picture can change chemical energy into electric energy or light energy.

mechanical (mə kan′ə kəl) **energy,** the energy an object gets from its motion.

chemical (kem′ə kəl) **energy,** energy that results from chemical changes.

Energy can change forms.

Lesson Review

1. If you try to turn a jar lid, but you cannot open the jar, are you doing work? Explain.
2. What is energy?
3. When does an object have kinetic energy? potential energy?
4. **Challenge!** From what does a sailboat get the energy it needs to move through water?

Study on your own, pages 386–387.

Use library books to learn about nuclear energy. Write a report that describes where this form of energy comes from. Include in your report how people use nuclear energy.

FIND OUT ON YOUR OWN

Measuring Work

Purpose
Measure the work done by a marble with different amounts of potential energy.

Gather These Materials
• cardboard about 10 cm wide and 28 cm long • file card • masking tape • centimeter ruler • marble

Follow This Procedure
1. Use a chart like the one shown to record your observations.
2. Fold the cardboard in half lengthwise. Fold the file card in half widthwise.
3. Stick two pieces of masking tape on a table top about 10 cm apart.
4. Rest the file card next to the tape on your left. The folded edge of the card should lie next to the edge of the tape as shown in the picture.
5. Place one end of the cardboard next to the edge of the other tape as shown. Raise the opposite end of the cardboard 1 cm above the table top.
6. Place the marble at the top of the cardboard track and let it roll into the folded file card.
7. Measure how far the folded edge of the card moved. Record your results. The farther the edge moved, the more work the marble did on the card.
8. Repeat steps 5–7, raising the track 3 cm, 6 cm, and 9 cm above the table top. Record your results.

Record Your Results

Height of marble	Distance file card moved
1 cm	
3 cm	
6 cm	
9 cm	

State Your Conclusion
1. At what height was the marble's potential energy the greatest?
2. How was the amount of work done affected by the marble's potential energy?

Use What You Learned
Some electric power plants use the energy of falling water to turn machines in the plants. Would you build a power plant near a high waterfall or a low waterfall? Explain.

Using Robots to Do Work

The Problem Imagine having to do the same thing over and over and over. Or imagine a job that is very dangerous. For many years people had no choice about jobs like these. The work needed to be done, and someone had to do it.

The Breakthrough More than 300 years ago in Europe, a few people made machines that could do things people could do. They made machines that could draw. More useful robots were not made until after computers were developed. By the 1960s, computers could guide a robot to walk down a hall, enter a room, pick up a book, and return to its starting point.

New Technology Today's robots are automatic machines with at least one arm. By 1986, about 20,000 robots were at work in the United States. The robots do different kinds of work. Many work in factories on assembly lines. The picture shows one robot that protects people from dangerous situations. It is one of several robots used by the New York City Police Department. The robot runs on two batteries.

The television camera on top rotates in a circle. A second camera lets the robot "see" what is going on behind it. The second camera can also be hooked to one of the robot's two arms to let the robot "look" under a car.

A 330-meter cable hooks the robot to a cart. The cart carries the equipment that controls the robot. A police officer uses a television screen to guide the robot.

The control cart also carries one end of a two-way sound system. Police use the sound system to talk to suspects. The robot also has electronic equipment that lets it "touch," as well as "see," "hear," and "speak" like a human police officer. In one case, the robot was called to the scene where an armed man held four hostages. Luckily, the suspect surrendered. But if he had not, the robot could have brought food to the suspect, taken his gun away, or even fired a gun at him. Meanwhile, the human police would have been a safe distance away.

What Do You Think?
1. Is a car a robot or a machine? Why?
2. What new kinds of jobs are created by using robots?

3 How Do Machines Use Energy to Do Work?

LESSON GOALS

You will learn
- what levers, inclined planes, and wedges are.
- what screws, wheels and axles, and pulleys are.
- what compound machines and complex machines are.

simple machine, a machine made of only one or two parts.

What kinds of machines do you use? Do you ever use a pencil sharpener, bicycle, skateboard, or hammer? You may not think of these things as machines, but they are. A machine is any tool that makes work easier to do.

Simple Machines: Lever, Inclined Plane, and Wedge

A **simple machine** usually has only one or two parts. The woman is using a simple machine called a lever to open the paint can. A lever is a stiff bar or board that is held up on a point called the fulcrum.

The lever in the picture is made up of a screwdriver and the edge of the paint can. Notice that the woman places one end of the screwdriver under the lid of the can. The screwdriver is held up by the edge of the can—or fulcrum. Then, the woman pushes down on the other end of the screwdriver. The fulcrum changes the direction of the force, causing the other end of the screwdriver to push up on the lid.

Using a lever

154

A ramp is a simple machine called an inclined plane. This machine is a flat surface with one end higher than the other end. People use inclined planes to gradually raise or lower objects. By using an inclined plane, the truck driver in the picture can easily raise the heavy box into the truck.

The wood below is being split with an axe. The head of an axe is a simple machine called a wedge. The sides of a wedge meet at a sharp edge or at a point. People use wedges to split or to pierce things. A nail and a knife are wedges.

Friction always wastes some of the energy put into a machine. A machine's **efficiency** compares how much work you get from a machine with how much energy you put into using the machine. High efficiency means you get a lot of work done for the amount of energy you use. Low efficiency means you get a small amount of work done for the amount of energy you use.

Friction wastes very little of the energy put into using a lever. Therefore, a lever's efficiency is high. The efficiency of an inclined plane depends on its surface and the surface of the object being moved. If both surfaces are smooth, the efficiency of the inclined plane is high. If both surfaces are rough, the efficiency is low.

efficiency (ə fish′ən sē), the amount of work a machine does compared to the amount of energy put into using the machine.

An inclined plane

The head of an axe is a wedge.

Simple Machines:
Screw, Wheel and Axle, and Pulley

A screw is a simple machine that holds things together. Many jar lids have a large, flat screw that holds the lid to the jar. People also use screws to hold wood or metal pieces together.

A screw is really an inclined plane wrapped around a rod. Compare the inclined plane around the pencil below to the screw. The colored edge of the inclined plane is like the ridge that runs around a screw.

Another kind of simple machine is the wheel and axle. Every time you turn a doorknob, you use a wheel and axle. Look at the doorknob in the picture. The knob is the wheel. The axle is the rod that goes through the door. The axle connects the two knobs.

When you turn a doorknob, you turn the axle. The axle then moves another part within the doorknob that makes the door open. You need to use less force to turn the axle using the wheel than you would need to turn the axle by itself.

A screw is an inclined plane wrapped around a rod.

A wheel and axle

The pulley in the picture on the right is a simple machine made of a wheel and a rope. The wheel has a groove around its rim. The rope passes over the groove. The people in the picture below are using a pulley to lift themselves. As they pull down on the rope, they move up the building. People use pulleys to move things up, down, and sideways.

Sometimes a number of pulleys are used to move objects. People use groups of pulleys to move heavy loads, such as boats, pianos, and safes. The more ropes used to hold the load, the stronger the force acting on the load.

A pulley's efficiency can be high or low. If the pulley does not turn easily, its efficiency is low. If the pulley turns easily, its efficiency is high.

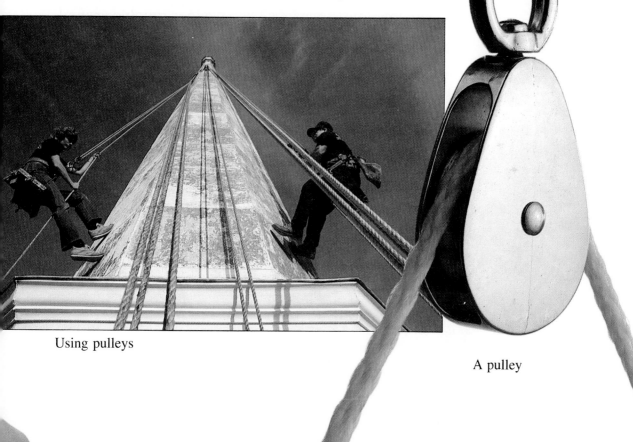

Using pulleys

A pulley

157

Compound and Complex Machines

A **compound machine** is made of two or more simple machines. An axe is a compound machine. Remember, the head of an axe is a wedge. The handle is a lever. Together, the wedge and the lever make up a compound machine.

Look at the hedge clipper in the picture. The clipper is really two levers. Each lever has one side that is a wedge. The pin that holds the levers together is the fulcrum.

Notice the simple machines that make up the pencil sharpener. The handle of the pencil sharpener is a wheel connected to an axle. The axle is also connected to wheels with teeth called gears. When you turn the handle, the axle moves the gears. The gears then move wedges. The wedges revolve around the pencil, cutting the wood away. Two screws hold the sharpener together.

compound (kom′pound) **machine,** a machine made of two or more simple machines.

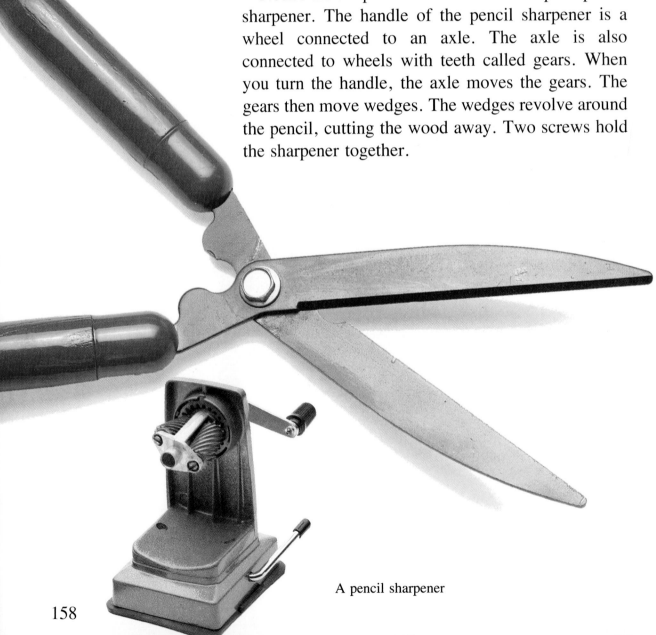

Hedge clipper

A pencil sharpener

158

A **complex machine** is made of many simple and compound machines. The car engine in the picture is a complex machine. Many complex machines, such as cars, have low efficiency. These machines have many moving parts. When the parts rub together, friction slows them down. Friction decreases the amount of work the machines do.

Even though complex machines have low efficiency, they are very important. Much more than half the gasoline put into a car is wasted. However, cars move people long distances quickly. Think about how different peoples' lives would be without complex machines.

More and more machines are electronic. These machines use electricity for energy and tiny computers to control motion. An electronic machine uses a computer to calculate how much force is needed. Then, electricity is used to provide the needed force.

complex (kəm′pleks) **machine,** a machine made of many simple and compound machines.

A car engine is a complex machine.

Lesson Review

1. Which simple machine has a fulcrum?
2. How do people use pulleys to do work?
3. How is a complex machine different from a compound machine?
4. **Challenge!** When you lift a ball in the palm of your hand, you use your arm as a lever. What is the fulcrum?

Study on your own, pages 386–387.

Simple machines are all around you. Look for objects within your home, school, and community that are simple machines. Make a list of all the objects you find. Next to each object, write down the kind of simple machine it is.

FIND OUT ON YOUR OWN

159

Skills for Solving Problems

Using Diagrams and Line Graphs

Problem: How do differences in the mass of objects affect how far a force can move them?

Part A. Using Diagrams to Collect Information

1. The diagrams show what happens when a ball rolls down an inclined plane and hits objects of different masses. What is the mass of one wooden block? two blocks? three blocks? four blocks?
2. How far did the force of the ball push the single wooden block? the stack of two blocks? three blocks? four blocks?

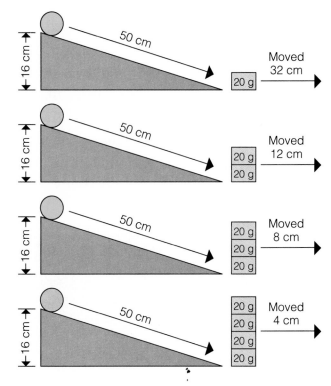

Part B. Using a Line Graph to Organize and Interpret Information

3. The line graph contains the information you collected in Part A. What do the lines on the left of the graph stand for? What do the lines at the bottom of the graph stand for?
4. Place your finger on the line at the bottom of the graph that stands for a 20 g object. Move your finger up the graph to the dot above this line. What does the line to the left of this dot stand for? The graph shows that the 20 g object was moved 32 cm.

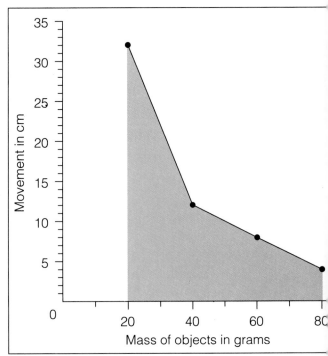

5. Find the other dots on the graph. How far did the ball move each of the other objects?

6. How does the mass of an object affect how far a force can move it?

Part C. Using Diagrams and Line Graphs to Solve a Problem

Problem: How do differences in the height of an inclined plane change the distance a ball rolling down it can move an object?

7. Use the diagram to collect the information you need to solve the problem. Make a line graph similar to the one in Part B to organize your information.

8. Look at your line graph. How do differences in the height of an inclined plane change the distance a ball rolling down it can move an object?

9. Predict what would happen if the height of the inclined plane was 30 cm.

10. You might want to do this experiment and use your own results to make a line graph.

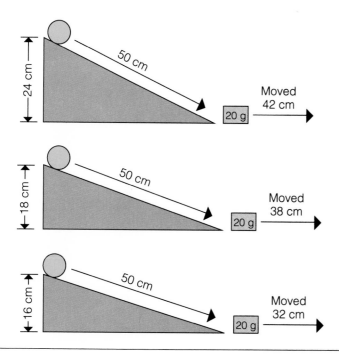

161

Chapter 6 Review

☑ Chapter Main Ideas

Lesson 1 • Forces change the motion of objects. • An object's speed is how far the object moves within certain periods of time. • Inertia tends to keep moving objects moving and still objects still. • Friction slows down moving objects.

Lesson 2 • Work is done only when a force moves something. • Energy is the ability to do work. • Kinetic energy is the energy of motion. • Potential energy is stored energy. • Energy can change from one form into another.

Lesson 3 • A machine is any tool that makes work easier to do. • A lever, an inclined plane, and a wedge are simple machines. A screw, a wheel and axle, and a pulley are other simple machines. • A compound machine is made of two or more simple machines. • A complex machine is made of many simple and compound machines.

☑ Reviewing Science Words

chemical energy
complex machine
compound machine
efficiency
energy

friction
gravity
inertia
kinetic energy

mechanical energy
potential energy
simple machine
work

Copy each sentence. Fill in the blank with the correct word or words from the list.

1. A ＿＿ is usually made of only one or two parts.
2. ＿＿ is the tendency of a moving object to stay in motion or a resting object to stay still.
3. ＿＿ results when two objects rub against each other.
4. ＿＿ is the result of a force moving an object.
5. ＿＿ is the force that pulls objects toward the earth.
6. ＿＿ is the ability to do work.
7. A ＿＿ is made of many simple and compound machines.
8. ＿＿ is the energy an object gets from its motion.
9. Stored energy is ＿＿.
10. ＿＿ is the amount of work a machine does compared to the amount of energy put into using the machine.
11. ＿＿ is a kind of potential energy stored in food.

12. Energy of motion is ▩.

13. A ▩ is made of two or more simple machines.

☑ Reviewing What You Learned

Write the letter of the best answer.

1. If you want to stop a moving object, you must use

   (a) speed.   (b) gravity.   (c) force.   (d) efficiency.

2. If a car's speed is 75 kilometers per hour, how many kilometers will the car travel in 20 minutes?

   (a) 20   (b) 50   (c) 25   (d) 75

3. When you move a box, you do

   (a) gravity.   (b) inertia.   (c) speed.   (d) work.

4. A skier who is standing still at the top of a hill has

   (a) potential energy.   (b) work.   (c) kinetic energy.   (d) speed.

5. A lever is made of a

   (a) wheel and wedge.   (c) pulley and rope.

   (b) bar and fulcrum.   (d) fulcrum and wheel.

6. If you use an inclined plane wrapped around a rod, you are using

   (a) a lever.   (b) a pulley.   (c) a wedge.   (d) a screw.

☑ Interpreting What You Learned

Write a short answer for each question or statement.

1. A small child and an adult are climbing a hill at the same speed. Who is doing more work? Explain your answer.

2. Suppose you throw a ball up into the air. When does the ball have potential energy only?

3. What forms of energy are released when coal is burned?

4. What does the efficiency of an inclined plane depend on?

☑ Extending Your Thinking

Write a paragraph to answer each question.

1. If you rub your hands together, you feel heat. What are three other examples you can think of that show friction produces heat?

2. A perpetual motion machine is a machine that could run forever without needing energy put into it. Explain why no one could ever build such a machine.

• For further review, use Study Guide pages 386–387.

7

Electricity and Magnetism

This girl is visiting a science museum. What is happening to her? She is touching a machine that gives her body a small amount of electricity. This electricity makes her hair stand on end.

164

Introducing the Chapter

Electricity can be exciting and fun. It can make your hair stand on end. In the activity below, you will make a small amount of electricity. This electricity is fun, but not useful. People can control larger amounts of electricity to make it useful. These amounts of electricity can be dangerous if not used safely.

Observing Electric Charges

Make about ten tiny pieces of white paper. Each piece should be as small as you can make it. Put the tiny pieces on a sheet of colored paper. Sprinkle a small amount of salt and pepper on the same paper. Slowly move a comb near the objects on the paper. Observe what happens.

Next, rub the comb back and forth a few times on a piece of wool cloth. Slowly move the comb toward the tiny pieces of paper, salt, and pepper. Observe what happens.

Talk About It
1. What happened the first time you moved the comb near the paper, salt, and pepper?
2. What happened the second time?
3. What do you think caused the change?

1 What Is Electricity?

LESSON GOALS

You will learn
- how an electric charge builds up.
- how a closed circuit is needed for an electric current to flow.
- how to use electricity safely.

electron (i lek′tron), a tiny bit of an atom that has a negative charge.

proton (prō′ton), a tiny bit of an atom that has a positive charge.

The clothes have a small electric charge.

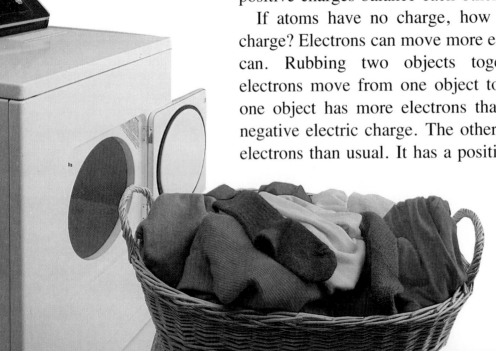

Imagine that you are sorting the clean laundry in the picture below. You might find that some pieces of clothing stick together when you take them out of the dryer. The clothes stick together because they have a small amount of electricity. Much larger amounts of electricity move through wires and make appliances like the clothes dryer work.

Electric Charge

You know that the clothes are made of atoms. Each atom is made of even smaller bits of matter. Some of these tiny bits are **electrons.** An electron has a negative electric charge. Electric charge is the amount of electricity in or on an object. Every electron in any kind of matter has the same amount of negative electric charge.

Some of the other tiny bits of matter that make up an atom are **protons.** A proton has a positive electric charge. Every proton in any kind of matter has the same amount of positive electric charge.

Atoms have no electric charge. They have one electron for every proton. Therefore, the negative and positive charges balance each other.

If atoms have no charge, how do objects get a charge? Electrons can move more easily than protons can. Rubbing two objects together can make electrons move from one object to the other. Then one object has more electrons than usual. It has a negative electric charge. The other object has fewer electrons than usual. It has a positive charge.

Two objects with opposite charges attract each other. The two objects pull together. Two objects with the same charge push away from each other.

What makes the clothes in the dryer stick together? The clothes rub against each other in the dryer. Some electrons move from one object to another. If one sock loses electrons, it has a positive charge. If another sock gains electrons, it has a negative charge. The two socks pull toward each other because they have opposite charges. The socks below have opposite charges. These opposite charges make them cling together.

Sometimes many extra electrons build up on an object. Have you ever walked across a rug and then felt a shock when you touched a doorknob? When you walk across a rug, your shoes rub against it. Your shoes gain electrons. The electrons spread out over your body. When you touch a metal object, the electrons jump to it. You feel a shock. Sometimes you can see a spark. The electrons jumping from you to the doorknob make the spark.

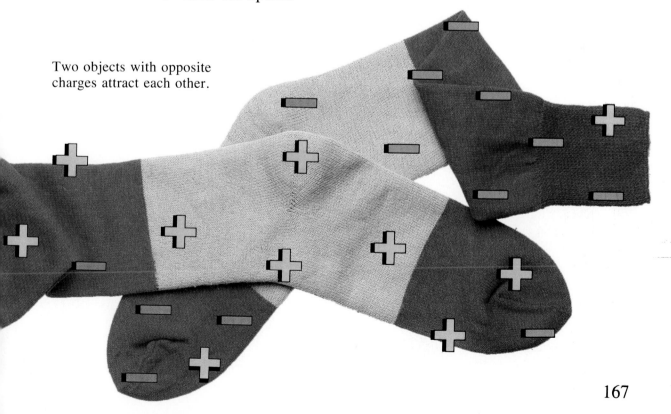

Two objects with opposite charges attract each other.

Electric Current

Sparks are moving electrons. Electrons can do more than jump from one place to another. Electrons can also flow smoothly through matter. Flowing electrons—or a flow of an electric charge—make electric current. People can control electric current to make electricity work for them.

Electric current passes easily through some materials. These materials are **conductors.** Many metals are good conductors.

Electric current does not pass easily through other materials. These materials are **insulators.** Air, rubber, glass, and plastic are insulators.

Look at the electric cord in the picture. The metal wire inside conducts—or carries—the current into an appliance. The rubber insulator on the outside keeps the current from flowing where it should not go.

Resistance measures how well electricity flows through a material. Good insulators have high resistance. Good conductors have low resistance. Superconductors have no resistance at all.

Resistance can be useful. Notice the glowing wire in the light bulb at the bottom of the next page. This wire is made from matter that has high resistance. The wire becomes very hot and glows as the electrons flow through it.

An electric cord

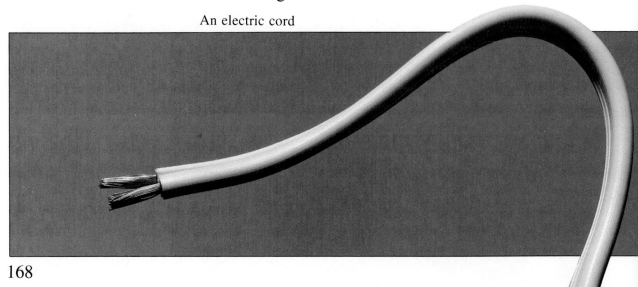

168

Electric current flows only when it can follow a closed path called a closed circuit. The circuit in the picture has three parts. First, something must push electrons through the path. The battery pushes the electrons. Second, an object in the circuit must allow the current to flow through it. The bulb lights up when current passes through it. Third, wires must connect the parts of the circuit. A wire connects the battery to the bulb. A wire also connects the bulb back to the battery.

What would happen if you took away one of the wires of the circuit in the picture? You would break the path that the electric current follows. You open the circuit. Because current can flow only through a closed circuit, the bulb would not light up.

A light bulb

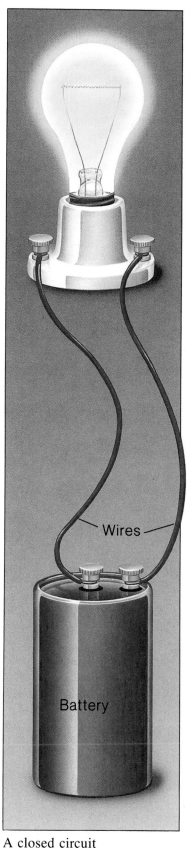

Wires

Battery

A closed circuit

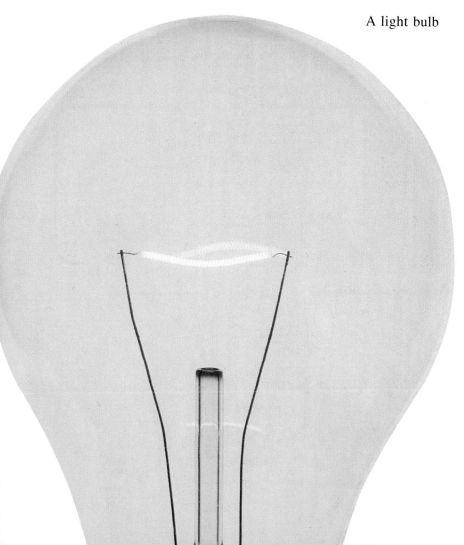

Light bulbs can be a part of two kinds of circuits—series circuits and parallel circuits. In a **series circuit,** the bulbs are in the same path. Find the two bulbs in the series circuit in the picture. If you remove or turn off either bulb, the circuit opens. Current cannot reach the other parts of the circuit. Think about what would happen if all the lights and appliances in your home were parts of a series circuit. Unless you had all the lights and appliances on, the circuit would be open. None of the lights and appliances would work.

In homes, lights and appliances are parts of **parallel circuits.** The electric current for each light and appliance has its own path. Find the two bulbs in the parallel circuit in the picture. Use your finger to trace the path of electric current for each bulb.

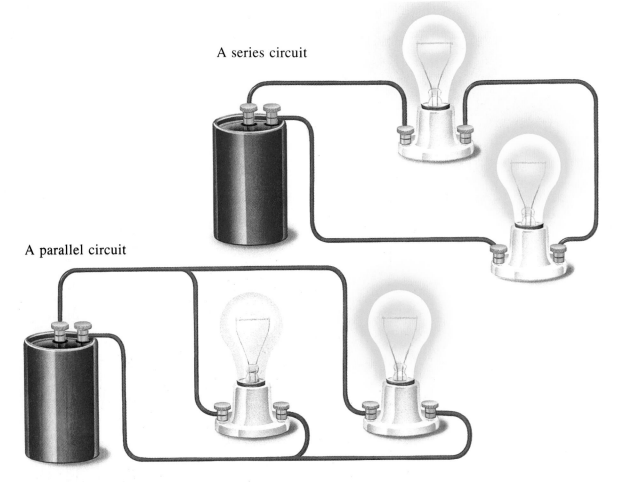

A series circuit

A parallel circuit

Using Electricity Safely

Electricity is dangerous if it is not used correctly. It can cause burns, shock, and death if it travels through a person's body. An important safety rule to follow is never touch anything electrical while you are wet. Water on your skin can conduct electricity. It can lead the electricity into your body.

Do not use electric lamps and appliances that have cords with worn, cut, or broken insulation around the wires. The electric current could easily travel to your body. The current also could start a fire.

People also need to be careful not to plug too many lamps and appliances into the same outlet. Too much electric current flowing through the outlet in the picture might make the wires in the wall hot enough to start a fire. However, most homes have a kind of switch that stops too much current from flowing through a circuit. This switch—a fuse or circuit breaker—opens the circuit when too much current flows through it. Then no current can flow through the circuit.

Do not plug too many cords into the same outlet.

Lesson Review

1. What causes sparks?
2. How does a light bulb make use of resistance?
3. What are two ways you can keep electric current from getting into your body?
4. **Challenge!** Why is it unsafe to run electric cords under a rug?

Study on your own, pages 388–389.

Electricity is electric energy. Electricity can be changed into light energy and heat energy. Look around your home and make a list of ways electric energy changed to light energy is useful. Make a list of ways electric energy changed to heat energy is useful.

**FIND OUT
ON YOUR OWN**

2 What Is Magnetism?

LESSON GOALS

You will learn
- how magnets act on objects and other magnets.
- the reason a compass points north.

magnet (mag′nit), an object that pulls iron and steel things to it.

magnetism (mag′nə tiz′əm), the force around a magnet.

pole (pōl), a place on a magnet where the magnetism is strongest.

Magnetism is strongest at the poles.

What does the word *magnet* make you think of? Do you think of a toy that can pick up paper clips? Do you think of objects that hold messages on your refrigerator door? You might not know that telephones, computers, and radio speakers all have magnets in them. Magnets have many important uses in your life.

A Force That Attracts Certain Metals

A **magnet** is anything that pulls iron and steel to it. The magnet in the picture is pulling iron filings to it. A force is something that pulls or pushes. **Magnetism** is the force around a magnet.

Magnets can be made in different shapes. However, magnets of all shapes have the same properties. You can see these properties most easily in a bar magnet. Notice where more iron filings stick to the bar magnet in the picture. Do more filings stick to the magnet's ends or to its middle? The magnet picks up more iron filings where magnetism is the strongest. The places on a magnet where magnetism is the strongest are the magnet's **poles.** A bar magnet's poles are at its ends.

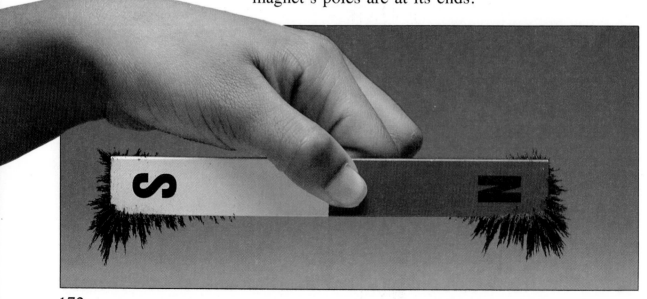

Notice that one pole of the bar magnet is labeled *N* and the other pole is labeled *S*. *N* stands for north pole. *S* stands for south pole. If you let a magnet turn freely, the north pole of the magnet always points north. The magnet's south pole always points south.

What happens if you put a north pole of one magnet near a north pole of another magnet? The two north poles push each other away. However, the north pole of one magnet attracts the south pole of another magnet. A north pole and a south pole stick together.

Notice in the picture how tiny pieces of iron are pulled to a magnet. Many of the iron pieces do not touch the magnet. However, they do all line up in a pattern around the magnet. The magnetism is acting on the iron pieces in the space around the magnet. This space around a magnet where magnetism acts is the **magnetic field.** Every magnet has a magnetic field. What places in the magnetic field have the most iron pieces?

magnetic field, the space around a magnet where magnetism acts.

A magnetic field

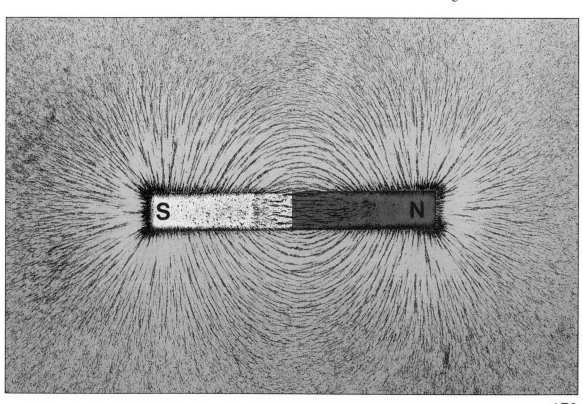

The place on the earth that people call the North Pole is the place that people use for the direction north. However, the magnetic north pole is about 1600 kilometers from this place. Special maps help people change the compass direction north to north on the earth.

compass (kum′pəs), a small magnet that can turn freely.

The Earth as a Magnet

Did you know that the earth is a magnet? The earth has a north magnetic pole and a south magnetic pole. A magnetic field surrounds the earth.

For almost 1000 years, people have used the earth's magnetic field to help them find directions. They discovered that one pole of a magnet that swings freely always points north. Using this idea, they made the first **compasses.** A compass is a small magnet that swings freely. The north pole of the magnet points to the earth's magnetic north pole. What direction is the compass below pointing?

A compass points north.

Lesson Review

1. What part of a bar magnet could pick up the most iron filings?
2. How does a compass work?
3. **Challenge!** How could you find the two poles of a magnet that has a different shape than a bar magnet?

Study on your own, pages 388–389.

FIND OUT ON YOUR OWN

Look up *magnet* in an encyclopedia. Find out what makes something become magnetic. Write a paragraph that explains what you learn.

Making a Magnetic Compass

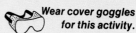
Wear cover goggles for this activity.

Purpose
Make a magnetic compass.

Gather These Materials
• sewing thimble • large sewing needle
• magnet • paper clip • sponge (2 cm ×
2 cm) • small plastic bowl • water
• detergent • spoon

Follow This Procedure
1. Use a chart like the one shown to record your observations.
2. Hold the thick end of the needle. Rub the thin end of the needle lengthwise along one pole of the magnet twenty times. Always stroke the needle in the same direction, and use the same pole of the magnet.
   CAUTION: Be careful not to stick yourself or others with the needle.
3. Test whether the needle is magnetic by trying to attract a paper clip with it. If the needle is not magnetic, repeat step 2.
4. Bend the sponge in half. Use a thimble to push the needle carefully through the sponge as shown.
5. Fill the bowl half full with water. Add two drops of detergent and stir.
6. Gently lower the sponge into the bowl. Keep the original magnet at least a meter away.
7. When the needle stops moving, it is pointing toward the earth's magnetic north pole. Give the sponge a little spin and observe what happens. Record your observation.

8. Hold the magnet next to the needle, and then move the magnet away. Record your observations.

Record Your Results

Position of needle	Observation
After spinning	
Magnet near needle	
Magnet away from needle	

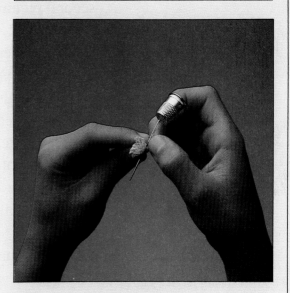

State Your Conclusion
1. Did the needle point in the same direction after you spun it? Why?
2. Explain the effect of the magnet on the needle floating in the water.

Use What You Learned
Use your needle and sponge to draw a map of your classroom that shows north, south, east, and west.

3 How Are Electricity and Magnetism Related?

LESSON GOALS

You will learn
- how a magnet can be used to make electricity.
- how electricity can be used to make a magnet.
- some uses of electromagnets.

generator (jen′ə rā′tər), a machine that uses an energy source and a magnet to make electricity.

About 170 years ago, scientists learned that electricity can make magnetism. They also learned that magnetism can be used to make electricity. Today, the electricity you use and many useful machines come from these discoveries.

Making Electricity from Magnets

Find the wire and magnet in the pictures. The wire is hooked to a device that measures electricity. Notice in the first picture that the pointer is on 0. The magnet is not causing any electric current to flow. In the second picture, the person moved the magnet through the loops of wire. Notice that the pointer shows an electric current moving through the wire. The magnet moving through the loops of wire makes electricity. You could also make electricity by moving the loops of wire instead of the magnet.

Electric **generators** are machines that use magnets and loops of wires to make electricity. Generators need energy to move the magnets or loops of wire. Coal, gas, oil, and moving water are some sources of this energy. Generators make almost all the electricity that people use.

The measuring device shows no electricity.

Moving the magnet causes electricity.

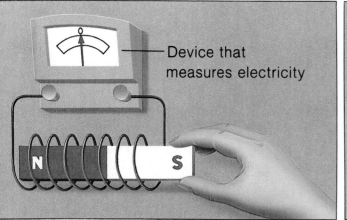

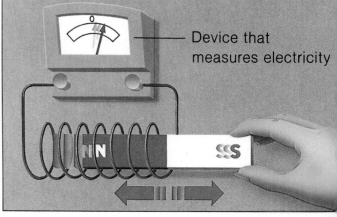

176

Making Magnets from Electricity

An electric current moving through a wire causes a magnetic field around the wire. If the wire is shaped into loops, the magnetic field gets stronger. Notice in the picture that the loop of wire has a north pole and a south pole. An electric current running through a loop of wire makes an **electromagnet.** If the electric current is shut off, the electromagnet is no longer magnetic. The electromagnet is turned off.

An electromagnet usually has a piece of iron in its center. When current runs through the wire, the wire and the iron become magnetic. The magnetic field of the iron is added to the magnetic field of the wire. The electromagnet becomes stronger.

The student in the picture is using electricity to make a magnet. She wrapped wire around a large nail. Then she connected each end of the wire to a battery. As you can see, the nail can now pick up paper clips. The student has made an electromagnet. What will happen to the nail when the wire is unhooked?

electromagnet
(i lek′trō mag′nit), a magnet made when an electric current flows through a wire.

A current makes the wire magnetic.

Making an electromagnet

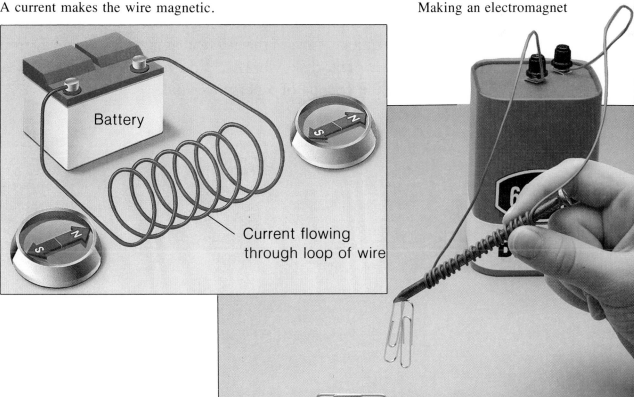

Battery

Current flowing through loop of wire

How Electromagnets Are Useful

Sometimes magnetism is needed only part of the time. Because electromagnets can be turned on and off, they are sometimes more useful than ordinary magnets. For example, a crane has an electromagnet on it. When current moves through it, the electromagnet can pick up scrap metal. When the current is off, the electromagnet loses its magnetism. The crane drops the scrap metal.

Electromagnets also have many uses in homes. When you push the button on a doorbell, you close a circuit. Current moves through a wire loop in the doorbell. The wire becomes an electromagnet. It pushes away an ordinary magnet. Something attached to the ordinary magnet hits a bell.

A telephone works because of an electromagnet. Find the electromagnet in the telephone below. Sound travels through the telephone wire as an electric current. This electric current changes as a person's voice changes. The electromagnet becomes stronger and weaker with the changing current. Find the metal disk in the telephone. The changing strength of this electromagnet causes the disk to move quickly toward the electromagnet and then away from it. The disk vibrates. You hear these vibrations as the sounds of a person's voice.

A telephone has an electromagnet

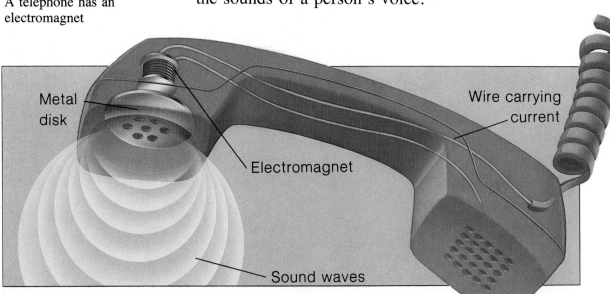

Metal disk

Wire carrying current

Electromagnet

Sound waves

Electric motors also use electromagnets. Factories use electric motors to run machines. You use electric motors of many sizes in your home. Hair dryers, refrigerators, and air conditioners have electric motors. Find the wires in the electric motor in the center of the hair dryer below.

Scientists also use electromagnets. Some of these electromagnets are each about 5 meters long. Scientists use more than 1000 electromagnets this size to help them study the tiny bits inside atoms.

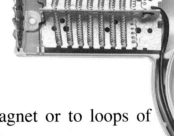

The inside of a hair dryer has an electric motor.

Lesson Review

1. What has to happen to a magnet or to loops of wire to make electricity?
2. Why do many electromagnets have iron centers?
3. What are three uses of electromagnets?
4. **Challenge!** One student made an electromagnet by wrapping ten loops of wire around a nail. Another student made an electromagnet by wrapping twenty loops of wire around a nail. Which electromagnet do you think is stronger? Explain your answer.

Study on your own, pages 388–389.

FIND OUT ON YOUR OWN

Use books in the library to find out about a famous scientist who made an important discovery about electricity or magnetism. You might find out about Michael Faraday, Hans Christian Oersted, Thomas Edison, Lewis Latimer, or another scientist. Write a paragraph telling about the scientist and the discovery.

Making an Electromagnet

Purpose
Infer that electricity produces magnetism.

Gather These Materials
• heavy, bare copper wire (50 cm) • pencil • iron filings • dry cell battery with terminals at the top • insulated thin copper wire (50 cm) with bare section in the middle • compass

Follow This Procedure
1. Use a chart like the one shown to record your observations.
2. Loop the bare wire several times around a pencil. Remove the pencil. *CAUTION: Handle the sharp ends of the wire carefully.*
3. Dip the wire loop into the iron filings. Observe what happens to the filings. Record your observations in the chart.
4. Connect the ends of the wire to the knobs on top of the dry cell. Repeat step 3. Then, disconnect the wire.
5. Place the compass on the table. Connect one end of the insulated wire to the dry cell. Place the bare part of the wire on top of the compass as shown in the picture. The wire should be in a line over the compass needle.
6. Connect the loose end of the wire to the dry cell. Observe what happens to the compass needle. Record your observations.

Record Your Results

	Wire with no current	Wire with a current
Iron filings		
Compass		

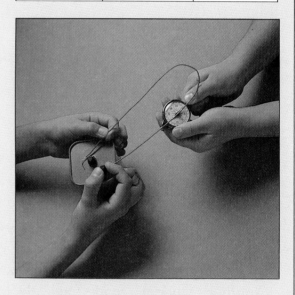

State Your Conclusion
1. When were the wires magnets?
2. What caused the magnetism?

Use What You Learned
Why do you think compasses on airplanes are kept away from electric circuits on the planes?

Making and Using Superconductors

The Problem When an electric current travels through a conductor, loose electrons move from atom to atom. As the electrons move, resistance slows or stops their flow. Resistance wastes energy and creates heat. Sometimes the heat of resistance is useful. For example, it toasts your bread for breakfast. More often the heat is unwanted. More than one-tenth of the energy sent through power-line wires is lost as heat.

The Breakthrough In 1911, a Dutch scientist used liquid helium to cool lead and mercury to -269 °C. This temperature is much colder than the coldest day in the coldest part of the world. At this temperature, lead and mercury began conducting an electric current without losing any energy at all to resistance. He had discovered superconductors. Scientists knew superconductors could be very useful. However, liquid helium is hard to work with and costs a lot of money. Scientists began looking for materials that would become superconductors at warmer temperatures.

New Technology In 1987 Dr. Paul Chu and other scientists made new kinds of materials that superconduct at -175 °C. These materials can be cooled in liquid nitrogen. Dr. Chu is holding a flask of liquid nitrogen in the picture. Liquid nitrogen is cheaper than milk and is much easier to use than liquid helium.

The new superconducting materials promise to have many uses. Computers

may use superconductors. Today's computers give off a lot of heat. Their parts would melt if packed together tightly. The distances needed between computer parts slow down the computer's work. Using superconductors in computers would mean faster, smaller computers. Scientists are looking for ways to use these new materials. Scientists also are hoping to find materials that will superconduct at room temperature.

What Do You Think?
1. How are superconductors different from other conductors?
2. Why would a material that superconducts at room temperature be useful?

Skills for Solving Problems

Using Diagrams and Line Graphs

Problem: How does the number of coils of insulated wire affect the strength of an electromagnet?

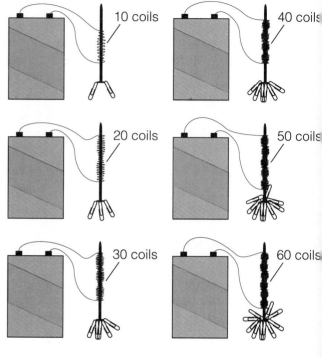

Part A. Using a Diagram to Collect Information

1. The diagrams show how a battery, insulated copper wire, and a steel nail make an electromagnet. You can measure the strength of the electromagnet by how many paper clips the nail picks up. In the diagram, how many paper clips are picked up by the electromagnet with 10 coils?

2. How many paper clips are picked up by the electromagnet with 20 coils? 30 coils? 40 coils? 50 coils? 60 coils?

Part B. Using a Line Graph to Organize and Interpret Information

3. The line graph contains the information you collected about how the number of coils of insulated wire affected the strength of the electromagnet. What do the lines on the left side of the graph stand for? What do the lines at the bottom of the graph stand for?

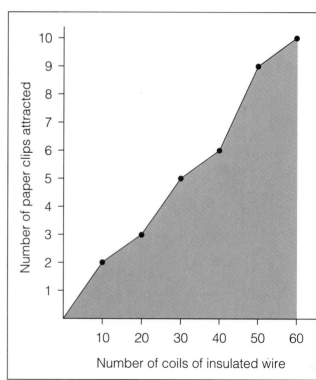

4. Find the line on the bottom of the graph that stands for 10 coils. Now find the dot above this line. What does the line across from this dot stand for? The graph shows that an electromagnet with 10 coils attracts 2 paper clips.

5. How many coils are wrapped around the electromagnet that picks up the most paper clips? How many coils are wrapped around the electromagnet that picks up the least paper clips? How does the number of coils of insulated wire affect the strength of an electromagnet?

Part C. Using Diagrams and Line Graphs to Solve a Problem

Problem: How does the number of coils of uninsulated wire affect the strength of an electromagnet?

6. Use the diagrams below to collect the information you need to solve the problem. Make a line graph similar to the one in Part B to organize your information.

7. Look at your line graph. What number of coils attracted the most paper clips? How does the number of coils of uninsulated wire affect the strength of an electromagnet?

8. Compare your graph with the graph in Part B. How does the strength of an electromagnet with insulated wire compare with the strength of an electromagnet with uninsulated wire?

9. You might want to do this experiment and use your own results to make a line graph.

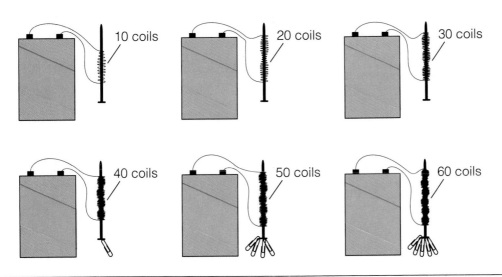

10 coils   20 coils   30 coils

40 coils   50 coils   60 coils

Chapter 7 Review

☑ Chapter Main Ides

Lesson 1 • An object gets an electric charge when it gains or loses electrons. • An electric current can flow through a closed circuit. • People need to use electricity carefully because it can be dangerous.

Lesson 2 • A magnet has a magnetic field that is strongest at its poles. • The earth is a magnet.

Lesson 3 • A magnet can be used to make electricity. • An electric current flowing through a wire makes a magnet. • An electromagnet has many uses.

☑ Reviewing Science Words

compass	insulator	pole
conductor	magnet	proton
electromagnet	magnetic field	resistance
electron	magnetism	series circuit
generator	parallel circuit	

Copy each sentence. Fill in the blank with the correct word or words from the list.

1. A circuit with objects connected in a single path is a ▦ .
2. The ▦ is the space around a magnet where magnetism acts.
3. An electric current does not pass easily through an ▦ .
4. A ▦ is a tiny bit of an atom that has a positive charge.
5. A ▦ is an object that pulls iron and steel things to it.
6. A small magnet that can turn freely and points north is a ▦ .
7. ▦ is how well electricity flows through a material.
8. A place on a magnet where the magnet is strongest is a ▦ .
9. An ▦ is a tiny bit of an atom that has a negative charge.
10. An electric current passes easily through a ▦ .
11. The force around a magnet is ▦ .
12. A circuit in which current has a separate path for each object is a ▦ .
13. A ▦ is a machine that uses an energy source and a magnet to make electricity.
14. A magnet made when an electric current flows through a wire is an ▦ .

☑ Reviewing What You Learned

Write the letter of the best answer.

1. What kind of circuit would you need to have one light bulb on and one off?
   (a) series   (b) magnetic   (c) generator   (d) parallel
2. Which pole of a magnet pulls the north pole of another magnet to it?
   (a) south   (b) north   (c) east   (d) west
3. An electric current can only flow through a circuit that is
   (a) open.   (b) magnetic.   (c) closed.   (d) charged.
4. If an object has extra electrons, what kind of charge does it have?
   (a) positive   (b) negative   (c) balanced   (d) none
5. If a wire is made into loops, the magnetic field that is made when electric current flows through the wire is
   (a) weaker.   (b) the same.   (c) balanced.   (d) stronger.
6. Air, rubber, glass, and plastic are good
   (a) conductors.   (b) magnets.   (c) insulators.   (d) circuits.
7. Many metals are good
   (a) conductors.   (b) generators.   (c) insulators.   (d) circuits.
8. What kind of circuit would cause all the lights on it to go out if one light went out?
   (a) parallel.   (b) series.   (c) magnetic.   (d) closed.

☑ Interpreting What You Learned

Write a short answer for each question.

1. How are electromagnets sometimes more useful than other magnets?
2. How does an object get a negative charge?
3. How do north poles and south poles of magnets act like electrons and protons?
4. What causes lightning?
5. How does a circuit breaker prevent fires?
6. Why does an electric generator need a source of energy?

☑ Extending Your Thinking

Write a paragraph to answer each question.

1. What do you think happens to the poles if you cut a bar magnet into three pieces?
2. How could you make an electromagnet from a steel screwdriver?

• For further review, use Study Guide pages 388–389.

Light and Sound

The leaf below has a row of clear balls along its edge. These balls are drops of water. If you look closely, you can see colorful flowers and leaves. The way that light travels causes these images.

Introducing the Chapter

You might think that light does not have any color, but it does. In the activity below, you will learn what colors make up light. In this chapter, you will learn more about light. You will find out how light travels and how people see colors. You will find out that sound and light are alike in some ways.

Making Colors with Light

Put a baking pan on a flat surface. Put water in the pan to a depth of 2 or 3 centimeters. Hold a small mirror so that most of it is under the water at a slant. Darken the room and shine a bright flashlight on the part of the mirror that is under the water. Look for a reflection of the light on the wall or ceiling. If you do not see different colors of light, move the flashlight around until you do.

When you do see the colors, put a piece of white paper between the mirror and the colors. Move the paper until you can see the colors on it.

Talk About It

1. What colors do you see on the paper?
2. What do these colors tell you about light?

What Is Light?

LESSON GOALS

You will learn
- what the visible spectrum is.
- what some sources of light are.

visible spectrum
(viz′ə bəl spek′trəm), light energy that can be seen and can be broken into the colors of light in the rainbow.

A prism breaks white light into colors.

Light is an important part of most people's lives. Without light, people could not see the world around them. Plants could not grow, and people would not have any food to eat.

Energy That You Can See

Light is a form of energy that you can see. Notice in the picture that light breaks up into all the colors of the rainbow. These colors are red, orange, yellow, green, blue, indigo, violet, and all the colors in between them. All these colors added together are called white light. White light and the colors of light in it are the **visible spectrum.**

Each color of light has its own special amount of energy. Bits of violet light have the most energy. Bits of red light have the least.

Sources of Light

Most objects you see do not make light. They are not sources of light. You see most objects because light bounces off of them and to your eyes.

The sun is the major source of light. Even moonlight is light from the sun bouncing off the moon. Which objects in the pictures are sources of light? Light bulbs, headlights on cars, flashlights, matches, and candles all make light.

Does your home or school have any electric lights like the tube in the middle picture? These tubes are filled with a gas. The inside of the tubes are covered with a special powder. When electricity flows through the tubes, the gas makes the powder glow. The glowing powder makes the light.

Car headlight

Electric light

Flashlight

Candles

Lesson Review

1. What is the visible spectrum?
2. What is the major source of light?
3. **Challenge!** What could you do to prove that an object is a light source or is not a light source?
   Study on your own, pages 390–391.

FIND OUT ON YOUR OWN

Another source of light energy is a laser. Laser light is a special kind of light that can be much more powerful than regular light. Scientists can even bounce a laser beam off the moon. Lasers have many uses. Some lasers help speed supermarket checkouts. Doctors use other lasers. Use books in the library to find out more about how people use lasers. Write a paragraph that tells what you learned.

2 How Does Light Travel?

LESSON GOALS

You will learn
- how light makes objects look the way they do.
- how flat and curved mirrors reflect light.
- how objects bend light.

ray, a narrow beam of light that travels in a straight line from a light source.

transparent (transper′ənt), allows light to pass through so that whatever is behind can be seen.

translucent (tran slü′snt), allows light to pass through but scatters it so that whatever is behind cannot be clearly seen.

opaque (ö päk′), does not allow light to pass through.

What happens when you shine a flashlight on a wall in a dark room? The light is brightest where you point the flashlight. The light travels in straight lines from the flashlight to the wall. Light travels from a light source in straight lines called **rays.**

Light and Materials

When rays of light hit different materials or objects, different things happen. Notice what happens when light hits the objects in the pictures.

Light passes through the glass in the first picture. The glass is **transparent.** You can see what is behind a transparent object. Clear glass, clean water, and clear plastic are transparent.

Light rays pass through the thin paper in the second picture. However, the paper spreads the light around in different directions. As a result, light can pass through, but you cannot see clearly what is behind the paper. This kind of material is **translucent.** Some kinds of glass are translucent.

Rays of light cannot go through the object in the third picture at all. This kind of material is **opaque.** You cannot see through an opaque object. Brick, wood, stones, and your body are opaque.

Transparent

Translucent

Opaque

People see colors because of what happens when light hits different objects and because white light is made of all the colors. Objects **absorb**—or take in—some of the light that hits them. Objects also **reflect**—or bounce back—some light.

An opaque object reflects whatever light it does not absorb. The color of the object is really the color of the light it reflects. The object in the picture on the left absorbs all the colors of light except red. It will reflect the red light. The red light bounces off the object and the object looks red. What color of light does a green object reflect? A black object looks black because it absorbs almost all the light that reaches it. What colors of light does a white object reflect?

Transparent and translucent objects are the color of the light they **transmit,** or let pass through. The piece of red glass in the picture on the right absorbs most of the colors of white light. It looks red because it transmits only red light. A piece of clear glass has no color because it transmits all the colors of white light.

absorb (ab sôrb′), to take in.

reflect (ri flekt′), to bounce back.

transmit (tran smit′), to pass through.

A red, opaque object reflects red light.

A red, transparent object transmits red light.

191

Mirrors and Reflections

You have learned that objects reflect light. You see reflected light when you look in a mirror. You are looking at a reflection that is an image of you.

Some surfaces form images better than other surfaces do. Mirrors have smooth, shiny surfaces that form good images. Look at the picture of light reflecting off the surface of a flat mirror. The light rays hit the mirror at a certain angle or direction. Notice that the rays reflect off the mirror at the same angle or direction. A good image will form.

Notice in the picture on the right that when light hits a rough surface, the rays reflect in many different directions. A wavy image might form, or no image might form.

Your image in a flat mirror is the same size that you are. Drivers often use flat mirrors to see the traffic behind them. When they see a car in a flat mirror, they know about how far away the car is.

Light reflecting from a flat mirror   Light reflecting from a rough surface

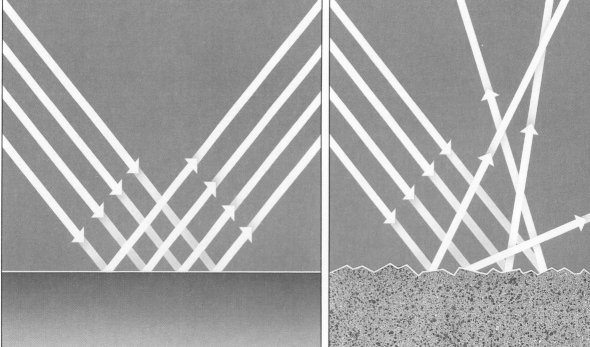

192

Other mirrors do not have flat surfaces. Instead, they have curved surfaces. The girl in the picture is looking at herself in a curved mirror. Images formed by curved mirrors are very different from images formed by flat mirrors. The images might be larger, smaller, or upside down. You cannot always tell the size or distance of an object by seeing its image in a curved mirror.

Each light ray that hits the surface of a curved mirror is reflected back at the same angle that it hit. Because the surface is curved, the light rays that hit the mirror in different places bounce off in different directions. Notice how the rays of light hit and bounce off of the curved mirror in the picture.

Curved mirrors can be fun, but they also have many uses. Curved mirrors in stores help clerks see much more of the store than a flat mirror would. Some cars also have curved mirrors to help the driver see more traffic than a flat mirror does.

Colors of light reflecting from a curved mirror

Image formed by a curved mirror

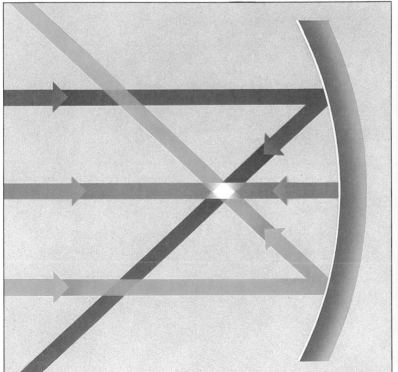

Bending Light

Why does the pencil in the glass seem to be broken in two? The pencil looks this way because light sometimes bends or changes direction.

Light travels at different speeds through different materials. When light changes speed, it also changes direction. Light bends when it moves from one material into another. Light travels faster through air than through water. When light moves from air into water, the light slows down and changes direction.

The light rays that reflect from the part of the pencil above water travel to your eyes through air. The rays do not bend. The light rays that reflect from the part of the pencil in the water travel back through the water before reaching the air. When these rays move into the air, they change speed and bend. The pencil looks broken.

Light also bends when it moves from air into a lens. A lens is a transparent object with at least one curved surface. Whenever light hits a lens, the light bends. Lenses bend light in a way that makes an image. Lenses have many uses.

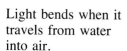

Light bends when it travels from water into air.

Some lenses bulge at the middle like a football. This kind of lens is a **convex lens.** A camera uses a convex lens to bring light rays to a point on the film. Each of your eyes has a convex lens. A magnifying glass has a convex lens that makes things look bigger. A microscope uses several lenses of this shape. Notice how the convex lens below bends light.

Other lenses are thinner in the middle than at the edges. This shape lens is a **concave lens.** A concave lens makes objects look smaller. Notice that the concave lens below spreads light rays apart.

SCIENCE IN YOUR LIFE

People use one kind of lens in small holes at eye level in doors. They can get a wide-angle view outside by peeking through this lens.

convex lens (kon veks´ lenz), a lens that is thicker in the middle than at the edges.

concave lens (kon käv´ lenz), a lens that is thinner in the middle than at the edges.

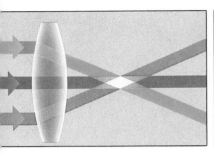

A convex lens

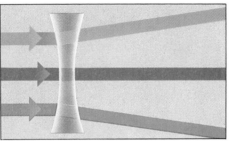

A concave lens

Lesson Review

1. What makes an object look white?
2. When drivers want to know how far away a car behind them is, would they probably use a flat mirror or a curved mirror?
3. What happens to light rays when they move from air into water?
4. **Challenge!** If you wanted to let light into a room but did not want people outside to see in, what kind of glass would you need?

Study on your own, pages 390–391.

Use an encyclopedia or other books in the library to find out how a color television makes a color picture. Try looking for information about mixing different colors of light under the word *color*. Write a paragraph telling what you found.

FIND OUT ON YOUR OWN

ACTIVITY

Observing Images in Mirrors

Purpose
Observe images reflected in a flat mirror and in curved mirrors.

Gather These Materials
• flat mirror • 2 file cards • pencil • shiny metal spoon

Follow This Procedure
1. Use tables like the ones shown to record your observations.
2. Write the capital letter *F* on a file card. Hold the card in front of the flat mirror. Observe the image of the letter *F* in the mirror. Draw the image in your table.
3. Write a backward *F* on the card. Hold the card up to the mirror. Observe the image in the mirror. Draw the image in your table.
4. Print your name on the other file card and hold it up to the mirror. Copy what you see in your table.

5. A spoon has two surfaces that can form images like curved mirrors. Look at your image in the back of the bowl of the spoon. Describe the image in your table. Look at your image in the front of the spoon. Describe the image in your table.

Record Your Results
Images in a Flat Mirror

	Image
Forward *F*	
Backward *F*	
Name	

Images in a Curved Mirror

	Image
Back of spoon	
Front of spoon	

State Your Conclusion
1. Describe the image of an object placed in front of a flat mirror.
2. What is the difference between an image in a flat mirror and an image in a curved mirror?

Use What You Learned
What kind of image would you see in a curved mirror if you placed a flat mirror in front of the curved mirror? Test your prediction.

196

Concentrating the Power of Light

The Problem For many years, people thought of light in very limited ways. They pictured light waves like a crowd of people going their different ways. The waves moved around in all directions. Light was also compared to noise. Just as noise is a jumble of sounds, ordinary light was thought of as a jumble of different colors. As ordinary light travels, the rays that make it up spread out. The light becomes less bright as it moves farther from its source. No one had been able to make light behave any differently.

The Breakthrough In 1917, Albert Einstein had a new idea about light. He showed that sometimes light passing by a gas can make the gas give off more of the same kind of light. In the 1940s and 1950s, Soviet and American scientists used Einstein's idea. They showed that it should be possible to make light waves march in step like a troop of soldiers. These waves would be like voices in a chorus singing the same note. The power of light would be concentrated. In 1960, American scientist Theodore H. Maiman made the first device that could produce strong light traveling in only one direction in a thin beam of a single color. He called the device a laser.

New Technology In recent years, scientists have found many ways to use lasers. Lasers can do jobs that ordinary light cannot do. Doctors use lasers in many ways.

Lasers are much better for performing surgery than knives. A laser makes an exact cut in one part of the body, without harming any nearby parts. Heat from the laser also cleans the area.

Lasers now play an important role in eye surgery. Sometimes the part of the eye sensitive to light, the retina, comes loose. A loosened retina can lead to blindness. In the past, retina surgery took hours. With lasers, the surgery has become a much shorter, simpler, and safer operation. You can see a laser beam in the picture. The beam is traveling through the eye and is focused on the retina. In a fraction of a second, the laser can seal the retina back in its proper place. Lasers can also unplug blocked arteries, destroy tumors, and remove birthmarks.

What Do You Think?
1. How is laser light different from ordinary light?
2. Machines guided by lasers often drill tunnels. What property of the laser light makes them useful for this job?

3 How Are Light and Sound Similar and Different?

LESSON GOALS

You will learn
- how light waves are different from sound waves.
- how light waves and sound waves travel.

wavelength
(wāv′lengkth′), the distance from a point on a wave to the same point on the next wave.

Look below at the waves made by a stone thrown into water. Notice that the waves move out in a circle. These waves are energy traveling through water. The waves get weaker as they move farther away from their source. Light and sound also are energy that travels in waves. They get weaker as they move farther away from their source.

Different Kinds of Waves

Light waves and sound waves are different. Find the drawing of a wave in water on the next page. Light waves move like waves in water. Unlike waves in water, light waves can travel through empty space.

The distance from the highest point in one wave to the next highest point is the light's **wavelength.** Different colors of light have different wavelengths. Other kinds of energy also have waves like light waves. Microwaves, X rays, and radio waves are like light waves. However, they do not have the same wavelengths as light, and people cannot see them.

Waves in water

Find the girl's hands making sound waves in the picture. First she slipped a rubber band over the doorknob. Then she pulled the rubber band tight. When she plucks the rubber band, it **vibrates**—or moves quickly back and forth. When the rubber band vibrates, it makes the air around it vibrate too. Sound is made when something vibrates. The air vibrates as it carries sound waves.

Sound waves are not like waves in water. Sound waves are more like waves that move through a wire spring. Notice in the drawing of waves moving through a spring that in some places the parts of the spring are closer together. The vibrations push the parts together. The wave travels through the spring as parts are pushed together and then move apart. The wavelength of a sound wave is the distance from where one part is squeezed together to where the next part is squeezed together. Different sounds have different wavelengths. People cannot hear sounds of all wavelengths.

All musical instruments have something that vibrates. A violin and piano have strings that vibrate. When you strike a drum, the material on the drum vibrates. When you play a trumpet, your lips make air inside the instrument vibrate.

vibrate (vɪ′brāt), to move quickly back and forth.

Making sound waves

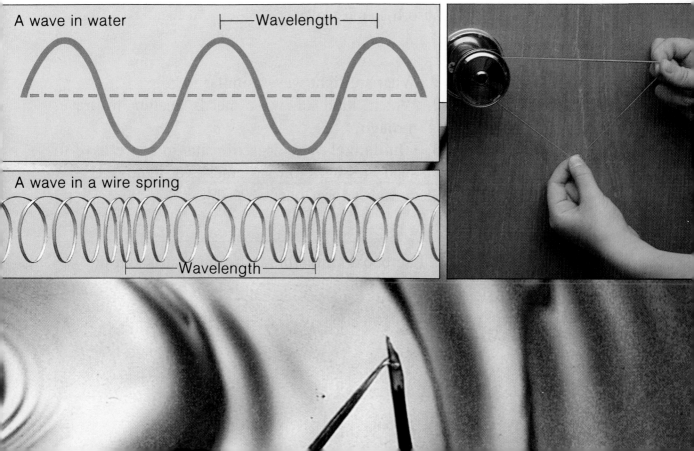

A wave in water |——Wavelength——|

A wave in a wire spring

|——Wavelength——|

How Waves Travel

Light waves travel fastest through empty space—or space that has no matter. Light waves move slower as they pass through matter. Light waves cannot pass through some matter at all.

Sound waves cannot travel through empty space. They must have matter to travel through, because matter can vibrate. Sound waves travel well through air. Sound waves travel even faster through solids and liquids.

Sound waves travel more slowly than light waves. Look at the lightning in the picture. If you saw this lightning in the sky, you would hear the thunder a little later.

You know that light waves can be absorbed, reflected, or transmitted by objects. Sound waves can also be absorbed, reflected, or transmitted. Smooth, flat surfaces, such as walls, reflect sound waves. If you have ever heard an echo, you have heard the reflection of sound waves. Curtains and carpets absorb sound waves.

You see lightning before you hear thunder.

Lesson Review

1. What are light waves similar to?
2. Which kind of wave needs matter to travel through?
3. **Challenge!** Why do astronauts in space have to send messages to each other over radios?

Study on your own, pages 390–391.

FIND OUT ON YOUR OWN

Use books in the library to find out about the pitch of sounds. What is pitch? What causes pitch? How can you change the pitch of a musical instrument? Write the answers to these questions. List some common sounds, and tell about their pitch.

Inferring How Sound Waves Travel

ACTIVITY

Wear cover goggles for this activity.

Purpose
Infer that sound waves are vibrations that travel through matter.

Gather These Materials
• large plastic-foam cup • pencil • 2 rubber bands • plastic food wrap • salt

Follow This Procedure
1. Use a chart like the one shown to record your observations.
2. Use the point of a pencil to punch a tiny hole in the bottom of the cup.
3. Cut the rubber band, and push one end through the hole. Tie a knot so the rubber band cannot be pulled out of the hole.
4. Stretch a piece of plastic wrap over the top of the cup. Use a rubber band to hold the plastic wrap tightly in place.
5. Sprinkle a few grains of salt on the wrap. Hold the cup while your partner slowly stretches the rubber band. Gently pluck the stretched rubber band and observe what happens to the salt. Record your observations in your chart.
6. Remove the plastic wrap.
7. Hold the cup near your ear while your partner slowly stretches the rubber band. *CAUTION: Do not hold the cup too close to your ear or stretch the rubber band so far that it breaks.*

8. Ask your partner to gently pluck the rubber band with one finger. Record your observations.
9. Switch places with your partner, and repeat steps 7 and 8.

Record Your Results

	Observations
Salt grains	
Cup placed near ear	

State Your Conclusion
1. Explain what happened to the salt.
2. What can you infer about sound waves based on your observations?

Use What You Learned
How was the plastic wrap in the activity similar to your eardrum?

201

Skills for Solving Problems

Using Light Meters and Bar Graphs

Problem: How is the amount of light reflected from different surfaces different?

Part A. Using Light Meters to Collect Information

1. The light meters below are measuring how much light is reflected from different surfaces. The pointer on the light meters moves to a higher number of units when more light is reflected. How far from the surfaces are the light bulbs?

2. In the pictures, light from 60-watt bulbs is reflected from three different surfaces. How many units does the light meter show for light reflected from aluminum foil? from brown cardboard? from white paper?

Part B. Using a Bar Graph to Organize and Interpret Information

3. The bar graph contains the information you collected in Part A about the amount of light reflected from different surfaces. Each bar of the graph stands for one kind of surface. What does the bar on the right stand for? What do the numbers at the left of the graph stand for?

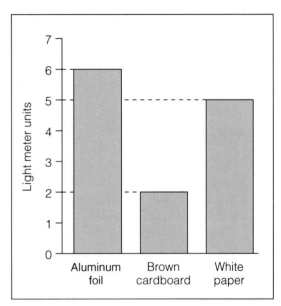

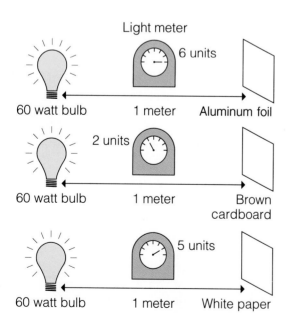

4. Place your finger at the top of the bar that stands for aluminum foil. Move across the graph to the line at the left. What is the number of units on the light meter for aluminum foil?
5. How is the amount of light reflected from each surface different?

Part C. Using Light Meters and Bar Graphs to Solve a Problem.

Problem: How is the amount of light reflected from a surface different when the surface is smooth, pleated, or wrinkled?

6. Use the pictures below to collect the information you need to solve the problem. Make a bar graph similar to the graph in Part B to organize your information.
7. Look at your bar graph. How is the amount of light reflected from a surface different when the surface is smooth, pleated, or wrinkled?
8. How would your results change if you used 100-watt bulbs but kept everything else the same?

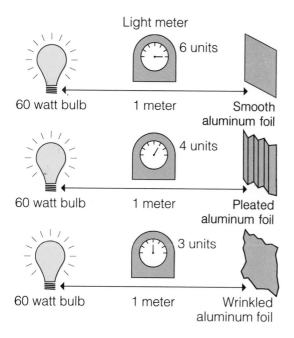

Light meter
6 units
60 watt bulb   1 meter   Smooth aluminum foil

4 units
60 watt bulb   1 meter   Pleated aluminum foil

3 units
60 watt bulb   1 meter   Wrinkled aluminum foil

Chapter 8 Review

Chapter Main Ideas

☑ *Lesson 1* • White light is made up of all the colors of the rainbow.
• The sun is the major source of light energy.

Lesson 2 • The amount of light that can pass through an object makes the object transparent, translucent, or opaque. • The color of an opaque object is the color of light it reflects. • Flat mirrors and curved mirrors form good images. • Light rays bend when they move from one material into another.

Lesson 3 • Light waves are similar to waves in water. • Sound waves are similar to waves in a wire spring. • Light waves are faster than sound waves and can travel through empty space. • Sound waves cannot travel through empty space.

☑ Reviewing Science Words

absorb	translucent
concave lens	transmit
convex lens	transparent
opaque	vibrate
ray	visible spectrum
reflect	wavelength

Copy each sentence. Fill in the blank with the correct word or words from the list.

1. The seven colors of the rainbow make up the ____ .
2. Transparent objects are the color of the light they ____ .
3. Any object you can see through clearly is ____ .
4. Each color has a separate ____ .
5. A magnifying glass has a ____ .
6. A beam of light that travels in a straight line is a ____ .
7. Red objects ____ all colors of light except red.
8. A ____ object lets light through but scatters it.
9. Opaque objects are the color of the light they ____ .
10. Objects make sound when they ____ .
11. Light cannot go through an ____ object at all.
12. An object looks smaller through a ____ .

☑ Reviewing What You Learned

Write the letter of the best answer.

1. A brick wall is
   (a) transparent.   (b) opaque.   (c) translucent.   (d) a mirror.
2. What makes up the visible spectrum?
   (a) white light   (b)microwaves   (c) black light   (d) radio waves
3. An object with a smooth, shiny surface makes a good
   (a) lens.   (b) light source.   (c) ray.   (d) mirror.
4. Light waves travel fastest through
   (a) solids.   (b) liquids.   (c) gases.   (d) empty space.
5. Sound waves travel fastest through
   (a) solids.   (b) the air.   (c) gases.   (d) empty space.
6. What does a black object do to light?
   (a) reflects all colors   (c) absorbs all colors
   (b) transmits all colors   (d) vibrates all colors
7. Which object makes use of light bending when it changes speed?
   (a) eyeglasses   (b) a flat mirror   (c) a curved mirror   (d) a window
8. Which of the following has waves that are like waves moving through a wire spring?
   (a) light   (b) sound   (c) X rays   (d) radio

☑ Interpreting What You Learned

Write a short answer for each question or statement.

1. Is the moon a source of light? Explain your answer.
2. What happens to light rays when they hit a rough surface?
3. Explain how sound waves are made.
4. How are sound waves different from light waves?
5. Explain how an opaque object makes a shadow.

☑ Extending Your Thinking

Write a paragraph to answer each question or statement.

1. Suppose you have an object that looks blue when it is in white light. How would the same object look if you put it in red light? Explain your answer.
2. If you wanted to catch a fish with your hands, what have you learned about light that would help you?

• For further review, use Study Guide pages 390–391.

Careers

When you toast a piece of bread or use a hair dryer, you are using energy to do work. Some people's careers involve figuring out how to best use energy to get work done.

Electrical engineers design and help build the equipment in a power plant. Some electrical engineers design robots that can help make various products. The engineer in the picture is working on a building.

Mechanical engineers design the engines that provide power for everything from cars to rockets. They also work on machines that use power. Some of these machines include refrigerators, air conditioners, and power tools. Electrical and mechanical engineers go to college for four years.

Mechanics keep machines running properly. A mechanic usually works on one type of machine. Some mechanics fix cars, while others work on household appliances or farm machinery. Mechanics learn some skills in high school or at a vocational school. They continue to learn on the job.

One important type of energy is light energy. Our eyes use light energy to see. Many people's eyes work better with the help of eyeglasses or contact lenses. **Dispensing opticians,** like the woman below, help customers choose eyeglass frames. Some dispensing opticians make the lenses that will go into the frames. Others prepare careful instructions so that laboratory technicians can make the lenses. When the eyeglasses are finished, opticians adjust them to fit the customer properly. Many opticians can also fit customers with contact lenses. Some dispensing opticians learn their skills on the job. Many opticians take classes at a vocational or technical school.

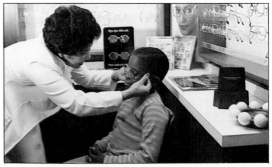

Photographers also work with light energy. They use a camera to capture light energy on film. A good photographer has an artistic sense. Some photographers take pictures of people. Others take pictures in nature of plants and animals. Some take photographs for advertisements or newspapers. Some photographers develop their own film in a special room called a darkroom. Photographers can go to college, take special classes, or learn by experience.

Cameras

Have you ever seen a moose on your way to school? You might have never seen a moose walking around, but you have seen a moose. You saw a picture of a moose on page 36. You see many things in pictures.

Cameras can take pictures of life in the ocean. Cameras on microscopes can take pictures of blood cels and other things too small for you to see. Cameras on telescopes can take pictures far away.

A photographer in the early 1800s needed much equipment, knowledge, and skill. Today, with a simple camera and film, you only have to push a button. The drawing below shows how a camera and film makes a photograph.

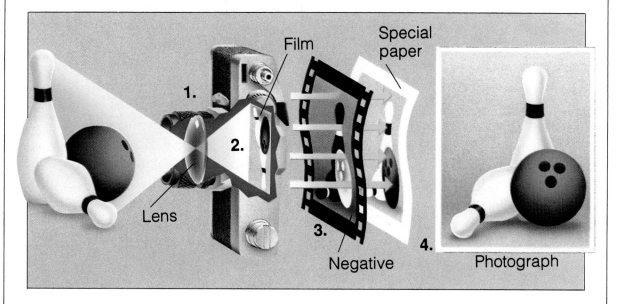

1 A camera uses light to make a picture. A camera is dark inside except for the light you let in when you push a button to take a picture.

Light passes through a lens that focuses an upside down image of the object on the film.

2 Film for pictures that are black and white is a thin layer of paper or plastic with a layer of silver salts on it. Light causes chemical changes in the silver salts. The more light an object reflects, the more the silver salts change. The different amounts of change create an image on the film. You cannot see the image, but it is stored on the film.

3 In a darkroom, chemicals are added to the film. The chemicals change the silver salts to metallic silver. Where the most light hit the film, the layer of metallic silver is thick and looks black. Where no light or little light hit, the layer is thin or not there at all.

The film now is called a negative. Light-colored objects look dark, and dark-colored objects look light.

4 Light passes through the negative to a special paper. The dark areas on the negative block out more light than the light and clear areas. The picture that is made is an image of what you took a picture of.

Unit 2 Review

Complete the Sentence

Fill in the blank with the correct word or words from the list.

atom	mixture
compass	opaque
density	proton
efficiency	reflect
energy	resistance
inertia	vibrate
mass	

1. The earth's magnetic field makes the arrow of a ____ point north.
2. The substances in a ____ can be easily separated.
3. A red object will ____ the red light that hits it.
4. People use different kinds of ____ to do work.
5. A 10-kilogram object has more ____ than a 5-kilogram object.
6. Eardrums ____ when sound waves strike them.
7. The ____ of an atom has a positive charge.
8. A person cannot see through material that is ____ .
9. An element contains only one kind of ____ .
10. The ____ of a material is how much mass it contains in a certain volume.
11. The ____ of a machine can be increased if friction between its parts can be reduced.
12. A person puts on the brakes to overcome the ____ of a car.
13. The ____ to an electric current is very high in an insulator.

Short Answer

Write a short answer for each question or statement.

1. Compare the shapes and volumes of the three states of matter.
2. How are the molecules in a compound different from the molecules in a mixture?
3. How can you measure the volume of a rock using a graduated cylinder?
4. Name three forces that act on an object that you throw.
5. Suppose you tried to push a heavy rock, but you could not move it. Would a scientist say that you did work? Explain your answer.
6. Why do people who repair electric wires use a special tape made of rubber?
7. One light bulb burns out and all the lights on a sign go out. What does this tell you about the sign's electric circuit?
8. How do you know that the North Pole of the earth is like the south pole of a magnet?
9. You look in a mirror and it makes you seem small. What shape is the mirror?

Essay

Write a paragraph for each question or statement.

1. Name four different kinds of simple machines. Tell how each one makes work easier.
2. Describe some of the differences between light waves and sound waves.

Science Projects

1. Make a mixture of solids by adding sand and iron filings or pieces of steel wool together. How might you separate these two solids? Make a mixture of two liquids by adding water to a cup and then olive oil or another cooking oil. Stir the two liquids. How might you separate the two liquids?

2. Use an empty milk or juice carton and a pinwheel to make a model of a windmill. Place your windmill outside and face it into the wind. What happens? Why? Is work being done? Explain. Use references to find out what windmills are used for.

3. Use a paper bowl, plastic straws, a wheel from an old toy, and glue to make a model of a wheelbarrow. Study your model and how it works. Is a wheelbarrow a simple machine or a compound machine? If it is a simple machine, what kind is it? If it is a compound machine, what simple machines help make it up?

4. Get several different shaped magnets, such as a round magnet and a horseshoe-shaped magnet. Place a piece of typing paper or notebook paper over each magnet. Then sprinkle iron filings or shreaded pieces of steel wool on the paper. Notice the patterns made by each magnet. How do these patterns compare with the patterns made by a bar magnet?

Science and Society

The Cost of Smashing Atoms Some scientists want to build a superconducting super collider (SSC). The SSC would be the largest atom smasher in the world. In fact, the SSC would be the largest machine in the world. People would be needed to fill jobs to build and take care of the SSC. Scientists would use the SSC to learn more about atoms. It will cost 4.5 billion dollars to build the SSC. Critics say the SSC costs too much. They think the nation could solve many problems with that money. Scientists point out that the machine is needed to make new discoveries in physics. The critics agree that scientific discoveries are good, but think these discoveries will not help people in any way. List some arguments for building the SSC. List some arguments against it.

Books About Science

Raceways: Having Fun with Balls and Tracks by Bernard Zubrowski. Morrow, 1985. Learn about velocity and acceleration through activities.

Introduction to Physics by Amanda Kent and Alan Ward. EDC Publishers, 1983. Learn about elementary physics, including electricity, sound, light, and magnetism.

Amazing Magnets by David Adler. Troll, 1983. Learn about magnets and magnetism.

Earth Science

You can see different layers of rocks in this canyon. The rocks formed over many years. The river also took many years to cut this path through the rocks.

The land is always changing. In this unit, you will discover different forces that change landforms on land and at the ocean bottom. You also will discover what causes changes in weather and how objects move in the solar system.

SCIENCE IN THE NEWS During the next few weeks, look in newspapers or magazines for stories about how the oceans are important to people. Also look for stories about people helping the oceans. Share the news with your class.

Chapter 9 Measuring Weather Conditions

Chapter 10 Changes in Landforms

Chapter 11 Oceans

Chapter 12 Movement in the Solar System

Chapter 9

Measuring Weather Conditions

Where these strawberries grow, the temperature dropped below freezing last night. A bright, sunny morning will bring warmer temperatures. The temperature will continue to change during the day as sunlight hits the earth.

Introducing the Chapter

You might have noticed that the way sunlight hits the earth changes during the day. In the activity below, you will observe different angles of light hitting a surface. In this chapter, you will learn how sunlight heats the earth. You will learn how heating the earth affects the weather.

DISCOVER!

Observing the Angle of Light

The angle that sunlight hits the earth causes different temperatures. You can use a flashlight and a sheet of black paper to observe different angles of light hitting a surface.

Tape one end of the paper to the top of a table or desk. Hold the sheet of paper straight up and down. Shine the flashlight directly at the paper. Notice the size and brightness of the lighted area on the paper.

Hold the flashlight in the same place. Now slowly move the top of the paper away from the light without bending the paper. The light should hit the paper less directly. Notice the size and brightness of the lighted area.

Talk About It
1. Which angle of light made the biggest lighted area?
2. If the light were sunlight, which direction would heat the paper the most?

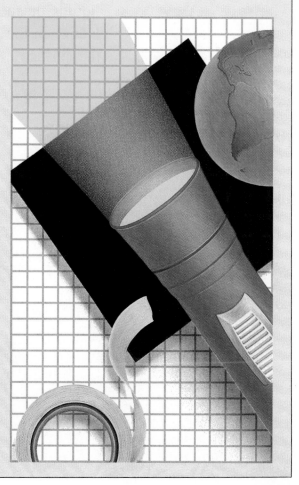

213

1 What Causes Different Air Temperatures Outside?

LESSON GOALS

You will learn
- how the angle of sunlight and number of daylight hours change air temperature.
- how different surfaces cause different air temperatures.
- how to measure temperature.

What is the weather like where you are today? Is the temperature hot, cold, warm, or cool? Is it sunny or cloudy? Is it raining or snowing? Your answers describe the weather.

The weather is always changing. It might be very different tomorrow or even later today. The weather might be different a few kilometers away from you. Changing air temperatures usually cause changes in the weather.

Sunlight Hitting the Earth

As sunlight passes through the air, it does not heat the air. The light energy from the sun hits solids and liquids on the surface of the earth and warms them. Notice in the picture below that the heat energy from the surface of the earth then heats the air above.

How sunlight hits the earth

Light energy

Liquids warm slowly.

Heat energy

Solids warm quickly.

Sunlight hits the earth at different angles. These different angles cause different air temperatures. The more directly sunlight hits the earth's surface, the higher the air temperature can become.

The angle that sunlight hits the earth changes during the day. Notice in the drawings below that sunlight hits the earth most directly around noon. It hits the earth less directly at sunrise and sunset. Air temperatures are often lowest before sunrise. Then air temperatures rise as the surface of the earth is heated. Sunlight heats the earth's surface most around noon. However, air temperatures are often the highest in the late afternoon. The surface takes this time to heat the air above it.

Different areas of the earth receive different angles of sunlight during a year. An area receives sunlight that is most direct during the summer. An area receives sunlight that is less direct during the winter.

The number of daylight hours also causes different temperatures. A summer day has more daylight hours than a winter day. The surface of the earth has more hours to heat up during a summer day.

Angle of sunlight around noon

Angle of sunlight in late afternoon

Different Surfaces

You know that the sun heats the earth's surface. Then the surface heats the air. Some surfaces absorb the sun's energy more quickly than other surfaces do. Land absorbs heat more quickly than water. Dark-colored surfaces absorb heat more quickly than light-colored surfaces. Such surfaces as blacktop, cement, and buildings absorb heat faster than grass and trees do.

A surface that absorbs heat quickly will also absorb more heat than other surfaces. A surface that absorbs more heat can heat the air above it more. Suppose you are walking barefoot on the surfaces in the picture on a hot summer day. How might each surface feel?

An ocean or a large lake can change the air temperature above the land near it. During a summer day, a large lake heats up more slowly than land nearby. The air above the lake will be cooler than the air above the land. This cool air often moves over the land. The air temperature above the land becomes cooler. Land away from the lake stays warmer.

Blacktop surface

Grass surface

Wood surface

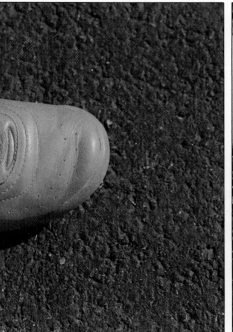

Measuring Temperature

How do you know if you need to wear a jacket outside? Knowing the outside air temperature would help you decide. A thermometer is a tool that measures temperature.

The pictures show two kinds of thermometers. One kind of thermometer is a tube that holds a liquid. Since heat causes matter to expand—or spread out—the liquid expands and moves up the tube as the air temperature gets warmer. The liquid moves down the tube if the air temperature gets cooler. Each mark on the thermometer on the right is for 2 degrees Celsius. What temperature does this thermometer in the picture show in degrees Celsius?

The other kind of thermometer is shaped like a circle. Inside this thermometer, pieces of metal expand as the temperature gets hotter. A pointer hooked to these metal pieces moves and points to the temperature. Each mark on the thermometer on the left is for 5 degrees Celsius.

SCIENCE IN YOUR LIFE

Air temperature should be measured in the shade. If the thermometer is in the sun, sunlight heats the matter that makes up the thermometer. The temperature shown on the thermometer will be the temperature of the thermometer—not the temperature of the air.

Two kinds of thermometers

Lesson Review

1. How is the earth's air heated?
2. Why might the temperatures above land and water be different?
3. What tool measures temperature?
4. **Challenge!** Why might people wear light-colored clothes in the summer?

Study on your own, pages 392–393.

Look in an encyclopedia to find out what climate is. How are climate and weather different? What is the climate like where you live? Write a paragraph that answers these questions.

FIND OUT ON YOUR OWN

2 How Does Temperature Affect Air Pressure and Wind?

LESSON GOALS

You will learn
- how temperature causes changes in air pressure and wind.
- how to measure air pressure.
- how to measure wind speed and direction.

air pressure, the amount that air presses or pushes on anything.

low-pressure area, an area where warm air rises and pushes down on the earth's surface with less pressure.

How air changes as you go higher above the earth

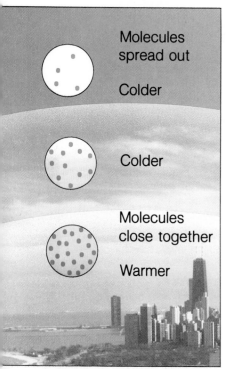

Molecules spread out

Colder

Colder

Molecules close together

Warmer

The earth is surrounded by a layer of air that presses down on the earth. This pressing down of air is called **air pressure.** You do not notice air pressure most of the time. However, you might have noticed a change in air pressure as you moved higher in the air. Have your ears ever popped as you rode in an elevator, in an airplane, or up a hill in a car? The sudden changes in air pressure at these times can make your ears pop.

Notice in the picture how air temperature changes as you go higher. Near the surface of the earth, the air is warmer. The surface heats the air above it. As you move higher and higher above the surface of the earth, the air gets colder.

Air pressure also changes as you go higher above the surface of the earth. The higher you are, the less air is above you. Less air presses down on you. The air pressure is lower.

Near the surface of the earth, the air molecules are close together. Higher above the surface, the air molecules are spread out more. The molecules of air get farther and farther apart.

Changes in Air Pressure and Wind

Air pressure on the earth's surface also changes. Changes in temperature cause changes in air pressure. You know that sunlight heats the surface of the earth. The surface then heats the air above it. As the air becomes warmer, its molecules move farther apart and the air becomes lighter. The warm air rises. Find the warm air rising in the picture on the next page. As it rises, the warm air pushes down on the surface of the earth with less pressure. A **low-pressure area** forms. What do you think happens to the temperature of the warm air as it rises?

Notice in the picture that cooler air moves in to take the place of the warm air that rises. Cooler air also sinks because it is heavier than warm air. The cool air pushes down on the surface of the earth with more pressure than warm air. A **high-pressure area** forms where cool air sinks.

Air moves from an area of high pressure to an area of low pressure. This moving air is wind. Find the direction of the wind in the picture.

You can use a balloon to show that wind blows from a place with high pressure to a place with low pressure. When you blow air into a balloon, you force air into the balloon. The air in the balloon has high pressure. This pressure gives the balloon its shape and makes its sides firm. What happens when you let the air out of the balloon? You can hear the wind as the air moves from a place of high pressure to a place of lower pressure.

The molecules of air are farther apart the higher a person travels up a mountain. People who visit places high in the mountains often get tired easily because they get less oxygen with each breath.

high-pressure area, an area where cool air sinks and pushes down on the earth's surface with more pressure.

Wind blows from an area of high pressure to an area of low pressure

Measuring Air Pressure

Knowing what the air pressure is in different places helps people predict the weather. A tool called a **barometer** measures air pressure. The pictures show two kinds of barometers.

One kind is made of a hollow tube that is closed at one end and open at the other end. The tube is filled with mercury. The open end of the tube is then placed in a dish of mercury. Notice in the picture on the left that the mercury no longer fills the tube. The mercury moves down the tube a little. Air pressure presses down on the mercury in the dish and holds the mercury in the tube at a certain level. As air pressure gets higher, it presses down more. The added pressure on the mercury in the dish pushes the mercury up the tube. When air pressure is lower, it presses less on the mercury in the dish. What do you think happens to the mercury in the tube then?

The other kind of barometer is like the one in the bottom pictures. This barometer has a box inside it. The box has a needle hooked to it. Some of the air has been taken out of the box. As a higher pressure pushes on the sides of the box, the needle points to a higher number on the front of the barometer. When air pressure gets lower, it presses less on the sides of the box. What do you think happens to where the needle points then?

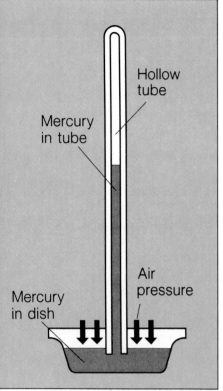

How a mercury barometer works

Another kind of barometer and how it works

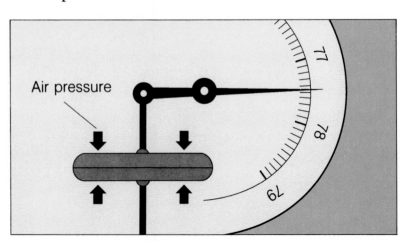

Measuring Wind Direction and Speed

A tool called a **wind vane** shows the direction the wind is coming from. Letters on the wind vane show which way is north, south, east, and west. An arrow turns to point into the wind. Find these parts on the wind vane in the picture.

If the arrow points north, the wind is from the north. If the arrow points between two directions, both directions are used to tell the wind direction. For example, the wind could be from the northeast or the southwest. A wind sock, like the one in the picture on the right, also shows wind direction.

wind vane (vān), a tool that shows wind direction.

A wind sock

A wind vane

221

anemometer
(an/ə mom/ə tər), a tool
that measures wind speed.

An **anemometer** measures the speed of the wind. Find the cups on the anemometer in the picture. The wind pushes these cups and makes this part of the anemometer spin. As the wind blows faster, the anemometer spins faster. The spinning part of the anemometer is attached to a dial that shows how fast the wind is blowing.

An anemometer

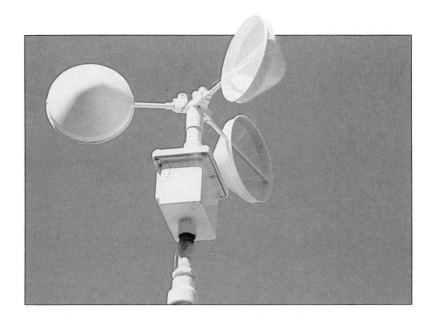

Lesson Review

1. How does air temperature cause a low-pressure area?
2. What tool measures air pressure?
3. What two tools measure wind?
4. **Challenge!** Why do you think the air high above the earth is cold?

Study on your own, pages 392–393.

**FIND OUT
ON YOUR OWN**

Look in an encyclopedia to find out how to guess wind speed by observing things around you. Make a chart of the information you learn.

Measuring Wind Speed

Purpose
Build a tool for measuring wind speed, and *measure* wind speed.

Gather These Materials
• protractor • ruler • clear tape • 25 cm of red thread • table tennis ball

Follow This Procedure
1. Use a table like the one shown to record your observations.
2. Tape the protractor to the ruler as shown in the picture.
3. Tape one end of the thread to the table tennis ball. Tape the other end of the thread to the protractor as shown. The thread should hang down the middle of the protractor.
4. Take your tool outside. Hold it still using the ruler as a handle. Point the ruler into the wind. Be sure the ruler is level with the ground.
5. When the wind blows the ball, it will move the thread on the protractor. Record the highest number on the protractor that the thread reaches.
6. Find the wind speed number in kilometers per hour under this number in the chart below. Record the wind speed in your table.
7. Measure and record the wind speed 3 times during the day.

Record Your Results

	1	2	3
Number on protractor			
Wind speed (km/hr)			

State Your Conclusion
1. What was the highest wind speed you measured?
2. How can you use a number on a protractor to find wind speed?

Use What You Learned
For a windmill to make electricity, wind speed must be at least 13 km/hr. Could windmills be used to make electricity where you live? Explain your answer.

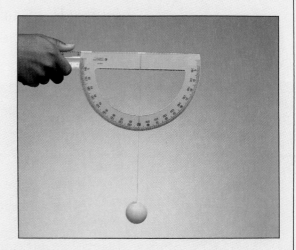

Number on protractor

90	95	100	105	110	115	120	125	130	135	140	145	150	155	160

Wind speed (km/hr)

0	9	13	16	19	21	24	26	29	31	34	37	41	46	52

3 How Does Temperature Cause Clouds and Precipitation?

LESSON GOALS

You will learn
- how clouds form.
- four kinds of precipitation.
- how to measure humidity and precipitation.

You know that water can be in three different states of matter. It can be the liquid water you drink. It can be solid ice. Water can also be a gas, called water vapor. Water vapor is needed for clouds to form.

Clouds

Water vapor gets into the air when liquid water evaporates. Water evaporates from oceans, rivers, puddles, the ground, or wherever water is. As warmer air rises, it carries the water vapor with it. When the air cools, the water vapor condenses—or becomes tiny drops of liquid water. These tiny drops are so small that they stay in the air. A cloud is made by these tiny drops of water.

Think about different clouds you have seen. You might have seen white fluffy clouds that look like cotton. These clouds are cumulus (kyü′myə ləs) clouds like the ones below. You often see these clouds in fair weather. However, they can grow larger, look dark, and bring rain.

Cumulus clouds

Cirrus clouds

You also might have seen white, feathery clouds like the ones in the picture. These clouds are cirrus (sir′əs) clouds. They are so high up in the air that they are made of tiny pieces of ice. You often see these clouds in fair weather.

A third kind of cloud you might have seen is in the picture on the right. These stratus (strā′təs) clouds form in layers that spread across the sky. You might see stratus clouds when it rains.

Precipitation

The tiny drops of water in clouds bump into each other and join together. They make bigger and bigger drops. Finally, the drops are heavy enough that they fall out of the clouds to the ground. Water that falls to the ground from clouds is **precipitation.**

What are some kinds of precipitation? You probably have seen precipitation that falls as rain. Snow, sleet, and hail are other kinds of precipitation. Snow forms in clouds that have a very cold air temperature. The water drops freeze and make the tiny ice crystals you know as snow. What do you think might happen to make snow fall as rain?

SCIENCE IN YOUR LIFE

Sometimes, people need rain but no precipitation falls. In some cases, people try to cause rain by "cloud seeding." They use airplanes to add substances to clouds. These substances help the water drops become large enough to fall as precipitation.

precipitation
(pri sip′ə tā′shən), moisture that falls to the ground from clouds.

Stratus clouds

Sleet forms when drops of rain freeze as they fall. Sleet is made of tiny pellets of ice. Hail is made of balls of ice. Hail forms when rain freezes and is pushed higher in the air by strong winds in clouds. As a piece of hail is blown higher, another layer of ice is added to it. Notice in the picture that the hail will keep getting bigger until it is too heavy for the wind to hold it in the air.

Measuring Humidity and Precipitation

Air has different amounts of water vapor in it at different times. The amount of water vapor that the air can hold changes with air temperature. Warm air can hold more water vapor than cold air can. If warm air holding a large amount of water vapor suddenly cools near the ground, fog forms. Fog is a cloud that forms near the ground.

Humidity is a measure of the amount of water vapor in the air. This amount is compared with the largest amount that the air can hold at that temperature. Humidity is usually given as a percent. If the humidity is fifty percent, the air has half of the water vapor that it can hold.

How hail forms

Layers of ice added.

Rain freezes.

Strong winds

Freezing temperatures

Hail becomes too heavy for wind to hold up.

226

A **hygrometer** is one kind of tool that measures humidity. One type of hygrometer uses a hair hooked to a pointer. The hair gets longer as it absorbs water vapor from the air. The pointer shows what the humidity is. What do you think happens to the hair as the humidity gets lower?

Another tool that measures humidity is made from two thermometers. The bottom of one thermometer is covered with a wet cloth. As water evaporates from this cloth, it cools the cloth. The temperature of this thermometer is lower than the temperature of the other thermometer. The less humidity in the air, the faster the water evaporates and the lower the temperature drops. Humidity is found by comparing the two temperatures on a special humidity chart.

A **rain gauge** is the tool that measures precipitation. A rain gauge is made of a tube like the one in the picture. The tube collects rain. Markings on the side show the amount of rain that has fallen.

hygrometer
(hī grom′ə tər), a tool that measures humidity.

rain gauge (gāj), a tool that measures precipitation.

A rain gauge

Lesson Review
1. How does a cloud form?
2. How does rain form?
3. What tools measure humidity and precipitation?
4. **Challenge!** How do you think you could measure the amount of snow that falls?

Study on your own, pages 392–393.

Keep a daily record of high and low temperatures, amount of precipitation, humidity, and kind and number of clouds. Measure and observe the information yourself or get it from a newspaper, radio, or television report. Make a chart and record the information in it. At the end of a week, describe what the weather was like for the week.

FIND OUT ON YOUR OWN

4 How Is Weather Predicted?

LESSON GOALS

You will learn
- how meteorologists get information about the weather.
- how meteorologists use information to make weather forecasts.

meteorologist
(mē/tē ə rol/ə jist), a person who studies weather.

The weather can help you decide what to do on a summer afternoon. Suppose the weather is hot and sunny without a cloud in the sky. You might be able to predict—or tell beforehand—what the weather will be like for the next hour. You might plan to go swimming. However, you do not have enough information to predict tomorrow's weather.

Meteorologists, like the people on these two pages, are people who study the weather. They predict what the weather will be like for the next few days. Before meteorologists can predict the weather, they must collect information.

Meteorologist and weather maps

228

Collecting Information

You know how to measure temperature, air pressure, precipitation, wind speed and direction, and humidity. Meteorologists collect this information from many places—not just where you live. The weather in other places helps meteorologists predict weather where you live. For example, the weather in California depends partly on weather over the Pacific Ocean. The weather in Texas depends partly on weather in Mexico. The weather in Maine depends partly on weather in other states and in Canada.

Many meteorologists get information from the **National Weather Service.** This government agency has weather stations collecting information all over the United States.

Weather balloons, radar, and satellites are three tools that collect information. Weather balloons like the one in the picture collect information from high in the air. Radar is a tool that sends radio waves into the air. These radio waves bounce off of rain and snow. Meteorologists use radar to find where precipitation is and where it is moving. The map below shows radar bouncing off of a tornado. Satellites high above the earth's air collect and send information about the weather all over the world.

National Weather Service, a government agency that collects information about weather from all over the United States.

Meteorologists releasing a weather balloon and studying weather maps.

A radar map

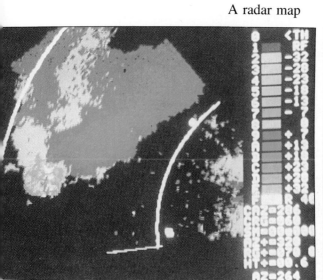

229

air mass, a large amount of air that has the same temperature and humidity.

front, the line where two air masses meet.

Meteorologists need information about air masses to predict weather. An **air mass** is a large amount of air that has the same temperature and humidity. An air mass can be warm or cold. It can have a large amount of water vapor or a small amount. Air masses are so large that two or three different air masses can cover most of the United States.

Meteorologists also need information about fronts to predict the weather. A **front** is the line where two air masses meet. The air masses do not mix together but stay separate. Find the cold front in the drawing. The cold air mass pushes the warm air up quickly. Notice that clouds form. A cold front often causes rain and thunderstorms.

Find the warm front below. The warm air mass runs into the cold air mass and slides up over the cold air. The clouds that form often cause a steady rain.

A cold front

A warm front

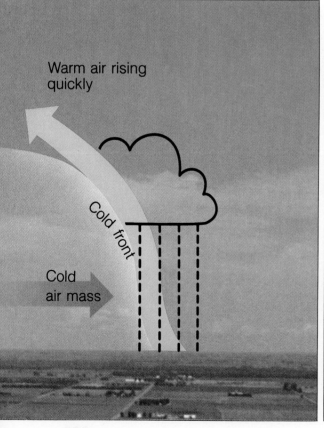

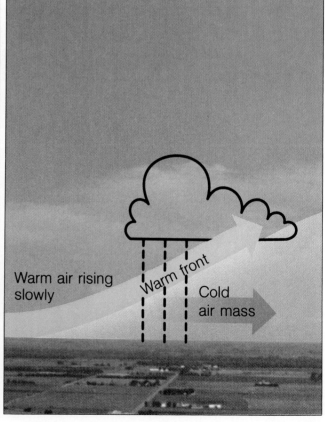

Using the Information to Predict Weather

Meteorologists use information about the weather to predict what the weather will be like. This prediction is a weather **forecast.**

In much of the United States, the air masses and fronts that cause weather usually move from west to east. They might move directly east. They also might move to the northeast or southeast. Depending on where you live, one way to predict weather might be to observe the weather west of where you are. In Indiana, tomorrow's weather might depend on today's weather in Iowa, Missouri, and Illinois.

Find the symbols for the weather maps below. The maps show the location of a cold front, rain, and snow on two days in a row. Notice that the cold front, rain, and snow have moved to the southeast.

forecast (fôr′kast′), a prediction of what the weather will be like.

The location of a cold front two days in a row.

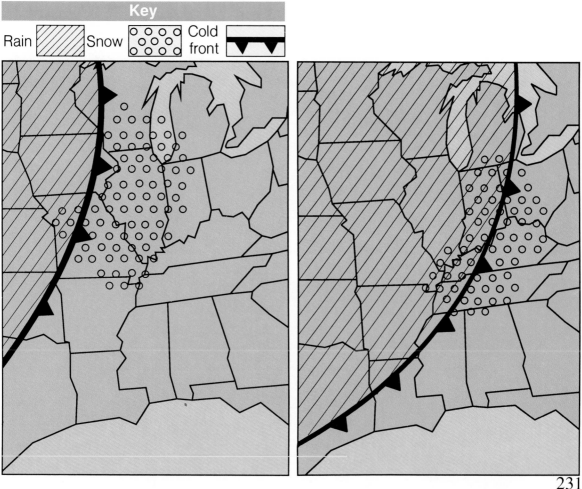

Key

Rain   Snow   Cold front

Meteorologists use computers to help them make weather forecasts. Computers use information about weather conditions. They make weather maps of where and how fast air masses and fronts will most likely move.

Meteorologists know the kinds of weather that often happen with certain air pressures, air masses, and fronts. High-pressure areas often have fair weather. Low-pressure areas often have clouds and precipitation. A warm air mass that comes from over the Gulf of Mexico might bring hot, humid weather on a summer day. A cold air mass from over Canada might bring cooler weather. Thunderstorms and snowstorms often happen at a cold front. Steady rain or snow often happens at a warm front.

Meteorologists study the direction air masses are moving. They study where high-pressure areas and low-pressure areas are moving. Meteorologists try to predict what air mass, front, and air pressure are moving into your area. Then they predict what the temperature, chances of precipitation, and wind might be.

Newspaper weather maps and forecasts

Lesson Review

1. How do meteorologists get information about the weather all over the United States?
2. How does knowing about air masses and fronts help a meteorologist make a forecast?
3. **Challenge!** If a bad storm was just west of you and clear, sunny weather was east of you, what weather might you predict for your area? Explain your answer.

Study on your own, pages 392–393.

The pictures on these two pages show some weather maps and forecasts. Collect weather maps from newspapers for a week. Look at the changes that take place in temperature, air pressure, air masses, fronts, and precipitation. Predict what the weather might be like where you live on the day after your last map. Write a paragraph explaining your forecast.

FIND OUT ON YOUR OWN

WEATHER ACROSS THE USA

HOW TO USE THIS PAGE
The color key shows today's high temperatures. The numbers below cities are today's forecast high and tomorrow morning's low. Temperatures are Fahrenheit.

LEGEND

Rain

Pacific Coast: Heavy rain, gale winds in morning along northern coast. Rain turning to snow in Wash., Ore. mountains.

Rockies: Showers in north spreading from west to east. Mostly sunny, mild from ern Utah, Colo. southw

South Central: Sunny from Kan. to Texas. Some afternoon clouds in Mo., Ark. Morning fog est Texas. Cold tonight.

North Ce over Min from N.I cold tonig

ACTIVITY

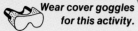
Wear cover goggles for this activity.

Making a Barometer

Purpose
To *make* and *use* a barometer.

Gather These Materials
• cut balloon • wide-mouth jar • rubber band • glue • toothpick • paper straw • sheet of cardboard • wood block

Follow This Procedure
1. Use a chart like the one shown to record your observations.
2. Stretch the cut balloon tightly over the mouth of the jar. *CAUTION: Be careful working with glass.* Hold the balloon in place with the rubber band. Make sure that the balloon is still stretched tightly over the jar.
3. Flatten the paper straw. Glue the toothpick to the end of the straw to make a pointer.
4. Glue the straw to the center of the balloon. Hold the straw in place until it dries. You have made a barometer.
5. Glue the cardboard to the block of wood as shown in the picture.
6. Place your barometer in front of the cardboard with the toothpick pointing at it. Draw a straight line across the cardboard where the toothpick points.
7. Check the barometer the next day. If the pointer is above the line, the air pressure has gone up. If the pointer is below the line, the air pressure has gone down. Record the change in air pressure in your chart. Also record what the weather is like that day.

8. Draw a new line where the toothpick is pointing. Write what day it is next to this line.
9. Repeat steps 7 and 8 for the next three days.

Record Your Results

	Air pressure	Weather
Day 1		
Day 2		
Day 3		
Day 4		

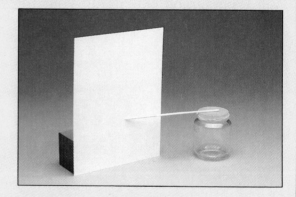

State Your Conclusion
1. How does your barometer show that air pressure is going up or down?
2. How did the weather change when the air pressure changed?

Use What You Learned
How do meteorologists use a barometer to predict weather changes?

Observing the Weather from Space

The Problem Severe storms can do millions of dollars of damage. Storms also take many lives. In 1955 Hurricane Diane killed 184 people as it swept from North Carolina to New England. The hurrican caused nearly $2 billion dollars in damage. Meteorologists were not able to forecast where the hurricane would hit and how strong it would be. Without that information, they could not tell people how to prepare for the storm.

Hurricanes form over tropical oceans. Thunderstorms that also cause great damage form high above the earth's surface. Meteorologists had many tools for collecting weather information from the earth's surface. However, these tools could not get enough accurate information to forecast hurricanes or thunderstorms.

The Breakthrough In 1960 the United States launched its first weather satellite. Its television cameras sent back pictures of the clouds above the earth. The pictures helped meteorologists find storms as they formed over oceans. Meteorologists could tell wind directions and speed by studying movements of clouds in satellite pictures.

Early weather satellites passed over the same spot on the earth twice a day. Modern weather satellites can stay over one spot on the earth. By the 1970s weather satellites took pictures of the earth's weather at night too. They measured heat given off by the earth.

New Technology New weather satellites have been launched that help scientists forecast severe storms. These satellites find signs of severe weather before any other methods. The satellites also can collect information about the winds surrounding a hurricane. The information helps meteorologists forecast exactly where the hurricane will hit land. Information from the new weather satellites lets meteorologists, like the one in the picture, learn more about the weather. They use what they learn to give more accurate forecasts.

What Do You Think?
1. How can weather satellites collect information about the weather at night?
2. How do weather satellites help save lives?

Skills for Solving Problems

Using Thermometers and Tables

Problem: How do different surfaces affect air temperature?

Part A. Using Thermometers to Collect Information

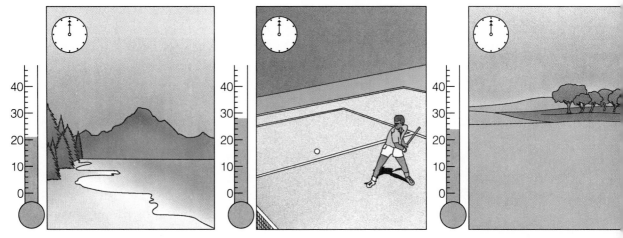

Thermometer A   Thermometer B   Thermometer C

1. Thermometer A above shows the temperature at the waterfront. Thermometer B shows the temperature at a concrete playing area. Thermometer C shows the temperature at a grassy area. What time of day do the clocks show?
2. Long lines on a thermometer measure every 10 degrees C. Short lines measure 2 degrees C. The temperature at the waterfront is 21°C. What is C an abbreviation for?
3. What is the temperature at the concrete playing area? at the grassy area?

Part B. Using a Table to Organize and Interpret Information

	Thermometer A	Thermometer B	Thermometer C
Location	Waterfront	Concrete area	Grassy area
Temperature	21°C	28°C	24°C

4. The table shows the information collected in Part A. What is the temperature at the waterfront? How does it differ from the temperatures at the other areas?
5. At which location is the temperature highest? How much higher is it than the other two temperatures?
6. What can you infer about the effect of different surfaces on temperature?

Part C. Using Thermometers and Tables to Solve a Problem

Problem: How does the temperature above different surfaces change as the sun goes down?

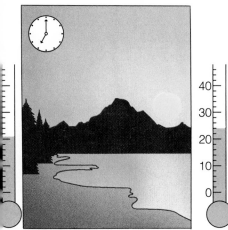

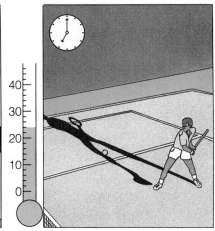

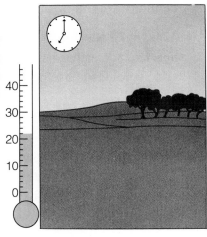

Thermometer A   Thermometer B   Thermometer C

7. Use the pictures to collect information you need to solve the problem. Make a table similar to the one in Part B to organize your information. Compare your table with the table in Part B. How does the time of day differ? How does the temperature at the waterfront in your table compare with the temperature at the waterfront in the table in Part B? How do the temperatures at the concrete area compare? at the grassy area?
8. What can you infer about how temperatures in different areas change as the sun goes down?
9. You might want to do this experiment and use your own results to make a table.

Chapter 9 Review

☑ Chapter Main Ideas

Lesson 1 • Air temperatures change as the number of daylight hours and the angle of sunlight hitting the earth change. • Different surfaces heat air at different speeds. • A thermometer measures air temperature.

Lesson 2 • Warm air rising causes a low-pressure area. • Cold air dropping causes a high-pressure area. • Air moves from an area of high pressure to an area of low pressure causing wind. • A barometer measures air pressure.

Lesson 3 • Clouds form when water vapor in the air condenses into tiny water drops. • When water drops in clouds get larger, they get heavy enough to fall to the ground as precipitation. • A hygrometer measures humidity. • A rain gauge measures precipitation.

Lesson 4 • Meteorologists get information from the National Weather Service. • Weather balloons, radar, and satellites collect information. • Meteorologists use patterns in weather to make a forecast.

☑ Reviewing Science Words

air mass	front	meteorologist
air pressure	high-pressure area	National Weather Service
anemometer	humidity	precipitation
barometer	hygrometer	rain gauge
forecast	low-pressure area	wind vane

Copy each sentence. Fill in the blank with the correct word or words from the list.

1. A ▨ is a tool that measures air pressure.
2. A ▨ is a tool that measures humidity.
3. ▨ is the amount that air presses on the earth.
4. A large amount of air that has a certain temperature is an ▨.
5. A ▨ is a tool that shows wind direction.
6. Rain and snow are two kinds of ▨.
7. A person who studies the weather is a ▨.
8. A ▨ measures the amount of precipitation.
9. A place where cool air is sinking is a ▨.
10. A ▨ is a tool that measures wind speed.
11. Meteorologists can get information from the ▨.
12. A place where warm air is rising is a ▨.

13. The amount of water vapor in the air is the ▨ .
14. The line where two air masses meet is a ▨ .
15. A prediction of what the weather will be like is a ▨ .

☑ Reviewing What You Learned

Write the letter of the best answer.

1. What kind of front is formed when a warm air mass moves into an area with a cold air mass?
   (a) warm   (b) high-pressure   (c) low-pressure   (d) cold
2. What does a barometer measure?
   (a) humidity   (b) wind speed   (c) air pressure   (d) rain
3. What does a thermometer measure?
   (a) humidity   (b) air temperature   (c) wind   (d) rain
4. The kind of precipitation that forms when rain freezes as strong winds push it higher in the air is
   (a) snow.   (b) rain.   (c) sleet.   (d) hail.
5. Air temperature is cooler when sunlight hits the earth's surface
   (a) for a longer time.   (c) over land.
   (b) directly.   (d) less directly.

☑ Interpreting What You Learned

Write a short answer for each question.

1. How are the changes in sunlight in one day like the changes in sunlight in one year?
2. What causes wind?
3. How does a cloud form?
4. What are three tools that collect information about weather conditions above the earth?

☑ Extend Your Thinking

Write a paragraph to answer each question.

1. Once the sun sets, a large body of water does not cool off as quickly as land does. At night, how might the air temperature of land near the water compare to the air temperature of land farther away from the water? Explain your answer.
2. What could happen to make nighttime warmer than daytime? Explain your answer.

• For further review, use Study Guide pages 392–393.

Chapter 10

Changes in Landforms

The volcano in the picture below is in Hawaii. You can see the hot, melted rock—or lava—shooting out of the volcano. You also can see this lava flowing across the land.

Introducing the Chapter

Lava can build up and form mountains as it cools and hardens. Mountains also can form as rocks inside the earth move closer together. The activity below will help you discover how the movement of rocks can cause mountains to form.

Making a Mountain Model

The earth is made of rocks. Forces in the earth make some of the rocks move. When the rocks move, they sometimes squeeze together. This movement of rocks can cause mountains to form.

You can make a model of a mountain forming. Flatten three pieces of clay as shown in the picture. The top piece of clay will be the earth's surface, or the land. The other two pieces of clay will be layers of rocks inside the earth.

Slowly squeeze the clay by pushing against the opposite sides. Observe what happens to the clay.

Talk About It
1. What happened to the clay when you squeezed it?
2. What happens to rocks inside the earth when they are squeezed?

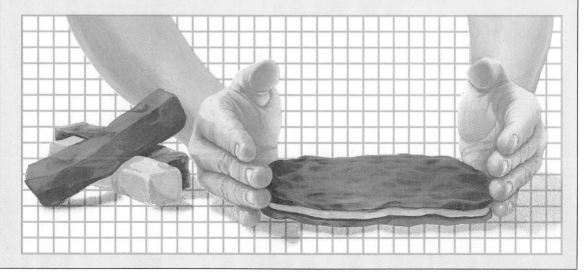

1 What Makes Up the Earth?

LESSON GOALS

You will learn
- three kinds of landforms.
- the earth's three layers.
- about the movement of plates in the earth's crust.

landform, a shape of the land, such as a mountain, plain, or plateau.

Imagine taking a trip across the United States. You could meet many interesting people and see many famous sights. You would also notice that the shape of the land changes. Sometimes you could see tall mountains. Other times you could see flat fields.

Landforms

Different shapes of land are called **landforms.** These pictures show three kinds of landforms: mountains, plains, and plateaus.

Mountains are parts of the land that rise at least 600 meters above the surrounding land. Mountains are often found in groups—or ranges. The line of mountains in the picture is a range.

Plains are flat parts of the land. However, plains are not always completely flat. They often have small hills. A plateau also is flat. A plateau is flat land that is higher than the land around it.

A mountain range

A plain

A plateau

The Earth's Three Layers

Landforms are on the surface of the earth. The picture shows what the inside of the earth looks like. Notice that the earth is made up of layers. How many layers do you see? The top layer is the **crust.** It is 8 to 65 kilometers thick. The crust is made of rocks and soil. Mountains, plains and plateaus are some landforms of the crust.

The layer below the crust is the **mantle.** It is about 2,800 kilometers thick. The mantle is mostly solid rock. However, some of the rock is partly melted.

The third layer of the earth is the **core.** It is about 3,500 kilometers thick. The core has two parts. The outer part is made of melted rock. The inner part of the core is solid rock.

SCIENCE IN YOUR LIFE

People can see a little way inside the earth's crust when they dig mines and wells. The deepest well ever dug is 9 kilometers deep. The deepest mine goes down about 4 kilometers. However, the center of the earth is almost 6,400 kilometers from the surface.

crust (krust), the top layer of the earth.

mantle (man′tl), the middle layer of the earth.

core (kôr), the center part of the earth.

Layers of the earth

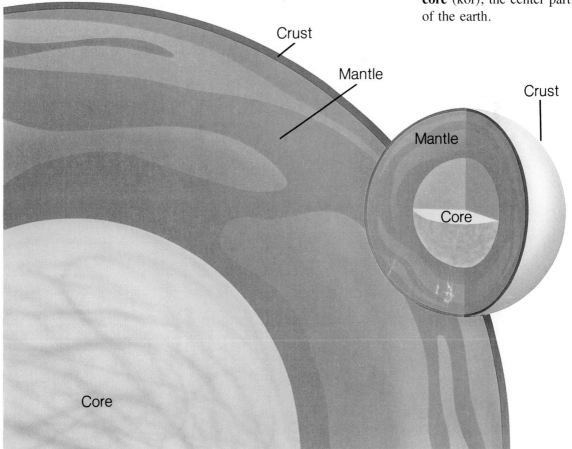

243

Plates That Move

Look at the picture of the continents. Notice that many of them seem to fit together like pieces of a giant jigsaw puzzle. Scientists think that millions of years ago, the continents were joined in one large piece of land. Then, the continents broke apart and moved away from each other. Today, the continents are still moving.

The continents move because the crust moves. The crust is made up of large sections of rock—or **plates.** The plates move over the melted rock in the earth's mantle. As the plates move, some of them move away from each other. Others bump into each other. Still others slide past each other.

The plates move all the time. People usually cannot feel the plates move because the plates move very slowly. They only move about 2 to 20 centimeters each year.

How continents fit together

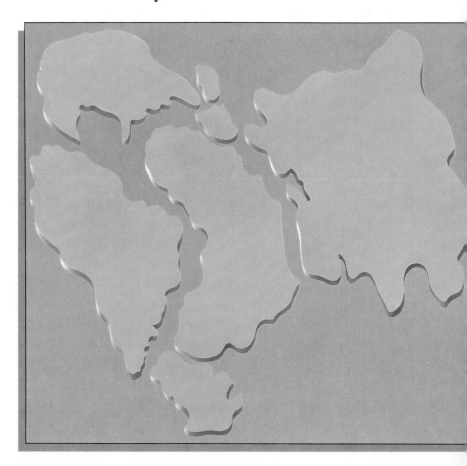

The red lines in the map below are places where two plates meet. Volcanoes often form near these places. As plates move, the melted rock under the plates moves up to the top and forms volcanoes. Most earthquakes also happen near the edges of plates. When the plates move past each other, rocks near the edges bend and break.

The red lines show where plates meet.

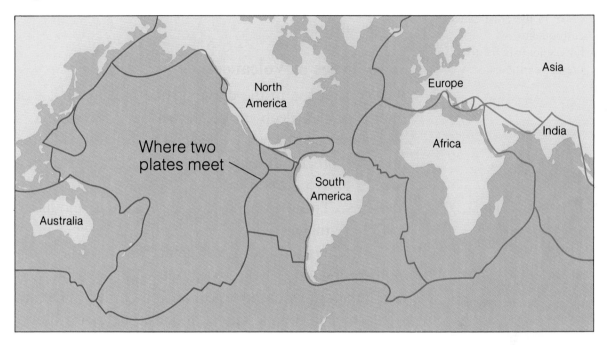

Where two plates meet

North America

Europe

Asia

Africa

India

South America

Australia

Lesson Review

1. How are a plain and a plateau different?
2. Describe the three layers of the earth.
3. What causes a continent to move?
4. **Challenge!** Some plates under the Atlantic Ocean are moving apart. Why do you think the Atlantic Ocean is slowly becoming wider?

Study on your own, pages 394–395.

A geyser is an opening in the ground from which hot water and steam burst out from time to time. Use books in the library to find out what causes geysers to erupt. Write a paragraph explaining what you learn.

FIND OUT ON YOUR OWN

2 How Do Volcanoes and Earthquakes Change Landforms?

LESSON GOALS

You will learn
- how volcanoes form.
- how the movement of rocks in the crust causes earthquakes.
- how scientists try to predict earthquakes.

As the plates in the earth's crust move, they change landforms. Some of these changes take place over thousands of years. Other changes take place quickly. Volcanoes and earthquakes can quickly change the shape of the land.

Two Types of Volcanoes

You can see in the drawing that melted rock—or magma—lies deep inside the earth. The magma is squeezed up through the crust. Sometimes, the magma breaks through the ground. Magma that comes above ground is called lava. As lava cools, it hardens. This hardened lava can build a mountain called a volcano.

Volcanoes erupt in different ways. When the volcano below erupts, it explodes. Lava, rocks, and ash burst out from the volcano. Sometimes, this kind of volcano erupts with so much force that it blows the top off of the volcano.

Lava

Magma

Lava, rocks, and ash exploding from a volcano

The volcano on the right erupts in a quieter way. Hot lava bubbles and oozes out of the volcano and flows down the sides. Rocks and ash do not explode from this kind of volcano.

The shape of a volcano depends on how the volcano forms. The volcano on page 246 was formed by eruptions that are like explosions. The lava, rocks, and ash that were thrown into the air fell back to the earth in a pile. Every time the volcano erupted, the pile grew higher and higher. Volcanoes formed in this way often have steep sides.

The volcano below formed by quiet eruptions. The lava that flowed out spread across the land and hardened into rock. After many eruptions, the lava formed a wide volcano with gentle slopes.

Volcanoes can be dangerous. Hot lava that flows from a volcano can burn people's homes. Rocks and ash can bury people. However, volcanoes are also helpful to people. After many years, some lava changes into a dark soil that is good for farming. In some countries, such as the United States and Japan, people are learning how to use heat from volcanoes to make electricity.

Lava flowing from a volcano

247

Earthquakes

fault (fôlt), a crack in the earth's crust along which rocks move.

In Lesson 1 you learned that plates of rock make up the earth's crust. When the plates move, they bend some of the rocks in the crust. Imagine bending a stick. If you bend the stick hard enough, the stick will break. In a similar way, rocks in the crust can break when they bend. When a rock breaks, it forms a crack in the crust. If the rock moves along the crack, the crack is called a **fault.**

Most faults are deep inside the earth. However, some faults can be seen on the earth's surface. The thin line in the picture is the San Andreas Fault in California. It is more than 1,000 kilometers long.

The drawings show how rocks move along a fault. Sometimes the rocks move from side to side. Other times the rocks move up and down.

The San Andreas Fault

Movement of rocks along faults

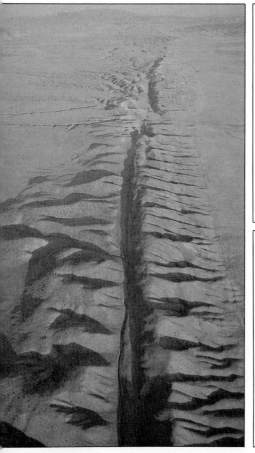

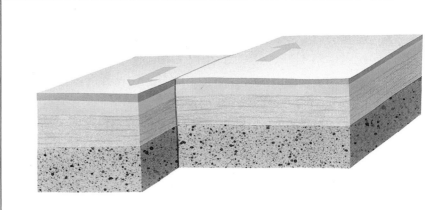

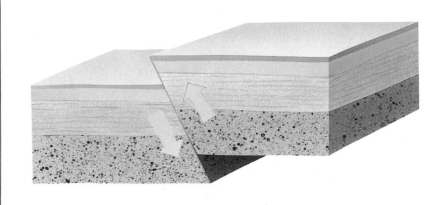

When the rocks at a fault move, the ground shakes. This shaking of the ground is an earthquake. Most earthquakes are so weak, people cannot feel them. Some earthquakes destroy buildings.

Scientists can measure the strength of an earthquake. They use an instrument—called a seismograph (sīz′mə graf)—that measures the movement of the ground. When an earthquake happens, the seismograph moves. Notice in the picture that the seismograph has a pen that records lines on the paper. Scientists measure the height of these lines to find the strength of the earthquake. The higher the lines are, the stronger the earthquake is.

Scientists give earthquakes a number from the Richter (rik′tər) scale. The stronger the earthquake, the higher the number the earthquake is given. An earthquake that is too weak to be felt by people might be a 1 or 2 on the Richter scale. A strong earthquake that destroys buildings might be a 6, 7, or 8 on the Richter scale. Each number represents an earthquake that is ten times stronger than the number below it.

SCIENCE IN YOUR LIFE

Many states require that new buildings be built to prevent as much damage from earthquakes as possible. Some kinds of buildings are safer than others. The picture below shows a test being done by making an earthquake in a laboratory. This kind of test helps people study how safe different kinds of buildings are.

Dr. Richter observing a seismograph

A laboratory test

Measuring with laser light

Laser light reflecting

Predicting Earthquakes

Scientists try to predict earthquakes by looking for signs that might mean an earthquake is going to happen. Many weak earthquakes—or tremors—could mean that a stronger earthquake will happen soon. Sometimes, the ground changes shape or rocks along a fault move slightly before an earthquake. Scientists use different tools to measure these changes. One of these tools uses laser light. The tool in the top picture is placed on one side of a fault. This tool sends a beam of laser light. The light bounces off a reflector on the opposite side of a fault. Find this light reflecting in the bottom picture. Any movement of the ground changes the time the light takes to travel to the reflector and back.

The water level in a nearby well also might suddenly change before an earthquake. Many people have noticed that some animals seem to act strangely before an earthquake takes place. Scientists use all these signs to try to predict earthquakes.

Lesson Review

1. What are two ways that volcanoes can form?
2. Why do earthquakes happen near faults?
3. What are two signs that might mean an earthquake is about to take place?
4. **Challenge!** Which of the two kinds of volcanoes described in this lesson is likely to be more dangerous to people? Explain your answer.

Study on your own, pages 394–395.

FIND OUT ON YOUR OWN

Tsunamis (sü nä′mēz) are caused by earthquakes that occur on the ocean floor. Use an encyclopedia to find out what a tsunami is. Write a report about what you learned. Include in your report how scientists predict tsunamis and how tsunamis can be dangerous to people.

Making Models of Faults

ACTIVITY

Purpose
Observe how rocks can move along faults and change the land's surface.

Gather These Materials
• 2 wooden blocks • clay • millimeter ruler • pencil

Follow This Procedure
1. Use a chart like the one shown to record your observations.
2. Place the wooden blocks next to each other on a table with the longest sides touching. Imagine that the blocks are rocks along a fault in the earth's crust.
3. Press the clay to make a sheet that is about 3 mm thick. Put the thin sheet of clay on top of the blocks. Press the clay down firmly. Imagine that the clay is the earth's surface.
4. Use the pencil to make a straight line from the side of one block to the side of the other block. This line is a road.
5. Press down firmly on the clay and rocks. Move the rocks very slowly past each other by pressing one of the blocks forward about 3 cm. The blocks should be touching at all times. Record in your chart what happened to the surface of the earth.
6. Return the blocks to their original position and press the clay into a flat sheet again. Repeat step 5 but this time move the rocks very quickly. Record what happened to the surface of the earth.

Record Your Results

	Changes in surface
Slow movement	
Quick movement	

State Your Conclusion
1. What can happen on the earth's surface when rocks along a fault move slowly?
2. What can happen on the earth's surface when rocks along a fault move quickly?

Use What You Learned
How might how fast rocks move along a fault affect people living near the fault?

3 How Does Weathering Change Landforms?

LESSON GOALS

You will learn
- how wind, water, and ice can weather rocks.
- how wind, water, and ice can cause erosion.
- how people can control erosion.

weathering
(weᴛʜ′ər ing), the breaking and wearing away of rocks.

Weathering has made these mountains smaller.

Volcanoes erupt and build up the land. They can form tall mountains. Other forces wear down these mountains.

Breaking Down Rocks

While volcanoes and earthquakes build up the land, wind and water wear it down. Look at the rocks and soil in the picture. At one time they were part of the mountains. Over the years, the rocks broke apart and wore away. Wind, water, and ice can break rocks apart. The breaking and wearing away of rocks is called **weathering.**

Water and ice weather rocks over thousands of years. Water seeps into tiny cracks in the rocks. When the weather gets cold, the water freezes inside the cracks. The ice presses against the sides of the cracks and pushes the rocks apart. When the ice melts, the rocks move back. Each time the water freezes, it pushes against the rocks. After many years, the rocks break apart. Mountains slowly crumble away.

Water can also weather rocks by eating away—or dissolving—the rocks. As water flows through the ground, it becomes a weak acid. Even though the acid is weak, over a long time it can dissolve some minerals in rocks. The acid changes the hard minerals into soft clay, and the rocks slowly break apart. Sometimes, the acid completely dissolves the minerals and leaves large holes in the rocks. Caves form when a large amount of rock under the ground has been dissolved.

Look at the arch in the picture. This landform is made of rocks that the wind has weathered. Wind carries sand. When sand hits a rock, it acts like sandpaper. The sand scrapes away some of the rock. Over thousands of years, the wind can weather rocks into many beautiful shapes.

Weathering shaped this arch.

The city of New Orleans in Louisiana is located on the Mississippi River Delta. This city is a very busy seaport. Thousands of ships dock in New Orleans every year.

---

erosion (i rō′zhən), the moving of weathered rocks and soil by wind, water, or ice.

sediment (sed′ə mənt), tiny bits of rocks, shells, and other materials.

delta (del′tə), land that is formed by sediments where a river empties into a lake or ocean.

Movement of Weathered Materials

Weathered rocks can be moved from one place to another. Water from rain and melting snow carries tiny rocks and soil as it flows across the land. Some of this water flows into lakes and streams. The water in the lakes and streams carries the tiny rocks and soil. Notice how the rocks and soil in the picture on the left make the water look brown. The moving of weathered rocks and soil by wind, water, or ice is called **erosion.**

As a river flows, it washes away tiny bits of rocks, sand, and soil—or **sediments**—that were once part of the land. The faster the river flows, the more erosion the river causes. The river will empty into a lake or ocean. There, the river will slow down, and the sediments will drop to the bottom. Over the years, the sediments might build up and form new land in the lake or ocean. This new land is called a **delta.** Notice how the delta in the picture on the right reaches out into the lake.

A river carrying sediments

A delta

Look at the ice in the picture on the left. It looks like a giant road through the mountains. This large area of ice—or **glacier**—formed from snow. High up in the mountains, the weather is cold all year. Some of the snow does not melt in the summer. As a result, layers of snow slowly built up. The top layers pressed the bottom layers of snow into ice. Over many years, the glacier formed.

Glaciers slowly move across the land. As a glacier moves, it moves rocks. When the glacier melts, it leaves rocks on the ground. The glacier in the middle picture moved the rocks and then left them behind.

The wind also causes erosion. The wind carries sediments, such as sand and soil. Strong winds can carry sediments over long distances. When the wind slows down, the sediments drop to the ground. Over time, large piles of sediments may form. You can see large piles of windblown sand—or **dunes**—near the mountains in the picture on the right. How did the mountains help form the dunes?

glacier (glā′shər), a large mass of ice that moves.

dune (dün), pile of sand formed by the wind.

A glacier

Rocks left behind by the glacier

Dunes

Strips of crops planted around hills

People Controlling Erosion

Erosion can be both helpful and harmful. In some places erosion helps build new land and add minerals to the soil. This land is good for growing crops. In other places erosion takes away land. Erosion can wash away farmland. It can also wash away the ground under houses and roads, making them unsafe for people to use.

One way people can slow down soil erosion is to plant new trees where trees have been cut down. Trees slow down erosion by protecting the soil from wind and rain. Tree roots help hold the soil in place.

To protect the land on their farms, farmers plant strips of grass or clover between strips of crops. The grass and clover hold rainwater better than the crops do. As a result, less water flows down the hill and erodes the soil. Farmers also plow their fields in rows that go around hills. Each row follows the shape of the hill and makes a kind of step on the hill. When it rains, much of the rainwater stays on the steps. The water then soaks into the land instead of flowing down the hill. The picture shows crops planted in strips around hills.

Lesson Review

1. How does weathering change the earth's surface?
2. How does erosion change the earth's surface?
3. How can people reduce erosion?
4. **Challenge!** Why is delta land especially good for farming?

Study on your own, pages 394–395.

FIND OUT ON YOUR OWN

Glaciers can make landforms called kettle holes. Use an encyclopedia to find out what a kettle hole is. Write a report about kettle holes. Include how kettle holes form and how a kettle hole can become a kettle lake.

256

ACTIVITY

Studying Weathering by Water

Purpose
Compare how water with and without sediment weathers solid materials.

Gather These Materials
• plastic spoon • fine sand • 2 plastic tubs with lids • waxed paper • white glue • paper • balance • water • 5 small rocks • masking tape

Follow This Procedure
1. Use a chart like the one shown to record your observations.
2. Place eight spoonfuls of sand in one of the tubs. Stir in enough glue to make a stiff mixture.
3. On the waxed paper, shape the mixture into two cubes that are the same size.
4. Put the cubes where they can harden one or two days. Wash out the tub.
5. Write the letter *A* on one piece of paper and the letter *B* on another. Put a hardened cube on each paper.
6. Measure and record the mass of cube A. Then place cube A back on paper A.
7. Repeat step 6 for cube B.
8. Half fill each plastic tub with water. Add five small rocks—or sediment—to one of the tubs. Place cube A in this tub. Put the lid on the tub and use tape to label the tub with the letter *A*.
9. Place cube B in the other tub. Put the lid on the tub and use tape to label the tub with the letter *B*.

10. Shake each tub fifty times while holding the lid tightly in place.
11. Measure and record the mass of each cube. Record how much mass each cube lost.

Record Your Results

	Cube A	Cube B
Mass before shaking		
Mass after shaking		
Amount of mass lost		

State Your Conclusion
1. Explain any differences between the cubes after shaking them.
2. Why did you measure the masses of the cubes before shaking the cubes?

Use What You Learned
Explain why a fast-moving river with sediment erodes the land faster than a fast-moving river without sediment.

4 How Are Rocks Made?

LESSON GOALS

You will learn
- how minerals are identified.
- how igneous rocks form.
- how sedimentary rocks form.
- how metamorphic rocks form.

mineral (min′ər əl), nonliving solid matter from the earth.

Imagine you are on a road going up the side of a mountain. The road is cut into the mountain. You might see different kinds of rocks as you ride along.

Minerals That Make Up Rocks

Rocks have different colors and shapes, but all rocks are made of one or more minerals. A **mineral** is nonliving, solid matter from the earth. Gold and diamond are minerals.

The atoms in a mineral join together in a certain pattern to make crystals. A crystal has a certain shape. Minerals do not all have the same shape of crystals. Notice in the picture that the shape of the salt crystal is different from the calcite crystals.

Minerals have different physical properties that help people identify them. Sometimes color helps people identify a mineral. The color of gold helps people identify it. However, most minerals are not always the same color. A mineral can have different colors depending on how it formed.

Salt crystal

Calcite crystals

258

Another property that helps people identify minerals is how light reflects from the mineral. Minerals, such as the pyrite (pī′rīt) in the picture, look like shiny metal. Other minerals, like the talc in the picture, do not look like metal.

A mineral can also be identified by how hard it is. A mineral is given a number from 1 to 10 for its hardness. Talc is the softest mineral and has a hardness of 1. Diamonds, like the ones in the picture, are the hardest mineral and have a hardness of 10.

Hardness of a mineral is found by trying to scratch it with different objects or with other minerals. A mineral can only be scratched by an object or other mineral that is harder. Testing the hardness of an unknown mineral can help identify it.

Talc

Pyrite

Diamonds

Igneous Rocks

Rocks form in different ways. Some rocks are made from magma deep inside the earth. These rocks are called **igneous rocks.** The magma slowly moves up through cracks in the earth's crust. As the magma rises, it cools and hardens. This hardened magma is igneous rock. Most of the earth's crust is made of igneous rock.

Some igneous rocks form under the ground. The granite (gran′it) in the pictures on the left is an igneous rock that forms under the ground. Other igneous rocks form above ground when magma pours out from a volcano or through cracks in the ground. When this magma—now called lava—cools, it hardens into igneous rock. Obsidian (ob sid′ē ən) in the pictures on the right is an igneous rock that forms above the ground.

Granite and a granite building   Obsidian and obsidian tools

Sedimentary Rocks

Some rocks are made from tiny pieces of rocks, sand, shells, and other materials. These tiny bits are sediments. Rivers and streams carry sediments into lakes and oceans. The sediments sink to the bottom of the water. Over the years, many layers of sediment collect on the lake or ocean floor. The top layers press down on the bottom layers. The bottom layers are pressed into rock. **Sedimentary rocks** are made from sediments that are pressed together. The sedimentary rock in the picture was once under water.

The sedimentary rock in the picture is shale. This sedimentary rock is made from layers of mud and clay. Traces of plants and animals—or fossils—are often found in sedimentary rocks. The organisms were trapped in layers of sediment. As the sediment hardened, the organisms' bodies decayed and left their traces in the rock. Find the fossils of the frog and leaf in the pictures.

SCIENCE IN YOUR LIFE

When you write with chalk, you might be using a sedimentary rock. A rock called chalk is made from tiny seashells that have been pressed together.

sedimentary
(sed′ə men′ tər ē) **rock,** a rock that is made from sediments that have been pressed together.

Shale and fossils

261

Metamorphic Rocks

Sometimes, one kind of rock changes into another kind. Rock that is buried under layers of other rock is under pressure. This pressure causes heat. Over many years, great heat and pressure can change igneous or sedimentary rock into **metamorphic rock.** The limestone in the picture is a sedimentary rock that becomes the metamorphic rock called marble. The head in the picture is made from marble.

metamorphic (met′ə môr′fik) **rock,** a rock that forms when igneous or sedimentary rock is changed by heat and pressure.

Marble

Limestone

Lesson Review

1. How do igneous rocks form?
2. How do sedimentary rocks form?
3. How are igneous and sedimentary rocks changed into metamorphic rocks?
4. **Challenge!** Scientists have found fossils of water plants and animals in rock high in mountains. What kind of rock are the fossils in and where did the rock form?

Study on your own, pages 394–395.

FIND OUT ON YOUR OWN

Copy the chart below on a sheet of paper. Use an encyclopedia to find out the missing information. Then, complete the chart.

Kind of rock	How rock forms	Uses for rock
Granite	from magma that cools and hardens	
Marble		statues, buildings, and furniture
Limestone	sedimentary	
Slate	metamorphic	
Pumice		scrubbing and polishing

Learning the Life Cycle of an Earthquake

Scientists usually do not know exactly where or when an earthquake will occur. Karen McNally is the scientist in the picture. She was sure she knew where an earthquake would happen. Dr. McNally had learned that Oaxaca had not had a large earthquake since 1928. Oaxaco is an area on the west coast of Mexico. Dr. McNally felt that it would have an earthquake soon.

In 1978, Dr. McNally and a scientist from Mexico visited the area. They set up seismographs in seven spots. For a month, only a few small tremors occurred. Then, many small quakes happened over a period of thirty hours. Next, all was quiet. Twelve hours later, a large earthquake rocked Oaxaca. It even caused damage in Mexico City, 402 kilometers away.

Since then, Dr. McNally has studied the small earthquakes that happen along Mexico's coast. She has noticed patterns that show the life cycle of Mexico's earthquakes. Over forty years, a pattern of small quakes and quiet periods ends with a large quake.

Dr. McNally thinks that scientists may be able to discover patterns for earthquakes in other parts of the world. Then, they could make better predictions. People would have a better chance to prepare for earthquakes.

What Do You Think?

1. What made Dr. McNally think that Oaxaca was likely to have an earthquake?
2. How might knowing the life cycle of an earthquake be useful to scientists?

Skills for Solving Problems

Using Balances and Bar Graphs

Problem: How does weathering change the mass of a rock?

Part A. Using Balances to Collect Information

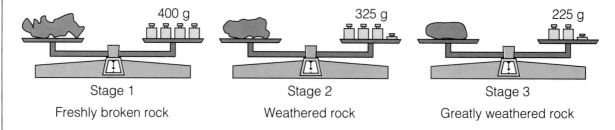

Stage 1	Stage 2	Stage 3
400 g	325 g	225 g
Freshly broken rock	Weathered rock	Greatly weathered rock

1. The pictures show a freshly broken rock and the same rock after it has been weathered. Find the freshly broken rock. This rock was placed on one pan of the balance. Objects of known mass were placed on the other pan of the balance. Objects with different masses were added to and taken off the pan until the two pans balanced. When the two pans balance, the mass of the rock is equal to the mass of all the objects on the other pan. What is the mass of the freshly broken rock?

2. What is the mass of the rock at Stage 2? at Stage 3?

Part B. Using a Bar Graph to Organize and Interpret Information

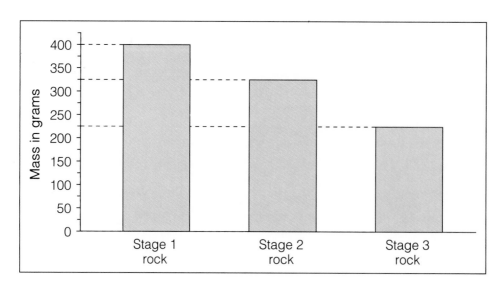

3. The bar graph contains information you collected about the rock. Each bar shows information about a different stage. Find the bar that stands for the rock at Stage 1. What does the line across from the top of this bar stand for?
4. How does the rock's mass at Stage 1 compare with its mass at Stage 2? at Stage 3?
5. How does weathering change the mass of a rock?

Part C. Using Balances and Bar Graphs to Solve a Problem

Problem: How does changing the shape of an object change its mass?

Clay cube rolled into a ball   . . . and then into a cylinder

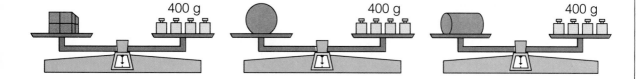

6. Use the pictures to collect the information you need to solve the problem. What is the mass of the clay cube? the clay ball? the clay cylinder? Make a bar graph similar to the one shown in Part B to organize your information.
7. Look at your bar graph. How does changing the shape of an object change its mass?
8. You might want to do this experiment and use your own results to make a bar graph.

265

Chapter 10 Review

☑ Chapter Main Ideas

Lesson 1 • Mountains, plains, and plateaus are three kinds of landforms. • The earth is made of three layers—the crust, mantle, and core. • The crust is made of plates that move over melted rock.

Lesson 2 • Eruptions that are like explosions form volcanoes with steep slopes. • Quiet eruptions form volcanoes with gentle slopes. • An earthquake is caused by the movement of rocks along a fault.

Lesson 3 • Weathering is the breaking apart of rocks by water, wind, or ice. • Erosion is the moving of weathered rocks and soil by water, wind, or ice • People are working to control erosion.

Lesson 4 • Minerals make up rocks. • Igneous rocks are made from hardened magma or lava. • Sedimentary rocks are made from sediments that were pressed together and then hardened. • Metamorphic rocks are made from other rocks that were changed by heat and pressure.

☑ Reviewing Science Words

core	glacier	plate
crust	igneous rock	sediment
delta	landform	sedimentary rock
dune	mantle	weathering
erosion	metamorphic rock	
fault	mineral	

Copy each sentence. Fill in the blank with the correct word or words from the list.

1. Strong winds can blow sand into a large pile called a ____.
2. The layer of the earth below the crust is the ____.
3. Igneous rock that is changed by heat and pressure becomes ____.
4. Landforms are part of the earth's ____.
5. Tiny bits of rocks, shells, and other materials that are carried by water are ____.
6. A ____ is a crack in the earth's crust along which rocks move.
7. As a ____ moves, it scoops up rocks and moves them along.
8. Nonliving solid matter inside the earth is called a ____.
9. A ____ can form where a river empties into a lake or ocean.
10. A mountain is a kind of ____.
11. ____ is the breaking and wearing away of rocks.

12. A large section of rock that makes up part of the earth's crust is a ▦ .
13. Magma or lava that has hardened is ▦ .
14. The ▦ is the center part of the earth.
15. ▦ is the moving of weathered rocks and soil.
16. ▦ is made from sediments that are pressed together.

☑ Reviewing What You Learned

Write the letter of the best answer.
1. Hardness is a property used to identify
   (a) minerals.   (b) earthquakes.   (c) ice.   (d) lava.
2. All rocks are made of
   (a) lava.   (b) magma.   (c) sediments.   (d) minerals.
3. What do scientists use to measure the strength of earthquakes?
   (a) heat   (b) seismographs   (c) sediments   (d) rulers
4. Deltas are made from
   (a) snow.   (b) ice.   (c) sediments.   (d) magma.
5. Which of the following is a sedimentary rock?
   (a) magma   (b) lava   (c) shale   (d) marble
6. How many layers is the earth made of?
   (a) two   (b) five   (c) one   (d) three

☑ Interpreting What You Learned

Write a short answer for each question or statement.
1. How can water dissolve rocks?
2. How does the shape of a volcano depend on how the volcano was formed?
3. How do scientists explain the movement of the continents?
4. What are two signs that might mean an earthquake is about to happen?

☑ Extending Your Thinking

Write a paragraph to answer each question.
1. The Teton Mountains in Wyoming are located near faults. What do you think caused these mountains to form?
2. How can an explosive eruption of a volcano be dangerous to people flying airplanes?

• For further review, use Study Guide pages 394–395.

Chapter 11

Oceans

The diver below is swimming in the ocean near a coral reef. Plants and animals that live in the oceans are different in many ways from plants and animals that live on the earth's land.

Introducing the Chapter

The oceans cover much of the earth. In the activity below, you will find out how much of the earth's surface is ocean water. In this chapter, you will learn where the oceans are and how they affect your life. You will also learn how ocean water moves and what the ocean floor is like.

Observing How Much of the Earth the Oceans Cover

DISCOVER!

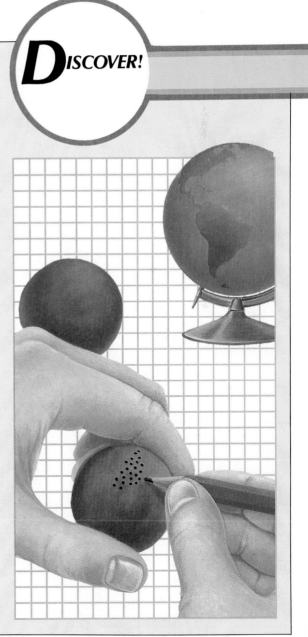

Use a piece of clay to make a ball about 4 or 5 centimeters across. Pretend this ball is the earth. Imagine that all the land on Earth were joined together. With a pencil, make dots on the ball over the amount of area you think all of the earth's land would cover.

Use another piece of clay to make a ball the same size as before. Pretend this second ball is also the earth. Make a circle around the ball with a pencil so that the ball is divided in half. Now use your pencil to make a line that divides one of the halves into two equal parts. Each of these smaller parts is one-fourth of the earth. Make dots with your pencil over one of these smaller parts. The area with no dots is about how much of Earth the oceans cover.

Talk About It
1. How did your first model compare with the second model?
2. About how much of the earth do the oceans cover?

1 What Are the Oceans and How Are They Important?

LESSON GOALS

You will learn
- the names of the four main oceans and their locations.
- what resources are found in the ocean.
- what resources come from the ocean floor.
- how oceans can become polluted.

If you could look at the Pacific Ocean from space, you would see the part of the earth that is made up mostly of ocean and small islands. You would see land only at the edges of the oceans. Almost all the earth's land is on the other half of the earth.

The Four Main Oceans

The four main oceans are the Pacific, the Atlantic, the Indian, and the Arctic. Find these four oceans on the map. The Pacific Ocean is the largest. This ocean is so large that all the land on the earth's surface could easily fit into it! The Pacific Ocean also is the deepest ocean. It averages more than 4,000 meters deep.

The four oceans are connected. Find the places on the map where water could move from one ocean to another. The four oceans are really part of one large world ocean.

The four main oceans

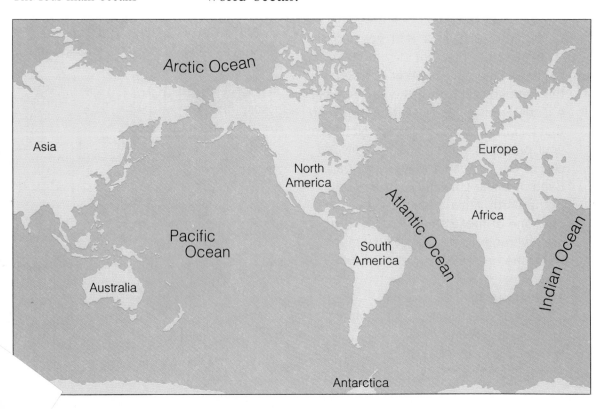

Resources in the Ocean

People use the oceans in many ways. Some people enjoy walking on the beach. Other people enjoy swimming, sailing, fishing, or diving.

The oceans have many **resources,** or materials people use and need. Most of the fish and other seafood people eat come from the ocean. Notice that the fishing boat below uses large nets to catch fish. In some countries, fish is a major source of food.

Ocean plants and other producers give off oxygen, a gas all animals need to live. Plants and other producers in the ocean are also used as food. Seaweed, like the ones in the picture, are eaten like lettuce. They are also dried, ground into flour, and used to make many different foods.

Have you ever swallowed some ocean water? The taste comes from salts in the water. When ocean water evaporates, the salts are left behind. People get many kinds of salts and minerals from ocean water. One kind of salt from the ocean is **sodium chloride,** or table salt. Some of the salt in your food might have come from the ocean.

A fishing boat

SCIENCE IN YOUR LIFE

Kelp, a kind of seaweed, is used in making many things people use. Ice cream, jellies, toothpaste, drugs, and salad dressing all have kelp in them.

resource (ri sôrs′), material that people use.

sodium chloride (sō′dē əm klôr′īd), table salt.

Kelp

271

Resources from the Ocean Bottom

nodule (noj′ül), lump of metals found on the ocean floor.

petroleum (pə trō′lē əm), liquid fuel made from living things that lived millions of years ago.

The ocean bottom has lumps of ores with metals such as manganese, iron, copper, and nickel in them. These lumps are called **nodules.** You can see a manganese nodule below. The metals in the nodules have important uses. However, people do not take many nodules from the ocean. Mining the metals from the land is less expensive than taking them from the ocean. People do use sand and gravel from the ocean floor to make buildings and roads.

People use the oil platform in the picture to drill for **petroleum** beneath the ocean. Petroleum is a liquid fuel made from living things that lived millions of years ago. About a fourth of the petroleum used comes from wells drilled under the ocean near the shore. Oil companies make gasoline, oils, waxes, and other things from petroleum.

Pollution in the Ocean

For many years, people have dumped wastes into the ocean. These wastes pollute the ocean water, or make it harmful to living things. Cities along the coast dump their sewage, or waste matter, into the ocean. Other cities dump sewage into rivers, which can carry it to the ocean. Chemicals from farms and factories sometimes end up in the ocean.

An oil platform

A manganese nodule

Sometimes oil spills from a large ship called a tanker. The oil kills living things in the ocean and along the shore. The boat in the picture cleans up oil spills. The oil is pushed under the middle of the boat where it is collected and removed.

Clean oceans are important to life on the earth. Many people work hard to protect the oceans from pollution. Many cities treat their waste to clean it before the waste is dumped into the water. Laws help keep people from dumping wastes into the ocean.

Lesson Review

1. What are the four main oceans?
2. What resources are found in the ocean water?
3. What resources come from the ocean floor?
4. What can cause the oceans to become polluted?
5. **Challenge!** What ways can you suggest to help keep the oceans clean?

Study on your own, pages 396–397.

Cleaning up an oil spill

Use an atlas or encyclopedia to find the height of mountains on land and the depth of the oceans. Compare the height of the tallest mountain on land to the depth of the deepest place in the ocean.

FIND OUT ON YOUR OWN

2 How Does Ocean Water Move?

LESSON GOALS

You will learn
- what a current is and where currents flow.
- what causes tides.
- how water moves in a wave.
- how waves can change beaches.

current (kėr′ənt), a river of water that flows through the ocean.

Suppose you were alone on an ocean beach like the one in the picture. What sounds would you hear? What would cause these sounds? Waves move to shore and crash against the beach. Water moves higher and lower along the shore at different times of the day. The water in the oceans is always moving.

Currents

Rivers of water—called **currents**—move through the ocean at different speeds. These currents can have different temperatures and different densities than the ocean water around them. For hundreds of years, sailors have known that currents move through the oceans. The sailors learned where the currents are and in what direction they flow. If ships sail against a current, the current slows them down. How could a current help ships move?

Ocean water is always moving.

274

The direction of winds and the movement of the earth cause the currents that flow at the surface of the ocean. Find some of these currents on the map. Notice that the arrows show the direction that the currents are flowing. Currents flowing from the North Pole or the South Pole move cold water. Currents flowing from the Equator carry warm water.

Satellites that circle high above the earth take pictures of the earth. These pictures show the different temperatures of the water in the oceans. Oceanographers can trace ocean currents using what they learn from these satellites.

The Gulf Stream is a warm current that moves north along the east coast of the United States. This warm current then moves east across the Atlantic Ocean to Europe. It warms the air that flows over Great Britain and northern Europe. Great Britain is as far north as Canada, but its winter weather is much warmer than Canada's.

A cold water current moves south along the western coast of the United States. This cold current cools nearby land in the summer.

Surface currents in the oceans

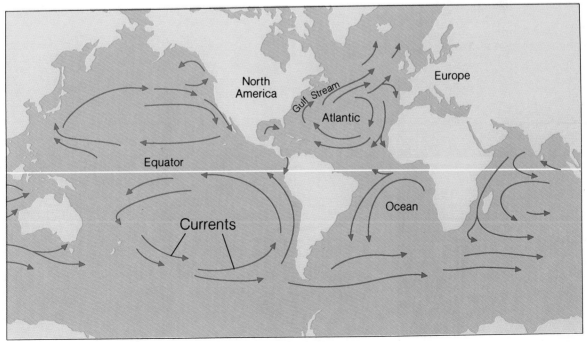

275

Tides can be used as a source of energy. Dams are built across a river or bay along the ocean coast. As the water rises for high tide, the water flows through the dam. It flows into a generator that makes electricity. As the water lowers for low tide the water flows out through the generator and makes more electricity.

tide (tīd) the rise and fall of the surface level of the ocean.

Tides

Look at the two pictures of an ocean beach taken at different times. How is the beach different? The pictures show a beach at high tide and at low tide. The **tide** is the rise and fall in the level of the water along the ocean shore. Most places along the ocean have tides twice a day.

Hundreds of years ago people learned that the moon causes the tides. People knew that two high tides and two low tides move onto a beach every 24 hours and 50 minutes. People also knew that the moon rises every 24 hours and 50 minutes.

The moon and the earth are attracted to each other by gravity. This gravity keeps the moon moving around the earth. The picture shows how the moon's pull on the earth causes high and low tides in the oceans. Notice that one arrow shows the moon's pull on the water. The other arrow shows the pull on the land. The difference in the pull from one side of the earth to the other causes tides.

High tide and low tide

The moon's pull on the earth

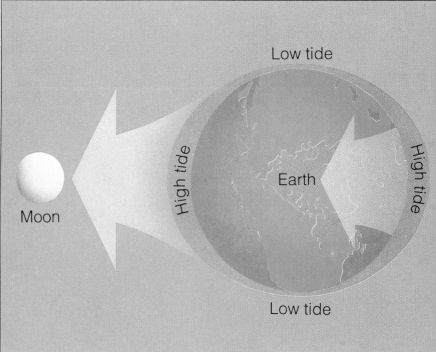

276

Waves

If you throw a rock into a pond, the rock disturbs the water. Waves spread out through the water. Winds that blow across the ocean's surface disturb the water and cause waves. Tides and earthquakes also cause waves.

All waves have the same main parts. Notice in the picture that the highest point of a wave is its **crest.** The lowest point is the **trough.** Find the distance from the crest to the trough. This distance is the **wave height.** The wave height of most ocean waves is about 3 meters. Storm waves can rise as high as 30 meters. Find the distance between the crest of one wave and the crest of the next wave. This distance is the wavelength.

You can see how a wave moves in water by seeing how a wave moves in a rope. One end of the rope in the picture is tied to a chair. A wave started at the other end. The rope moves up and down as a wave moves forward along the rope. The rope does not move forward. Like the rope, water moves up and down as a wave moves forward on the surface of the ocean. The water does not move forward.

crest (krest), the highest point of a wave.

trough (trôf), the lowest point of a wave.

wave height, distance between the crest and the trough.

The parts of a wave

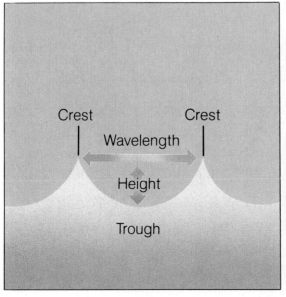

The rope does not move forward with the wave.

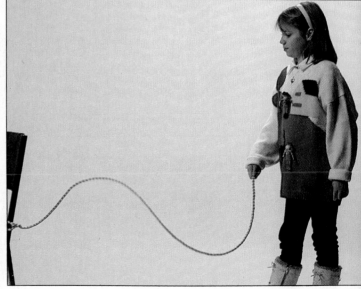

277

How Moving Water Changes Beaches

Moving water can change a beach over time. Waves pound on the beach day after day. During a storm, strong waves crash high on the beach. Rocks and sand bump into each other and wear away surfaces. Notice in the pictures how waves wore away parts of the shore. Waves also can move sand to different places and build up land.

Lesson Review

1. What is a current?
2. What causes tides?
3. How does water move in a wave?
4. How can water change a beach?
5. **Challenge!** How could the tides affect living things on a beach?

Study on your own, pages 396–397.

Changes caused by waves

FIND OUT ON YOUR OWN

El Niño (el nē′nyō) is a warm current that sometimes moves south down the coast of South America. Look in an encyclopedia or a book about oceans to find out how El Niño affects the people who live in Peru and the fish that live along the coast.

Making Waves and Currents

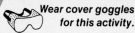
Purpose
Observe the effects of waves and currents on water.

Gather These Materials
• large basin • warm water to fill basin
• centimeter ruler • sharpened pencil
• plastic-foam cup • small pieces of
ice • cold, colored water • small pieces
of cork • drinking straw

Follow This Procedure
1. Use a chart like the one shown to record your observations.
2. Add warm water to the basin until the water is 3 cm deep.
3. Use the point of the pencil to punch eight small holes near the bottom of the plastic-foam cup.
4. Fill the cup with ice. Place the cup in the middle of the basin.
5. Add colored water to fill the cup. The cold water is like a current in the warm water. Observe where the colored water moves. Record your observations in your chart.
6. Place the pieces of cork in the basin of water.
7. Above the water, blow air through the straw to make waves on the surface of the water. Do not blow on the cork.
8. Observe how the waves move the cork. Record what you observe.
9. Observe how the waves affect the movement of the colored water. Record your observations.

Record Your Results

	Observations about movement
Effect of adding cold water	
Effect of waves on cork	
Effect of waves on colored water	

State Your Conclusion
1. Where does a current of cold water move when it is in warm water?
2. Why do you think the waves moved the cork but not the colored water?

Use What You Learned
Explain why currents mix ocean water more than waves do.

3 What Is the Ocean Bottom Like?

LESSON GOALS

You will learn
- what the ocean bottom is like.
- how the ocean bottom changes.
- how scientists study the ocean bottom.

People have sailed the oceans for thousands of years. Sailors of long ago used ropes to measure how deep the ocean was. They tied weights to long ropes. Then they lowered the ropes until the weights hit bottom. The sailors could tell how deep the water was by measuring the length of the wet rope. How could measuring this way sometimes be incorrect?

Mapping the Ocean Bottom

Scientists today use sound to map the ocean bottom. They send sound waves from ships down toward the ocean bottom. The sound waves bounce off the ocean floor and return to the surface. The scientists measure how long the sound waves take to return to the surface. Scientists use this time to find how deep the ocean is. Because scientists know how fast sound travels through water, they can tell how far the sound travels. They can measure even very deep parts of the ocean this way.

The Ocean Bottom

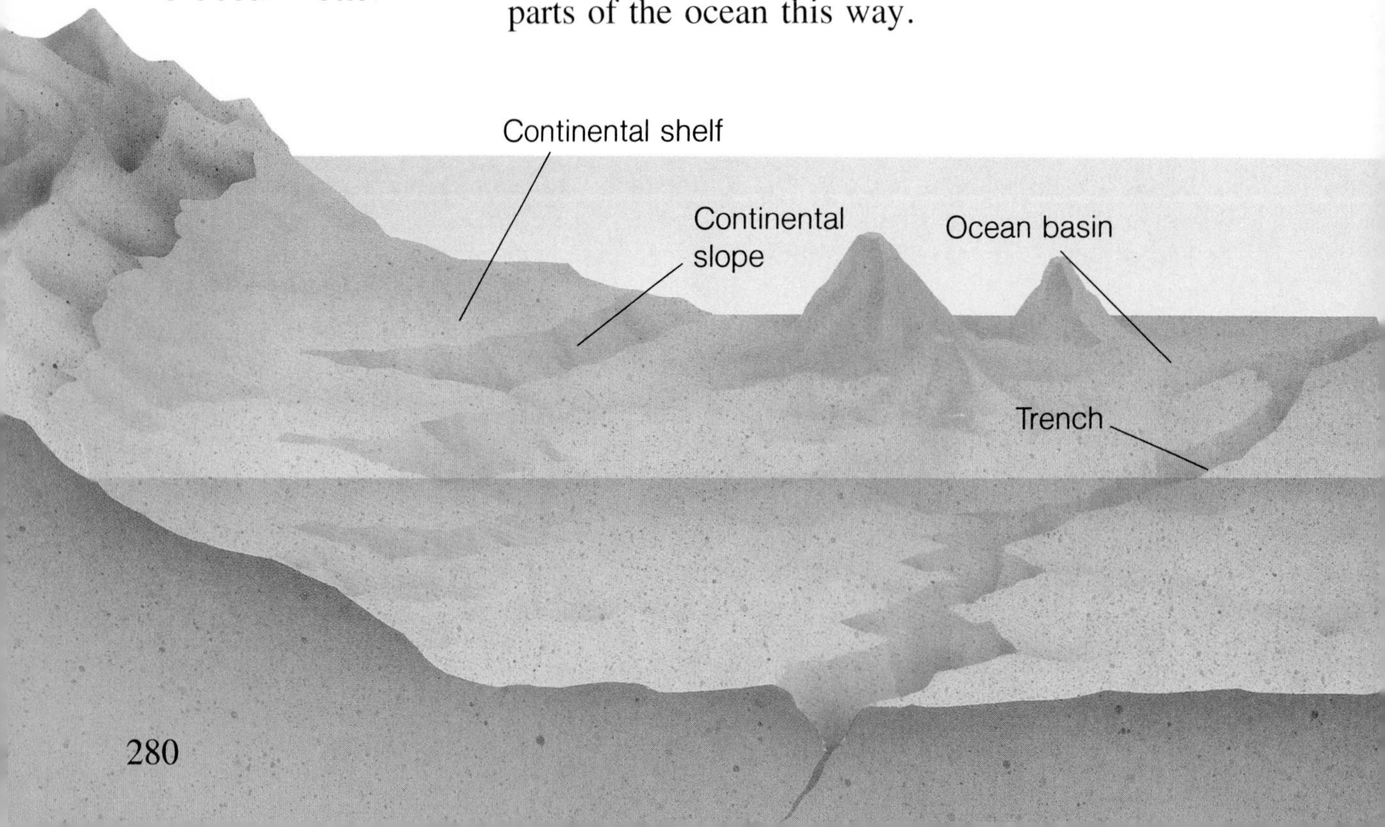

Continental shelf
Continental slope
Ocean basin
Trench

The picture on page 280 and 281 shows the shape of the bottom of the ocean. Find the **continental shelf** near the shoreline. At the continental shelf, notice that the shallow bottom of the ocean drops gently from the shore. The ocean is an average of 135 meters deep on the continental shelf.

Now find the **continental slope,** which is farther from the shore. The ocean bottom drops sharply at the continental slope. Beyond the continental slope lies the deep **ocean basin.** Here, the ocean is about 4,000 or 5,000 meters deep.

Look at the picture to find some features of the ocean basin. Notice that the bottom of the ocean is not flat. It has hills, mountains, and deep valleys. Some mountains in the ocean are taller than any mountains on land. **Trenches** are very deep valleys in the bottom of the ocean. They are deeper than any valleys on land.

Find the **ridge** in the picture. Ridges are long chains of mountains found in some parts of the ocean basin. One of these mountain chains is called the Mid-Atlantic Ridge.

continental (kon′tə nen′tl) **shelf,** the shallow part of the ocean floor close to the edge of a continent.

continental slope, the land from the continental shelf to the ocean basin.

ocean basin, the deep ocean floor.

trench (trench), a deep, narrow valley in the ocean floor.

ridge (rij), a chain of underwater mountains.

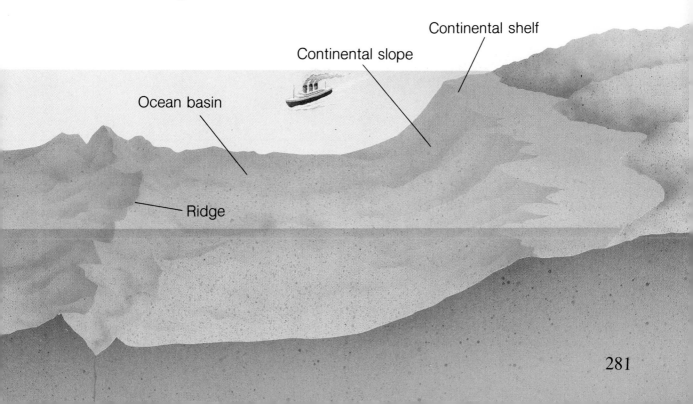

Continental shelf

Continental slope

Ocean basin

Ridge

How the Ocean Bottom Changes

You learned in Chapter 10 that the surface of the earth is always changing. Volcanoes and earthquakes change the shape of the land. They can also change the land at the bottom of the ocean. Volcanoes on the ocean bottom build underwater mountains. Sometimes these mountains rise above the level of the sea and form islands. Earthquakes under the ocean can change the shape of the ocean bottom.

You have also learned that moving plates make up the earth's crust. Scientists first learned about the earth's plates by studying the ocean bottom. Ridges are found where plates move apart. Magma from inside the earth pushes up between the plates. This magma hardens to form new crust. The Mid-Atlantic Ridge is one place where the ocean bottom is getting wider. The parts of the ridge are moving apart about a centimeter a year. Find the ridges in the map below.

Trenches are the deepest places in the ocean floor. They form where two plates come together. One plate moves down and under the other plate. Trenches can be as deep as 10 kilometers. Find the trenches below.

Ridges and trenches

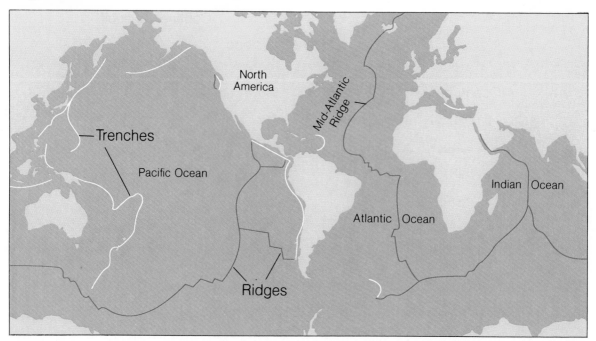

282

Exploring the Ocean Bottom

An **oceanographer** is a scientist who studies the ocean. Oceanographers use many tools to study the ocean's bottom. Underwater research ships carry scientists as deep as 4 kilometers below the surface of the ocean. Robot ships that carry only instruments can go even deeper. Some ships have tools that can drill holes in the ocean bottom and bring up samples for oceanographers to study. These samples show some of the layers of rocks and sediments that make up the ocean floor.

Lesson Review

1. What are the features of the ocean bottom?
2. How does the ocean bottom change?
3. How do people study the ocean bottom?
4. **Challenge!** How can studying the ocean bottom be useful to people?

Study on your own, pages 396–397.

SCIENCE IN YOUR LIFE

A robot ship took television pictures of the ship *Titanic* on the ocean floor. Other robot ships inspect undersea pipes and cables and can collect samples of the ocean bottom.

oceanographer
(ō′shə nog′rə fər), scientist who studies the oceans.

Deep in the ocean, oceanographers found hot water and minerals shooting up through holes. These holes are like chimneys in the ocean floor. Oceanographers found living things that had never been seen before, such as the tube worms in the picture. Look in books about life in the oceans to find out about the strange things that live near the warm chimneys.

FIND OUT ON YOUR OWN

Making a Model of Sediment Layers

Purpose
Compare how quickly different sizes of sediments settle and form layers.

Gather These Materials
• piece of paper • large, clear-plastic container with lid • half cup of sand • half cup of soil • half cup of fine gravel • half cup of pebbles • water

Follow This Procedure
1. Use a chart like the one shown to record your observations.
2. If the container has a small opening at the top, make a funnel out of a piece of paper. Use the funnel to add the sediments without spilling. Place about half a cup each of sand, pebbles, gravel, and soil into the plastic container.
3. Fill the container with water to about 2 cm below the top of the container. Screw the lid tightly on the container.
4. Shake the container, mixing the materials inside completely.
5. Put the container down, and observe the materials inside for 5 minutes. Notice the order in which the materials settle to the bottom. Record your observations by numbering the sediments from 1 to 4 in your chart. The sediment that settles first is 1.

Record Your Results

Sediment	Order in which sediments settled to bottom
Sand	
Gravel	
Pebbles	
Soil	

State Your Conclusion
1. Which sediment settled first? last?
2. Explain why the sediments settled the way they did.

Use What You Learned
When a fast-moving river enters the ocean, what kind of sediment is deposited first?

Conquering the Ocean Depths

The Problem The storm of 1728 was one of the worst ever. The crashing waves tossed the little ship like a piece of driftwood. Finally, one mighty wave hit the ship and capsized it. Its heavy cargo of silver bars dragged it to the bottom of the sea more than 150 meters down. The cargo was lost. Divers could not bring the cargo to the surface because the pressure of the deep water would crush them.

The Breakthrough For centuries, inventors tried to make diving suits to protect people from the pressure in deep water. Most suits were made of wood and leather. None would work below 60 or 90 meters. Finally, in the early 1900s, a man named Joseph (Pop) Peress built a suit from a special mixture of metals. Pop's suit weighed more than 360 kilograms, but it could work 120 meters below the surface. The water pressure at 120 meters could not crush the suit. Divers could now go deeper into the ocean than ever before.

New Technology With the discovery of mineral riches on the ocean floor in the 1950s, diving deeper into the sea became even more important. Scientists asked Pop Peress to help them invent a new kind of diving suit, using special kinds of plastic. The "Jim" suit, shown in the picture, was built. A diver wearing this suit can walk on the ocean floor more than 425 meters below the surface. In 1986, new equipment was used to find the *Titanic,* a ship that sank in more than 3,900 meters of water.

"Jason, Jr.," a kind of swimming eyeball, was sent down to take pictures of the wreck. "Alvin," a tiny two-man submarine with remote-controlled arms, was able to pick up objects from the wreck and carry them back to the surface.

What Do You Think?
1. What makes oceans difficult to study?
2. What kinds of objects might "Alvin" pick up?

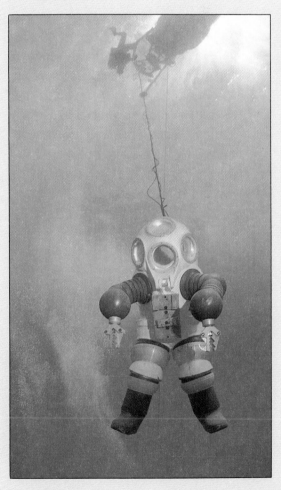

Skills for Solving Problems

Using Hydrometers and Line Graphs

Problem: How does the amount of salt in water affect an object floating in it?

Part A. Using Hydrometers to Collect Information

1. A hydrometer is a weighted object that floats upright in water. The hydrometer in the pictures is made from a drinking straw and clay. A scale on the straw measures changes in the level the hydrometer floats in the water. Hydrometer A is floating in plain tap water. What unit on the scale of the hydrometer is level with the surface of the water?

2. Ten grams of salt were added to the water in which hydrometer B is floating. What unit on hydrometer B is level with the water? on hydrometer C? D? How much salt was added to the water in C? D?

Part B. Using a Line Graph to Organize and Interpret Information

3. The line graph contains the information you collected in Part A. What do the lines on the left of the graph stand for?

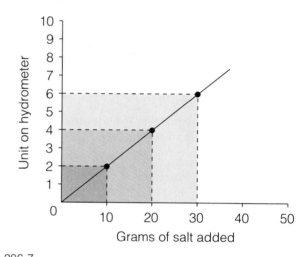

286-7

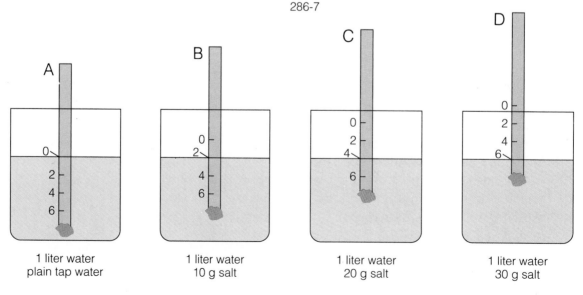

A	B	C	D
1 liter water plain tap water	1 liter water 10 g salt	1 liter water 20 g salt	1 liter water 30 g salt

286

4. The bottom line of the graph shows the different amounts of salt that were added to the water. The dots on the graph show the units on the hydrometer for the different amounts of salt added to the water. Find the dot above the line for 10 grams of salt. What was the unit on the hydrometer for the water with 10 grams of salt added? 20 grams? 30 grams?

5. What would be the unit on a hydrometer floating in a liter of water with 40 grams of salt added?

6. How does increasing the amount of salt in water affect an object floating in the water?

Part C. Using Hydrometers and Line Graphs to Solve a Problem

Problem: How does the amount of sugar in water affect an object floating in it?

7. Use the pictures below to collect the information you need to solve the problem. Make a line graph similar to the one shown in Part B to organize your information.

8. Look at your line graph. How does the amount of sugar in water affect an object floating in it?

9. You might want to do this experiment and use your own results to make a bar graph.

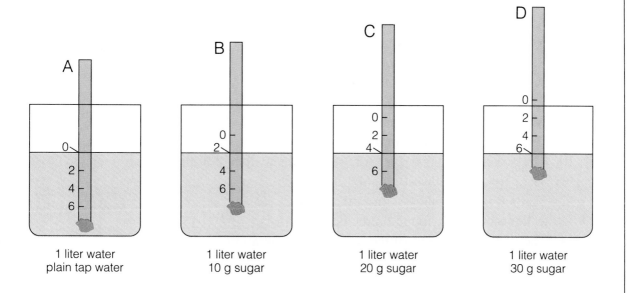

A	B	C	D
1 liter water plain tap water	1 liter water 10 g sugar	1 liter water 20 g sugar	1 liter water 30 g sugar

Chapter 11 Review

☑ Chapter Main Ideas

Lesson 1 • Four main oceans cover about three-fourths of the earth's surface. • Fish, ocean plants, and sodium chloride are resources in the ocean. • Nodules and petroleum are resources from the ocean bottom. • Dumping wastes causes pollution in the ocean.

Lesson 2 • Ocean water moves in currents. • The pull of the moon causes tides. • Waves have the same main parts. • Moving water can change beaches.

Lesson 3 • Features of the ocean bottom include the continental shelf, the continental slope, the ocean basin, trenches, and ridges.
• Movement of the earth's plates changes the ocean bottom.
• Oceanographers study the ocean bottom using underwater ships.

☑ Reviewing Science Words

continental shelf	ocean basin	sodium chloride
continental slope	oceanographer	tide
crest	petroleum	trench
current	resource	trough
nodule	ridge	wave height

Copy each sentence. Fill in the blank with the correct word or words from the list.

1. The highest point on a wave is its ▨ .
2. Hills, mountains, and valleys are found on the deep ▨ .
3. A ▨ moves like a river through an ocean.
4. You measure ▨ from the highest to the lowest point of a wave.
5. People drill beneath the ocean for ▨ , a liquid fuel.
6. A high ▨ is the rise of the level of the ocean water.
7. The ▨ is the bottom of the ocean nearest the land.
8. An ▨ is a scientist who studies the ocean.
9. One kind of salt found in ocean water is ▨ .
10. The ocean becomes deeper past the continental shelf at the ▨ .
11. The ▨ is the lowest point of a wave.
12. Seafood is a useful ▨ from the ocean.
13. A lump of metals found on the ocean floor is a ▨ .
14. The very deepest part of the ocean bottom is a ▨ .
15. A chain of underwater mountains is a ▨ .

☑ Reviewing What You Learned

Write the letter of the best answer.

1. Certain metals are found on the ocean floor in the form of
   (a) petroleum.   (b) nodules.   (c) sodium chloride.   (d) salts.
2. The ocean floor nearest to the land is the
   (a) ocean basin.   (c) continental slope.
   (b) continental shelf.   (d) Mid-Atlantic Ridge.
3. Scientists map the ocean bottom using
   (a) ropes and weights.   (c) sound waves.
   (b) water waves.   (d) satellites.
4. The deepest ocean is the
   (a) Indian.   (b) Pacific.   (c) Atlantic.   (d) Arctic.
5. Storm waves have greater than usual
   (a) wave heights.   (b) nodules.   (c) low tides.   (d) ridges.
6. What has a different temperature than the water around it?
   (a) a tide   (b) a wave   (c) a current   (d) a crest

☑ Interpreting What You Learned

Write a short answer for each question.

1. How are the four oceans related to each other?
2. In what ways are the living things in the ocean useful to people?
3. In what ways is a water wave similar to a wave on a rope?
4. What tools might an oceanographer use to study the ocean?
5. Where on the ocean bottom would you expect to find volcanoes and earthquakes?

☑ Extending Your Thinking

Write a paragraph to answer each question.

1. How can polluted ocean water affect the resources people get from the ocean?
2. How do the changes on the ocean's bottom relate to the movements of the plates on the earth's crust?

• For further review, use Study Guide pages 396–397.

Movement in the Solar System

This huge ball of glowing gases is the sun at the center of the solar system. This star supplies light energy for the earth and other planets that move around it. Without this light energy, the earth would be a cold, dark planet.

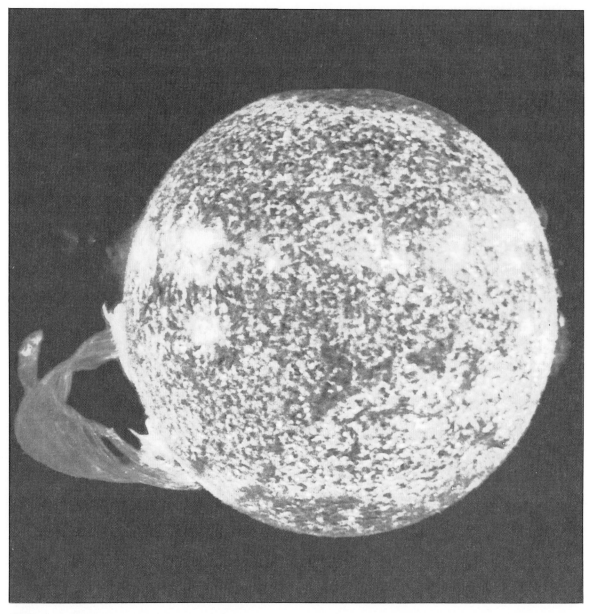

Introducing the Chapter

You might have seen beautiful sunrises or sunsets. What makes the sun appear to rise every morning and set every night? The activity below is an easy way to find out what causes sunrises and sunsets. In this chapter you will learn how the earth, the moon, the planets, and other objects appear to move in the sky. You will also learn how they really move.

Making a Model of the Sun Rising and Setting

DISCOVER!

You are going to use your body and a light bulb to find out what causes sunrises and sunsets. Stand facing a light bulb that is turned on. Pretend that your head is the earth. Your eyes see what a person standing on the earth would see. Pretend that the light bulb is the sun.

Stand facing the light bulb. When the sun and the earth are in this position, it is noon for you. Start turning your body around slowly to your left. Keep your head and eyes straight ahead. As you turn, the light bulb will begin to go out of your sight. When you have turned so that you can no longer see the light bulb, the sun has set. Night has begun. Keep turning slowly. When the light bulb comes back into view, it is sunrise.

Talk About It

1. How are the light bulb and the sun alike?
2. What causes sunrises and sunsets?

1 How Does the Earth Move?

LESSON GOALS

You will learn
- how the earth's rotation causes nighttime and daytime.
- how the earth moves around the sun.
- what causes the seasons.

axis (ak′sis), an imaginary line through a spinning object.

rotation (rō tā′shən), one full spin of an object around an axis.

A ball spins on an axis.

Long ago, people watched the sun rise, move across the sky, and then set. They thought that the earth was not moving and that the sun moved around the earth. If you did the activity on page 291, you know that the sun only appears to rise and set. The turning of the earth causes sunrises and sunsets.

Spinning on an Axis

The ball in the picture is spinning—or rotating. Imagine a line drawn from the finger up through the ball. The ball is rotating around this line, called an **axis.** Each time the ball makes one full spin around its axis, it has made one **rotation.**

The earth is like the ball that spins on an axis. As the earth spins, the part of the earth that faces the sun is lighted by the sun and has daytime. Find what part of the earth has daytime in the picture. The part of the earth that faces away from the sun has nighttime. What you know as one daytime and one nighttime together make one full day. The length of time for one rotation is one day. On the earth, the day is divided into twenty-four hours.

The earth spins on an axis.

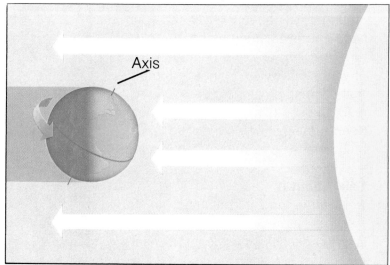

Axis

Revolving Around the Sun

As it spins, the earth also moves around the sun. This moving of the earth around the sun is called revolving. The earth's **orbit** is the path the earth takes as it is revolving around the sun. One full orbit around the sun is one **revolution.** The earth takes one year or about 365 days to make one revolution. Find the path of the earth's revolution in the picture.

The earth revolves around the sun because of gravity. This force keeps the earth from moving straight ahead into space. The sun's gravity pulls the earth back toward the sun.

Movement and Tilt Combined

If the earth's axis were straight up and down, sunlight would always hit the earth at the same angle. Sunlight also would hit different parts of the earth the same way. However, the earth's axis is tilted. Notice in the picture on page 292 how sunlight hits the earth. The northern part of the earth is getting more direct sunlight than the southern part. Since sunlight is the source of energy that heats the earth, the northern part of the earth in the picture has summer while the southern part has winter.

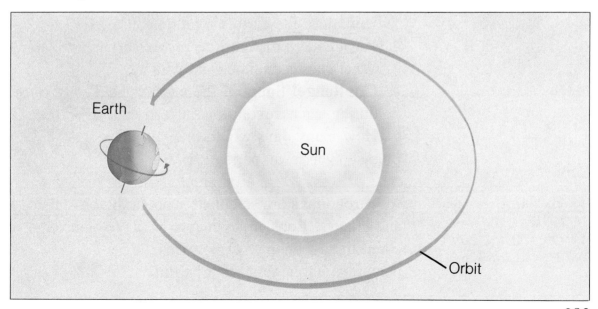

Earth

Sun

Orbit

293

The picture shows how sunlight hits the earth at two times during a year. How many months apart do you think these times are? Notice the earth stays tilted in the same direction. As the earth revolves around the sun, different parts of the earth get the most direct sunlight. Which picture of the earth shows the northern part during its summer?

Sunlight hitting the earth at two times of the year

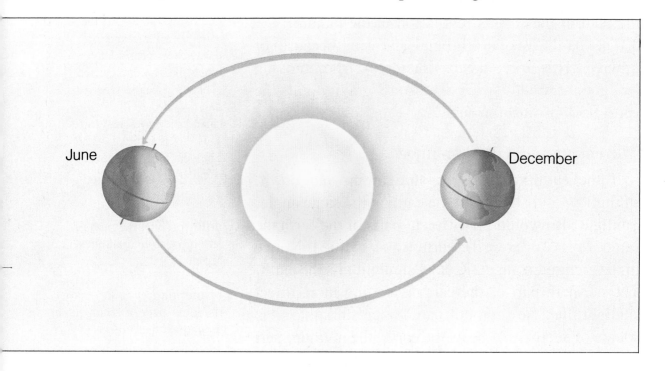

June

December

Lesson Review

1. How does the earth's rotation cause days?
2. What causes the earth to revolve around the sun?
3. What causes summer and winter?
4. **Challenge!** Suppose the earth rotated only once during each revolution instead of 365¼ times. How many days would one year have?

Study on your own, pages 398–399.

Study on your own, pages 398–399.

FIND OUT ON YOUR OWN

Astronomers are scientists who study the stars and planets. Look in an encyclopedia to find out about the astronomer Copernicus. Write a paragraph explaining what he did.

Observing the Earth's Tilt

Purpose
Observe how the earth's tilt affects how directly sunlight reaches different parts of the earth.

Gather These Materials
• plastic-foam ball • pencil • tape
• marker • flashlight

Follow This Procedure
1. Use a chart like the one shown to record your observations.
2. Push the pencil through the center of the ball. The ball is the earth.
3. Place a piece of tape on the ball next to the eraser end of the pencil. Mark an *N* on the tape. That end of the pencil will be the axis at the North Pole. The other end will be the axis at the South Pole.
4. Using a marker, draw the Equator half way between the Poles.
5. Hold the axis so that the North Pole is tilted toward you as shown in the picture. Have your partner sit across from you and hold the flashlight about 20 cm from the earth, shining the light on the Equator. The light will be sunlight.
6. Move the earth in a circle around the flashlight. Keep the North Pole tilted toward you. Be sure your partner shines the light on the Equator. Observe whether the northern or southern part of the earth gets more direct sunlight when the North Pole is tilted toward the sun.

7. Observe which part gets more direct sunlight when the South Pole is tilted toward the sun. Record your observations in the chart.

Record Your Results

	Part of Earth getting more direct light
North Pole tilted toward sun	
South Pole tilted toward sun	

State Your Conclusion
1. How does the earth's tilt affect how directly sunlight reaches the different parts of the earth?
2. When the northern part is tilted toward the sun, what season of the year is it in the United States?

Use What You Learned
Explain the reason that countries near the Equator do not have seasons.

2 What Does the Moon's Movement Cause?

LESSON GOALS

You will learn
• how the positions of the earth, sun, and moon cause the moon's phases.
• how the positions of the earth, sun, and moon cause eclipses.

satellite (sat′l īt), an object that revolves around another object.

The brightness of a full moon can light a dark night with moonlight. However, the moon does not make its own light. Moonlight is really sunlight reflected from the moon.

The moon is a **satellite** of the earth. A satellite is an object that revolves around another object. The earth is a satellite of the sun.

Sunlight lights half the earth and half the moon. The other half of the earth and half of the moon are dark. People can only see the moon when at least part of the lighted half of the moon is facing the earth.

Phases of the Moon

Although the moon is really shaped like a ball, its shape appears to change from day to day. The different shapes are the moon's phases. Sometimes the moon appears as a whole circle. This phase is a full moon. Find the location of the moon, sun, and earth when the moon appears to be full.

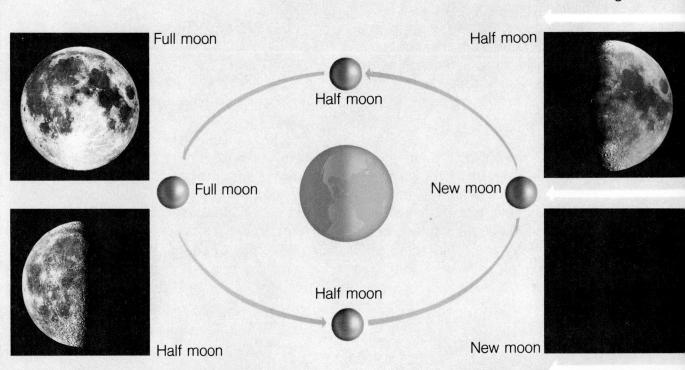

Sunlight

Full moon

Half moon

Half moon

Half moon

Full moon

New moon

Half moon

Half moon

New moon

As the moon continues to revolve around the earth, a part of the dark side of the moon faces the earth. Each day more of the dark side faces the earth and people see less of the moon. The moon slowly changes from a circle to a half circle. When people on the earth see the moon as a half circle, they see half the lighted side and half the dark side of the moon. This phase of the moon is sometimes called the half moon. Find this phase of the moon.

After a while, only the dark side of the moon faces the earth. The moon does not appear in the sky. This phase of the moon is called the new moon even though it is not really new. The moon is just beginning a new set of phases. The new moon takes place a little more than two weeks after a full moon.

Then the moon slowly changes from the new moon back to a full moon. The changes from a full moon, to a new moon, and back to a full moon take 29⅓ days. The moon takes this long to revolve around the earth once.

Eclipses of the Moon and Sun

As the moon revolves around the earth, the earth usually does not come between the sun and the moon. Notice in the picture what happens when the earth does come between the sun and the moon. The moon passes through the earth's shadow, which causes a **lunar eclipse.** Find the earth's shadow in the picture of a lunar eclipse. What do you think the moon looks like from earth during a lunar eclipse?

A lunar eclipse

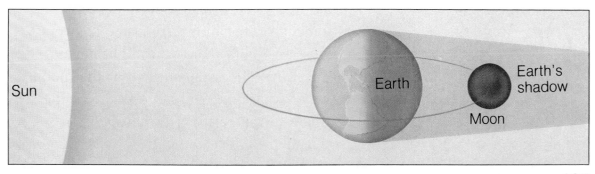

Sun   Earth   Moon   Earth's shadow

297

solar eclipse (sō′lər
i klips′), the blocking of
sunlight by the moon as the
moon passes between the
sun and the earth.

A solar eclipse

The moon usually does not come between the earth and the sun. When it does, the moon blocks some sunlight from the earth, and a **solar eclipse** takes place. The moon makes a small shadow on the earth. From this shadow, the sun appears to get covered slowly. Find the moon's shadow on the earth in the pictures of a solar eclipse.

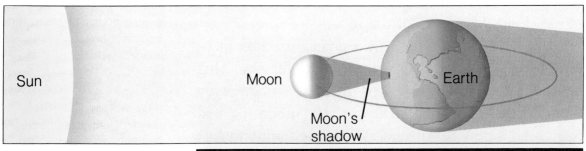

Sun   Moon   Earth

Moon's
shadow

How the sun looks during a
solar eclipse when it is only
partly covered by the moon

Lesson Review

1. What causes the phases of the moon?
2. What causes a lunar eclipse and a solar eclipse?
3. **Challenge!** Can more people on earth see a lunar eclipse or a solar eclipse? Explain your answer.

Study on your own, pages 398–399.

Study on your own, pages 398–399.

**FIND OUT
ON YOUR OWN**

Go to the library and read about the people who first landed on the moon. Find the answers to these questions and others you might have: Who were they? What is the surface of the moon like? How do the gravity and atmosphere of the moon compare to the earth's? Write a story telling about their visit to the moon.

Making a Model of the Moon's Phases

Purpose
Observe how the moon's phases change.

Gather These Materials
• ball • flashlight

Follow This Procedure
1. Use a chart like the one shown to record your observations.
2. Hold the ball in front of you and slightly above your head, as shown in the picture.
3. Ask your partner to stand 2 meters in front of the ball, and shine the light on the ball as shown. You are the earth, the ball is the moon, and the light is sunlight.
4. The moon is now in Position A, as the diagram shows. Observe how much of the part of the moon that you can see is lighted while in Position A. Observe how much is dark. Record your observations in your chart by shading in the part of the moon that is dark.
5. Keep the moon at the same height and turn to your left to Position B. Be sure your partner continues to shine the light directly on the moon. Observe how much of the part of the moon that you can see is lighted. Observe how much is dark. Record your observations.
6. Repeat step 5 for Positions C and D.

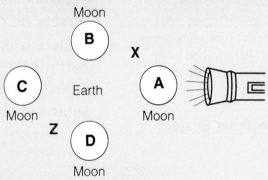

Record Your Results

How the Moon Looks			
A	B	C	D
◯	◯	◯	◯

State Your Conclusion
1. Which position represents a full moon?
2. Explain what causes the moon's phases.

Use What You Learned
Predict how the moon looks at Positions X and Z on the diagram. Test your prediction.

3 How Do the Planets of the Solar System Move?

LESSON GOALS

You will learn
- how the revolutions and rotations of the other planets compare to Earth's.
- the names of the planets and their order from the sun.

solar (sō′lər) **system,** the sun, the nine planets and their moons, and other objects that orbit the sun.

The Solar System

For thousands of years, people have watched the stars at night. The stars appear to rise and set slowly as the night goes on. The stars are like the sun and make their own light.

From night to night, some points of light seem to move among the stars. These points of light are planets. Like the earth and the earth's moon, planets do not make light. They reflect light from the sun.

People have known for five hundred years that planets are satellites of the sun. The orbits of the nine planets from the sun outward are Mercury, Venus, Earth, Mars, Jupiter, Saturn, Uranus, Neptune, and Pluto. These planets and the sun make up most of the **solar system.**

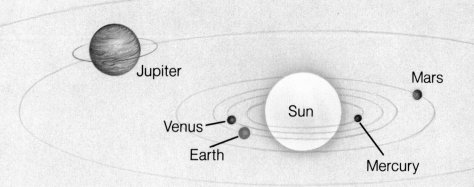

Neptune

Jupiter

Venus

Earth

Sun

Mars

Mercury

Uranus

Movements of the Planets

Find the earth's path in the picture. Planets such as Mars and Jupiter are farther away from the sun than Earth is. These planets take longer to make one revolution. They have farther to go, and they do not move as fast.

The orbits of the planets are almost circles. They are really **ellipses,** or circles that have been flattened a little. Find the orbits of Mars and Jupiter in the picture. Notice that the orbits around the sun get longer as the ellipses get larger.

Pluto is known as the farthest planet from the sun because it has the longest orbit. However, Pluto's orbit sometimes crosses Neptune's orbit. Pluto will be closer to the sun than Neptune is until 1998.

ellipse (i lips′), the shape of a circle that has been flattened a little.

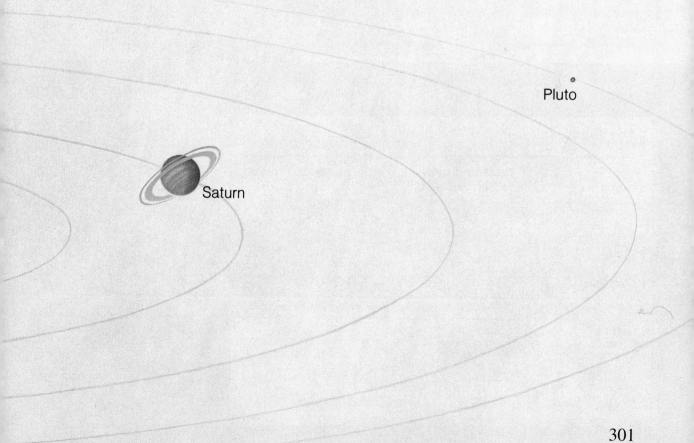

Pluto

Saturn

301

You know that a year on the earth is how long the earth takes to orbit the sun. A year on any planet is how long that planet takes to orbit the sun. The length of time for each planet's orbit is listed in the table. A year on Mars is almost two of Earth's years. How long is one year on Mercury? What planet has the longest year? Notice that the length of a year gets longer as the distance from the sun gets greater.

You know that a day on the earth is how long the earth takes to rotate once. A day on any planet is how long that planet takes to rotate once. The table shows that Jupiter rotates in ten hours. A Jupiter day is only ten Earth hours long. What planet has the longest day?

A Voyager space probe

The Planets

Name	Time for 1 orbit (in Earth time)	Time for 1 rotation (in Earth time)
Mercury	88 days	176 days
Venus	8 months	127 days
Earth	1 year	1 day
Mars	1.9 years	25 hours
Jupiter	12 years	10 hours
Saturn	29.5 years	11 hours
Uranus	84 years	17 hours
Neptune	165 years	18 hours
Pluto	250 years	6 days

Exploring the Planets

People learn more about the planets and their moons by sending spacecraft, like the one in the picture, close to the planets. Each planet is different from the other planets in some ways. Mercury, Venus, Earth, and Mars are all rocky planets. Jupiter, Saturn, Uranus, and Neptune are made mostly of gases. Pluto might be made of frozen materials. Compare the sizes of these planets, how far they are from the sun, and their moons by studying the table. Which planet is the smallest? Which two planets are the largest? Notice that Pluto is forty times farther from the sun than Earth is. Which planet is closest to the sun?

As the picture shows, Mercury is covered with large holes called craters. The craters could have formed when Mercury was hit by huge rocks from space. Because Mercury is close to the sun, it is very hot. The temperature on Mercury can reach 425° Celsius. Notice in the table that Mercury is less than half the size of Earth and has no moons.

Mercury

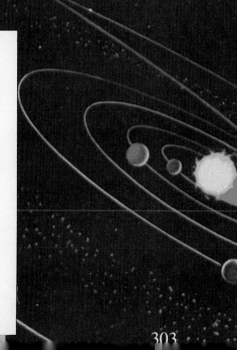

The Planets

Name	Distance from sun (compared to Earth)	Diameter in kilometers	Number of known moons
Mercury	0.4	4,878	0
Venus	0.7	12,104	0
Earth	1	12,756	1
Mars	1.5	6,794	2
Jupiter	5.2	142,796	16
Saturn	9.5	120,000	17
Uranus	19.2	52,290	15
Neptune	30	48,600	2
Pluto	40	2,300	1

If you see a very bright object in the western sky after sunset or in the east before sunrise, it is probably Venus. Venus is often called the "evening star" or the "morning star." However, Venus is a planet, not a star. Jupiter is the only other planet that gets very bright in the earth's sky.

Venus is the closest planet to Earth. It is also about the same size as Earth. Venus is always covered with clouds, as it is in the picture. These clouds are made of drops of acid. The air on Venus is mostly carbon dioxide. The clouds and carbon dioxide make Venus a very hot planet. A few spacecraft have landed on Venus and sent back pictures of the rocks under the clouds. Venus has giant volcanoes.

Viewed from space, Earth always has some clouds. Oceans and land can also be seen from space. Find the oceans in the picture of Earth.

Notice in the picture below that Mars is covered with reddish dust and rocks. Winds blow the dust into the air and make the sky pink. Mars has giant volcanoes. Find the volcano in the picture on the next page. Mars also has a giant canyon much larger than the Grand Canyon on Earth. The temperature on Mars is usually lower than on Earth.

Jupiter is the largest planet. Some of its moons are bigger than some planets. One of Jupiter's moons even has volcanoes.

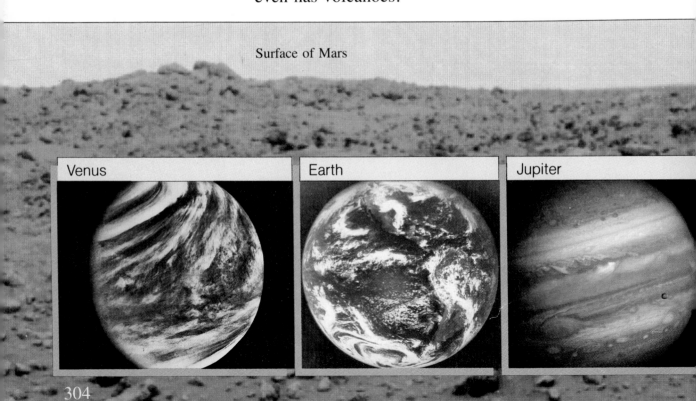

Surface of Mars

Venus

Earth

Jupiter

304

As you see in the picture on page 304, Jupiter has bands of colorful clouds. Jupiter has a ring around it that is hard to see. Jupiter also has storms. The Giant Red Spot is a storm that is larger than Earth. Unlike the other planets you have read about, Jupiter gives off energy that heats the gas above it.

Mars

Uranus

Neptune

Pluto

Saturn

Saturn is the second largest planet. Like Jupiter, Saturn has many moons. One of them is bigger than the planet Mercury. Saturn also has storms and gives off energy that heats the air above it. Saturn has bands that are harder to see than Jupiter's bands. Saturn has beautiful rings. These rings can be seen from Earth with a telescope. Find these rings in the picture. Each ring is made up of thousands of thinner rings.

Uranus is about four times bigger than Earth. It is so far from the sun that it is very cold. Notice what color Uranus is in the picture. Uranus is a blue-green color because of a gas that surrounds it. Uranus has at least ten narrow rings.

Find the pictures of Neptune and Pluto. Not much is known about these two planets. Neptune is a large planet that looks greenish. Pluto is the smallest planet. It is about the size of Earth's moon. Scientists will keep learning more about these planets and their moons as spacecraft send back more information. Scientists will also learn more as they continue watching the planets through telescopes on Earth.

Lesson Review

1. How does the length of one orbit on Venus compare to one revolution on Earth?
2. What are the planets in the order of their orbits from the sun?
3. **Challenge!** How old would you be now in Jupiter years?

Study on your own, pages 398–399.

Use books in the library to find out who discovered Uranus, Neptune, and Pluto. Also find out what year each was discovered. Make a table of the information you find.

FIND OUT ON YOUR OWN

4 What Other Objects Move in the Solar System?

LESSON GOALS

You will learn
- what an asteroid is.
- what a meteor is and when a meteor becomes a meteorite.
- what a comet is.

asteroid (as′tə roid′), a rocky object orbiting the sun between the planets.

Nine planets and their moons orbit the sun in the solar system. Thousands of other objects also orbit the sun. Some of these objects light up the sky each August. Once people on the earth see other objects, many years pass before people can see them again.

Asteroids

Thousands of objects made of rocks orbit the sun in between the planets. They are known as **asteroids.** The largest asteroid is about the same size across as the state of Texas.

Find the orbits of asteroids in the picture. Most asteroids are between the orbits of Mars and Jupiter. Some asteroids have orbits closer to the sun. These asteroids sometimes cross the orbit of the earth.

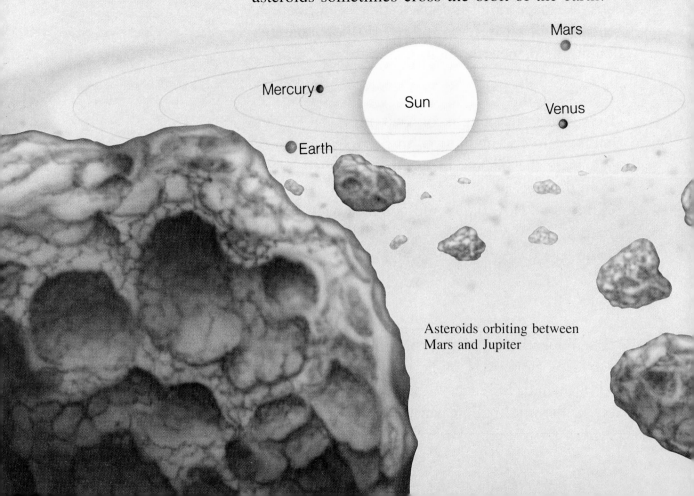

Asteroids orbiting between Mars and Jupiter

Meteors

Besides asteroids, other smaller pieces of rocks and dust orbit the sun. Sometimes, a small piece gets close to the earth and enters the earth's air. As the rock or dust passes through the earth's air, friction causes it to heat up and burn. This burning piece of rock or dust is a **meteor.** People see meteors as flashes of light crossing the sky. Although meteors are not stars, some people call them shooting stars because of the way they look in the sky.

Some meteors are large enough that not all of them burn up before reaching the earth. Any part of a meteor that reaches the ground is a **meteorite.** The students in the picture below are touching a meteorite. The largest meteorites that have been found weigh several tons.

A large meteorite

SCIENCE IN YOUR LIFE

Every night, a meteor flashes across the sky about every ten minutes. On a few nights each year, many more meteors can be seen. The best of these meteor showers takes place on August 12.

meteor (mē′tē ər), a piece of rock or dust from space burning up in the earth's air.

meteorite (mē′tē ə rīt′), a rock from space that has passed through the air and landed on the ground.

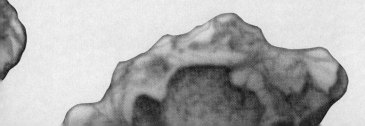

Comets

comet (kom′it), a frozen chunk of ice and dust that orbits the sun.

Large chunks of ice and dust also orbit the sun. These chunks are **comets.** Comets have orbits that are much longer and flatter than the orbits of planets. Notice that a comet's orbit takes it far away from the sun for most of its orbit. Comets cannot be seen from the earth when they are far away.

When comets are far away from the sun, they do not get much heat from the sun. As comets move closer to the sun, the sun's energy begins to heat them. Some of the ice becomes a gas. The sun pushes the gas and dust into a long tail. The tail extends from the bright part of the comet known as the head. Find the comet's head and tail in the picture. A comet's tail can be millions of kilometers long.

Lesson Review

1. What is an asteroid?
2. When does a meteor become a meteorite?
3. How is a comet's orbit different from the orbit of a planet?
4. **Challenge!** If comets had shorter orbits, would they be seen more or less often from Earth? Explain your answer.

Study on your own, pages 398–399.

FIND OUT ON YOUR OWN

About every five years people on the earth can see a comet without a telescope. The most famous comet is Halley's Comet. A computer added the colors to the picture of Halley's Comet. The different colors show different levels of brightness. Use an encyclopedia or other books to find out about Halley's Comet.

Halley's Comet

Flying into the Future

The planet Mars is our next-door neighbor, but it is still very far away. A spaceship would take about nine months to fly there. The long distances to other planets makes them difficult to study. If rockets could go faster, exploring space would be easier.

Dr. Franklin Chang-Diaz is a scientist who is working to design rockets that can go faster. He knows that such rockets would need special fuel. Also, they must be made of special metals that are not harmed by the high heat during flight.

Designing rockets is only part of the work of Dr. Chang-Diaz. He is also a NASA astronaut. In the picture, he is training to go on a space flight. When he recently flew in an orbit around the earth, he did experiments on rocket metals, on light, and on living things. On the same flight, Dr. Chang-Diaz gave a spaceship tour in Spanish that was shown on live television. He showed how astronauts live and work. He also showed how the space program helps people here on the earth. As a result, Spanish-speaking people in the United States and in other countries could learn more about the space program.

Dr. Chang-Diaz hopes that many countries will take part in space travel and research in the future. He also hopes that all countries will share what is gained from exploring space. Through his rocket research and his spaceship tour, Dr. Chang-Diaz is working to bring outer space a little closer to home.

What Do You Think?

1. Earth is 150 million kilometers from the sun. Mars is 225 million kilometers miles from the sun. When Earth and Mars pass close to each other, how close are they?
2. If people wanted to travel to Mars, how would having a faster rocket make the trip easier?

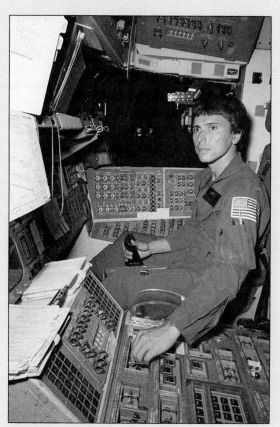

Using Diagrams and Line Graphs

Problem: How does a planet's distance from the sun affect the time needed to make one revolution?

Part A. Using Diagrams to Collect Information

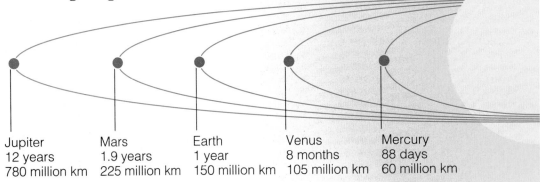

Jupiter
12 years
780 million km

Mars
1.9 years
225 million km

Earth
1 year
150 million km

Venus
8 months
105 million km

Mercury
88 days
60 million km

1. The diagram above shows five of the planets in the solar system. The first number under each planet is the time that planet takes to make one revolution around the sun. How long is one revolution for each of the planets?
2. The second number under each planet is that planet's distance from the sun. Notice that Mercury is 60 million kilometers from the sun. How far is each of the other planets from the sun?

Part B. Using a Line Graph to Organize and Interpret Information

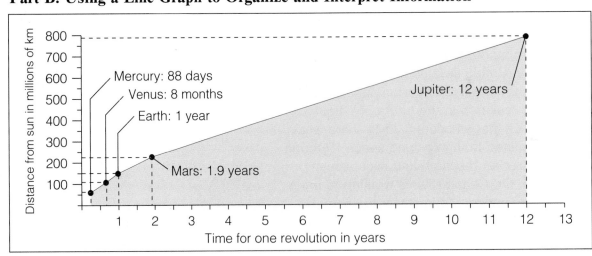

3. The line graph contains the information you collected in Part A. What do the lines at the bottom of the graph stand for? What do the lines at the left of the graph stand for?

4. Find the line at the bottom of the graph that stands for a revolution of 1 year. Now find the dot above this line. What planet does the dot stand for? What does the line across from this dot stand for?

5. Find the other dots on the graph. What happens to the time for one revolution as the distance from the sun gets larger?

Part C. Using Diagrams and a Line Graph to Solve a Problem

Problem: How does the length of time for a planet to make one revolution relate to the planet's diameter.

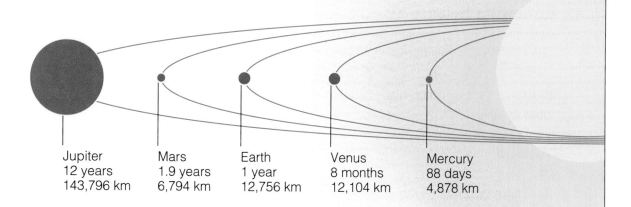

Jupiter	Mars	Earth	Venus	Mercury
12 years	1.9 years	1 year	8 months	88 days
143,796 km	6,794 km	12,756 km	12,104 km	4,878 km

6. The diagram above gives different information about the planets. The first number under each planet is the time for one revolution. The second number is that planet's diameter. Use the diagram to collect the information you need to solve the problem. Make a line graph similar to the one in Part B to organize your information.

7. Look at your graph. How does the time for a planet to make one revolution relate to its diameter?

Chapter 12 Review

✓ Chapter Main Ideas

Lesson 1 • One rotation of the earth on its axis is one day. • The revolution of the earth around the sun takes one year. • The tilt of the earth and the earth's revolving around the sun cause seasons.

Lesson 2 • As the moon revolves around the earth, different amounts of the moon's lighted half face the earth. • A lunar eclipse occurs when the earth passes between the sun and the moon. • A solar eclipse occurs when the moon passes between the sun and the earth.

Lesson 3 • One year on a planet is how long that planet takes to complete one orbit. • One day on a planet is how long that planet takes to rotate around its axis once. • Nine planets orbit the sun.

Lesson 4 • An asteroid is a rocky object that orbits the sun between the planets. • A meteorite is a meteor that hits the ground. • A comet is a frozen chunk of ice and dust that orbits the sun.

✓ Reviewing Science Words

asteroid	meteor	rotation
axis	meteorite	satellite
comet	orbit	solar eclipse
ellipse	revolution	solar system
lunar eclipse		

Copy each sentence. Fill in the blank with the correct word or words from the list.

1. The moon blocks some sunlight from the earth during a ____.
2. An imaginary line through a spinning object is an ____.
3. The earth completes one ____ every twenty-four hours.
4. The moon gets dark during a ____.
5. A circle that has been flattened a little is an ____.
6. The path of an object around another object is an ____.
7. The earth takes one year to complete one ____.
8. The moon is a ____ of the earth.
9. The nine planets and the sun are parts of the ____.
10. A ____ is a frozen chunk of ice and dust.
11. An ____ is a rocky object that orbits the sun between planets.
12. A piece of rock from space that burns up is a ____.
13. A rock from space that lands on the ground is a ____.

✓ Reviewing What You Learned

Write the letter of the best answer.

1. The rotation of the earth causes
   (a) years.   (b) days.   (c) seasons.   (d) eclipses.
2. What force keeps the earth orbiting the sun?
   (a) the moon   (b) rotations   (c) Venus   (d) gravity
3. What season is the northern part of the earth having if the southern part is having summer?
   (a) winter   (b) spring   (c) summer   (d) fall
4. The earth is a satellite of
   (a) the moon.   (b) the sun.   (c) the planets.   (d) Mars.
5. The planet that has the longest orbit is
   (a) Venus.   (b) Neptune.   (c) Pluto.   (d) Mars.
6. What planet is between Mars and Saturn?
   (a) Uranus   (b) Jupiter   (c) Earth   (d) Mercury
7. What is a shooting star?
   (a) a meteor   (b) a comet   (c) an asteroid   (d) a planet
8. What causes a comet to have a tail?
   (a) gravity   (b) the earth   (c) asteroids   (d) the sun

✓ Interpreting What You Learned

Write a short answer for each question.

1. Is a comet, a meteor, or an asteroid closest to the earth? Explain your answer.
2. What are two ways the earth moves?
3. How are a lunar eclipse and a solar eclipse different?
4. How is the length of one year on planets close to the sun different from one year on planets farther away from the sun?
5. How does a meteor become a meteorite?

✓ Extending Your Thinking

Write a paragraph to answer each question.

1. You look for the moon at two o'clock in the morning, but you do not see it. What are some possible reasons you do not see the moon?
2. How might the seasons change where you live if the earth's axis were tilted the same amount but in the opposite direction from the sun?

• For further review, use Study Guide pages 398–399.

Careers

People who are very interested in rocks are sometimes called rockhounds. If you are a rockhound, you might want to become a geologist. **Geologists** study rocks and rock layers. Some geologists make maps of the earth's landforms. The geologist below is studying maps. Other geologists study fossils—remains of animal or plant life in rocks.

Geology technicians assist geologists in their work. They set up equipment, help conduct laboratory experiments, and record information gained during field research. Geology technicians study in college for at least two years. Geologists go to college for at least four years.

Geologists who study the ocean bottom might spend a great deal of time at sea. **U.S. Coast Guard members** also spend much of their time on the water. Their job is to make the oceans safe. Coast Guard members rescue people whose boats have sunk. They also warn ships about icebergs in the area. They may stop criminals fleeing in boats. The Coast Guard is part of the military service. When a person joins the U.S. Coast Guard, he or she will spend nine weeks at a training camp.

Oceanographers are interested in the oceans. Some oceanographers explore the ocean bottom to look for signs of oil, gas, or mineral deposits. They might ride in a special submarine while observing the ocean floor. The oceanographer below is studying living things in the ocean. Others study ocean currents and tides. Some plot maps of the ocean bottom. You must graduate from college and take special classes to be an oceanographer.

Some people are interested in ocean travel, and others are interested in space travel. The people who design spacecraft are called **aerospace engineers.** They also design jets, helicopters, and missiles. To become an aerospace engineer, you need to go to college for four years.

Weather Satellites

"Tomorrow will be sunny and warmer. Then, clouds will move into the area. You can expect rain for the rest of the week."

You might have seen television weather maps with storms moving across the land. The pictures you see are made of many pictures taken by satellites that orbit the earth. Each picture was taken at a different time of day. When the pictures are shown one after the other, the storm appears to move.

The United States has two weather satellites that keep watch on the earth every day of the year. Here is how the satellites collect and send weather information back to earth.

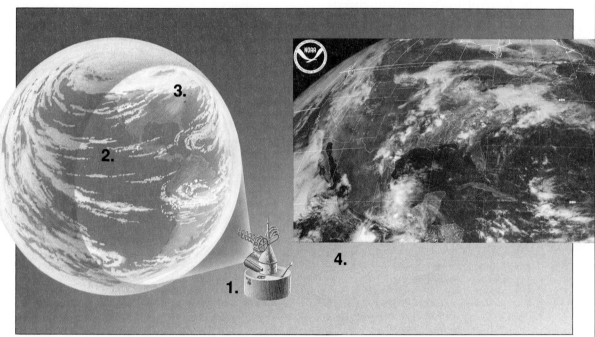

1 The satellites, nicknamed GOES, orbit the earth at a height of about 36,000 kilometers. At that height, each satellite travels in its orbit at the same speed that the earth rotates. As a result, each satellite stays in its same track above a certain part of the earth.

2 From its orbit, each GOES can see about one-fourth of the earth. The satellites contain many scientific instruments, including television cameras. The instruments can make pictures of the earth in the daylight. Also, other instruments sense heat from clouds, allowing them to make pictures of the clouds during the day or night.

3 These pictures are then sent using radio waves to receiving stations on the ground.

4 Computers collect all the pictures sent back by GOES. Then, the computers put the pictures together to make moving-picture weather maps like the ones you see on a television weather report.

Unit 3 Review

Complete the Sentence

Fill in the blank with the correct word or words from the list.

air pressure   meteorologist
anemometer   nodules
asteroids   orbit
axis   precipitation
current   revolution
igneous rock   sediments
mantle   tide

1. The level of the ocean will rise or fall with the _____ .
2. The earth rotates on its _____ .
3. An _____ moves faster as the wind blows faster.
4. The earth's path around the sun is called the earth's _____ .
5. Rain and snow are different forms of _____ .
6. A _____ flows through the ocean like a river.
7. A person who studies the weather is a _____ .
8. When _____ changes quickly, a person's ears might pop.
9. _____ is formed from magma deep inside the earth.
10. The ocean bottom contains clumps of metals called _____ .
11. Over many years _____ build up to form new land in a lake or ocean.
12. Thousands of _____ orbit the sun between the planets.
13. The earth will make one _____ around the sun in one year.
14. The _____ is the middle layer of the earth.

Short Answer

Write a short answer for each question or statement.

1. How does a large body of water affect the air temperature over nearby land?
2. Why do differences in air pressure cause the wind to blow?
3. What happens to warm air with large amounts of water vapor as it rises?
4. What information do meterologists use to forecast the weather?
5. Describe what might happen when rocks move along a fault.
6. In what kind of rock would scientists search for fossils? Explain why.
7. What is the difference between where a cold ocean current and a warm ocean current come from?
8. What landform on earth is similar to a ridge in the ocean?
9. What causes the earth to have seasons?
10. What is the order of the planets in size, from smallest to largest?
11. How are asteroids different from comets?

Essay

Write a paragraph for each question or statement.

1. Describe how pieces of rocks from mountains can become part of new land in the ocean?
2. Suppose the moon were larger. How would this difference in size affect a solar eclipse?

Unit Projects and Books

Science Projects

1. Traces of plants and animals, or fossils, are often found in sedimentary rocks. Find sedimentary rocks in your area and look for fossils in them. If you cannot find any fossils, then study pictures of fossils in books. You might even wish to visit a natural history museum in your area. Such a museum often has a fossil display.

2. One kind of fossil is called a mold. A mold is an impression left in sedimentary rock. Make a mold by pressing an object, such as a shell, into clay. Remove the shell.

3. Sometimes a mold is filled with sand or other material that has hardened. When this happens, a cast is formed. A cast is another kind of fossil. To make a cast, fill the clay mold you made in the project above with plaster of Paris that is about as thick as thick soup. Allow the plaster to harden before you remove the cast from the clay mold.

4. Look through old magazines to find pictures of products that come from the ocean. Cut out these pictures. Arrange them on a poster board to make a collage.

5. The three main kinds of telescopes are refracting, reflecting, and radio telescopes. Use references to find out about these telescopes. How is each kind of telescope different from the other kinds? How are they the same?

Science and Society

Offshore Resources The Department of Energy (DOE) has to decide if drilling for oil should be allowed in the ocean off the Oregon coast. Many people favor the drilling plan. They point out how badly this nation needs oil and natural gas. Other people are against the plan. They remember other disasters. Leaks in offshore wells coated the water and shoreline with oil. Many plants and animals died. The people who want to drill say, "We cannot let shortages of oil and gas slow this country down." Critics say that offshore drilling threatens the jobs of fishers and other people. What would an oil-driller argue? What would a fisher argue?

Books About Science

Mountains by Martin Bramwell. Watts, 1987. Learn about mountains—folding, faulting, and weather.

Monster Seaweeds: The Story of Giant Kelp by Mary Daegling. Dillon, 1986. Examine the structure, life cycle, and ecosystem of giant kelp.

River in the Ocean: The Story of the Gulf Stream by Alice Thompson Gilbreath. Dillon, 1986. Learn about the warm river flowing in the ocean.

The Comet and You by E. C. Krupp. Macmillan, 1985. Learn about comets in relation to other celestial bodies and familiar things.

The Human Body

The objects in the picture give your blood its red color. These objects are red blood cells. These cells carry oxygen everywhere in your body.

Your blood does much more than carry oxygen. In this unit, you will discover the many different jobs of your blood. You also will discover how your digestive system works and how your sense organs gather information about your surroundings.

SCIENCE IN THE NEWS During the next few weeks, look in newspapers or magazines for new discoveries about the health of the circulatory system. Also look for news about the health of the digestive system. Share the news with your class.

Chapter 13 Digestion and Circulation

Chapter 14 Your Brain and Your Sense Organs

Digestion and Circulation

Find the tube-shaped part in the picture below. This part of the body is one of the parts that changes the food you eat. The blood inside the red vessels in the picture carry this changed food to your body cells.

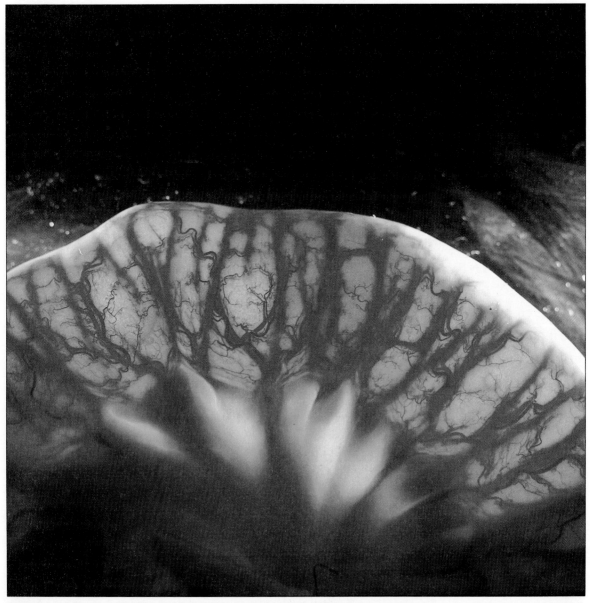

Introducing the Chapter

You breathe and eat to get oxygen and food into your body. Certain body parts work together to change the food. Other body parts take oxygen and this changed food to your body cells. In the activity below, you will learn how chewing helps change the food you eat.

Observing Different Sizes of Food Disappear

When you take a bite from an apple, you start chewing. Most foods are easier to swallow if you chew them well. Chewing helps break food into smaller pieces. Besides being easier to swallow, smaller pieces can be digested faster.

You can see the difference size makes. Get two glasses that are the same size. Fill both glasses about half full with the same amount of water. Grind up a sugar cube by putting it in a plastic bag and stepping on it. Drop a whole sugar cube into one of the glasses. At the same time, empty the crushed sugar cube into the other glass. Stir both glasses with drinking straws. Time how long the sugar takes to disappear in each glass.

Talk About It
1. How is grinding up the sugar cube like chewing?
2. How does the size of food affect the time liquids take to change the food?

pure cane
SUGAR

1 How Does Your Digestive System Work?

LESSON GOALS

You will learn
- what the digestive system does to food.
- what happens to food in the mouth and esophagus.
- what happens to food in the stomach and small intestine.
- what happens to food in the large intestine.

nutrient (nü′trē ənt), a material your body gets from food to use for energy, growth, and repair.

digestion (də jes′chən), the breaking down of food into forms that the body can use.

enzyme (en′zīm), a chemical that helps the digestive system change the food you eat.

The watermelon in the picture is too large to fit inside your body cells. However, your cells need materials that are in watermelon and other foods. Your cells use these materials—or **nutrients**—for growth, repair, and energy.

Changing Food for the Body to Use

Your digestive system changes foods into a form that your body cells can use. Food enters your digestive system when you put food in your mouth. The food is moved from one part or organ of the digestive system to another. Along the way, the food is broken down and changed. This changing of food into a form that your body cells can use is called **digestion.** Chemicals called **enzymes** cause most of the changes of digestion.

Watermelon has nutrients.

324

The Mouth and Esophagus

Think about biting into an apple. Imagine how crisp and tasty it is. Biting is the first step in breaking down food for your body. When you chew food, your teeth grind and cut it into smaller pieces. The more you chew, the smaller the pieces become.

As you chew, your tongue helps mix the food with **saliva,** the liquid in your mouth. Salivary glands near your mouth make saliva. Tiny tubes carry the saliva to your mouth. Saliva makes your food wet and easy to swallow.

An enzyme in saliva begins to break apart some of the materials that make up food. For example, a cracker is made of starches. Simple sugars are joined together to make up starches. Saliva begins to break the starches into the sugars that they are made of. When you chew such foods as crackers and bread, you might notice a sweet taste. This taste tells you that the enzyme in saliva is at work.

After you chew your food, your tongue moves it to the back of your mouth. You swallow, and the food enters a tube called the **esophagus.** Muscles in the esophagus push the food along. Notice in the pictures how these muscles squeeze the food toward the stomach.

saliva (sə lī′və), the fluid in the mouth that makes chewed food wet and begins digestion.

esophagus (ē sof′ə gəs), the tube that carries food and fluids from the mouth to the stomach.

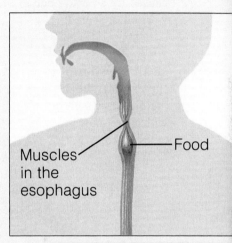

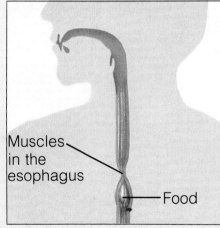

Muscles in the esophagus squeeze food toward the stomach.

325

Most people get stomachaches at one time or another. Often, the pain is really in the small or large intestine—not the stomach. Stomachaches can be caused by something a person ate or by an illness. Stomachaches also can be caused by a person being worried or scared.

small intestine
(in tes′tən), the organ of the digestive system in which the most digestion takes place.

The Stomach and Small Intestine

The stomach is like a sack that receives food. Cells in the lining of the stomach make juices. The wall of the stomach is made of muscles that squeeze and mix food with the juices. This mixing by the stomach soaks every tiny piece of food with juices. Enzymes in these juices break down more of the food. The food is a thick liquid by the time it leaves the stomach.

The stomach squeezes the food into the **small intestine.** This organ is a long tube. The muscles in the small intestine push food along.

Most digestion takes place in the small intestine. Juices made in the lining of the small intestine mix with the food. Nearby organs called the liver (liv′ər) and the pancreas (pan′krē əs) also make juices. Tiny tubes carry these juices to the small intestine. Different kinds of enzymes in all the juices break down the food into forms that the body cells can use.

The next job of the small intestine is to send these nutrients to the rest of the body. Blood vessels fill the wall of the small intestine. The nutrients move through the thin lining of the small intestine. Then they move through the thin walls of the blood vessels into the blood. The blood carries these nutrients everywhere in the body.

The picture on the next page shows the parts of the digestive system. Find the salivary glands in the picture to the right of the girl's head. Use your finger to trace the path that food takes from the girl's mouth to the small intestine. Name the parts the food passes through. Notice that the food moves from the small intestine into another tube. What is the name of this tube? You will read about this part of the digestive system on page 328.

The Digestive System

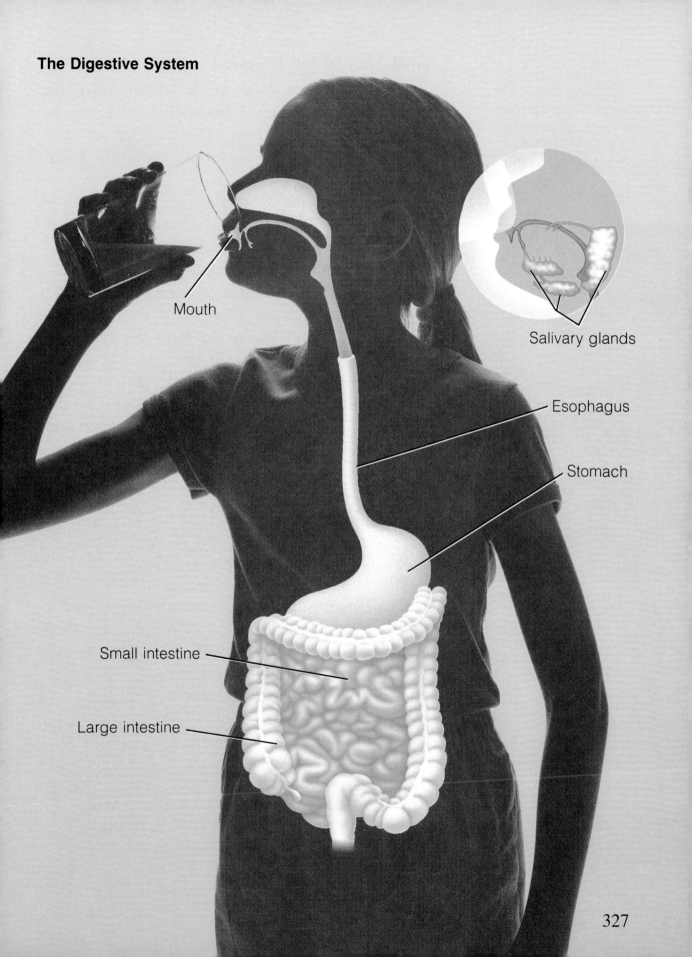

Mouth

Salivary glands

Esophagus

Stomach

Small intestine

Large intestine

327

Food That Is Not Digested

large intestine, the last organ of the digestive system, which removes water and stores the waste material.

Not everything in food can be broken down into the parts that make it up. Fibers such as the strings in celery are not broken down. These undigested parts of food move from the small intestine to the **large intestine.**

The material that enters the large intestine is mostly liquid. The large intestine removes much of the water in this liquid. The water passes through the thin lining of the large intestine into blood vessels. The undigested food is an almost solid waste by the time it reaches the end of the large intestine. The picture shows an X ray of the large intestine with waste in it. The backbone and the hips look greenish-yellow in the background. The tube is the large intestine. Find the brightly colored waste in the large intestine. The large intestine stores this waste until it leaves the body.

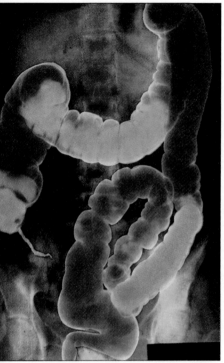

X ray of the large intestine

Lesson Review

1. What does your digestive system do?
2. What does saliva do?
3. Where does most digestion take place?
4. What are two jobs of the large intestine?
5. **Challenge!** Sometimes, doctors must remove a person's stomach. The esophagus is then connected to the small intestine. The person can still live a healthy life. Explain how.

Study on your own, pages 400–401.

FIND OUT ON YOUR OWN

Look in books to find out about ulcers. Write a paragraph telling what an ulcer is, what causes ulcers, and where most ulcers form in the digestive system.

328

Observing Changes in Milk

Wear cover goggles for this activity.

Purpose
Observe how an acid and an enzyme change milk.

Gather These Materials
- 4 clear plastic cups • masking tape
- milk • plastic wrap • 4 rubber bands
- 4 plastic spoons • water • enzyme
- weak acid

Follow This Procedure
1. Use a chart like the one shown to record your observations.
2. Label 4 cups 1 through 4 by putting the numbers on masking tape and putting the tape on the side of each cup.
3. Put 3 spoonfuls of milk in each cup.
4. Use a clean spoon to add 2 spoonfuls of water to cup number 2 and stir.
5. Use a clean spoon to add 2 spoonfuls of acid to cup number 3 and stir.
6. Use a clean spoon to add 2 spoonfuls of enzyme to cup number 4 and stir.
7. Cover each cup with plastic wrap. Use a rubber band to hold the plastic wrap in place.
8. Wait for 1 minute and observe the milk. Record what the milk looks like.
9. Wait for 1–2 hours and observe the milk. Record any changes.

Record Your Results

Cup number	Changes after 1 minute	Changes after 1-2 hours
1. Milk		
2. Milk and water		
3. Milk and acid		
4. Milk and enzyme		

State Your Conclusion
1. Describe how water, an acid, and an enzyme change milk.
2. What difference did you notice in the way the acid and the enzyme acted?

Use What You Learned
The enzyme in this activity is from a meat tenderizer. People sometimes buy meat tenderizer in the grocery store. They use it on meat to make the meat more tender. Why do you think meat tenderizer can make meat more tender?

2 How Does Your Circulatory System Work?

LESSON GOALS

You will learn
- what the different parts of blood do.
- the differences among the three kinds of blood vessels.
- the path of blood through the heart.

Can you feel your heart beating? Your heart is a strong muscle. With each beat, your heart pumps blood through your body. Every minute, almost 4 liters of blood pass through your heart.

Your heart is only one part of your circulatory system. Your blood is another part. Place the tips of your fingers over your wrist. Push firmly and move your fingers around until you feel a beat. You are feeling blood in a blood vessel as it is pumped by your heart. The blood vessels are another part of your circulatory system. The blood vessels carry blood to all parts of your body.

Your circulatory system has many jobs. It carries nutrients, oxygen, and water to all your body cells. It picks up the wastes that body cells make. The circulatory system carries these wastes to body organs that get rid of them. The circulatory system also protects your body from sickness and helps you get well when you do get sick. It stops bleeding when you get a cut or scratch.

Blood cells and platelets

Red blood cells

Parts of Blood

The test tube on the left in the picture has blood in it. What color is the blood? This test tube of blood was spun very fast. The test tube on the right shows what happened to the blood. The top part in the test tube is the clear, watery part of blood called **plasma.** In your body, nutrients, blood cells, and other things float in the plasma. The bottom part of blood in the test tube is all the blood cells.

Blood has the red blood cells, white blood cells, and platelets shown in the pictures on these two pages. **Red blood cells** are small cells that give blood its color. These cells carry oxygen. **White blood cells** are larger than red blood cells. They protect the body from sickness. Your body has different kinds of white blood cells. The picture below shows one kind. You can see other kinds of white blood cells in the picture on page 330. White blood cells destroy germs and make chemicals that kill germs. Some white blood cells can move through the walls of blood vessels to protect the body. **Platelets** are only tiny parts of cells. Platelets help stop bleeding and make blood clots.

plasma (plaz′mə), the watery part of blood that carries nutrients, wastes, and blood cells.

red blood cell, the kind of cell that carries oxygen from the lungs to the rest of the body.

white blood cell, the kind of cell that fights germs.

platelet (plāt′lit), a tiny part of a cell that helps stop bleeding.

Test tubes of blood

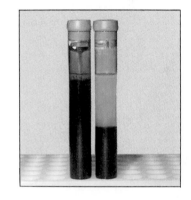

One kind of white blood cell

Platelets

artery (är′tər ē), a blood vessel that carries blood away from the heart.

capillary (kap′ə ler′ē), a tiny blood vessel with thin walls through which oxygen, nutrients, and wastes pass.

vein (vān), a blood vessel that carries blood back to the heart.

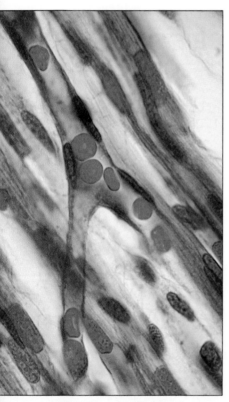

Red blood cells moving single file through a capillary

Kinds of Blood Vessels

The circulatory system has three kinds of tubes that carry blood. These tubes are called blood vessels. Blood flows through blood vessels from the heart to all parts of the body and back to the heart. Each kind of blood vessel is different and has its own job. Find each kind of blood vessel in the picture on page 333 as you read about it.

When you felt the blood moving in your wrist, you were pushing on an **artery.** This kind of blood vessel carries blood away from the heart. The wall of an artery has muscles. This kind of wall allows arteries to stretch as the heart pumps blood through them.

The arteries that are connected to the heart are large. These arteries branch into smaller and smaller arteries. Blood in the smallest arteries flows into tiny blood vessels called **capillaries.** These blood vessels are so small that red blood cells go through them in single file. Find the red blood cells in the capillary in the picture on the left. Capillaries have thin walls. Oxygen and nutrients move out of the blood and through the thin capillary walls into body cells. Wastes from the body cells move out of body cells and through the thin capillary walls into the blood.

The third kind of blood vessels are **veins.** These blood vessels carry blood from capillaries back to the heart. The blood in capillaries flows into tiny veins. These veins join together to make larger and larger veins. The largest veins empty blood into the heart. The walls of veins have less muscle than artery walls. Veins have something that arteries do not have. They have valves, which are like one-way doors. They keep blood from flowing backwards through the vein.

The drawing on the next page shows some of the blood vessels in the circulatory system. Blood vessels that are shown as blue really carry blood that is dark red. Blood that is dark red has less oxygen in it than bright red blood does.

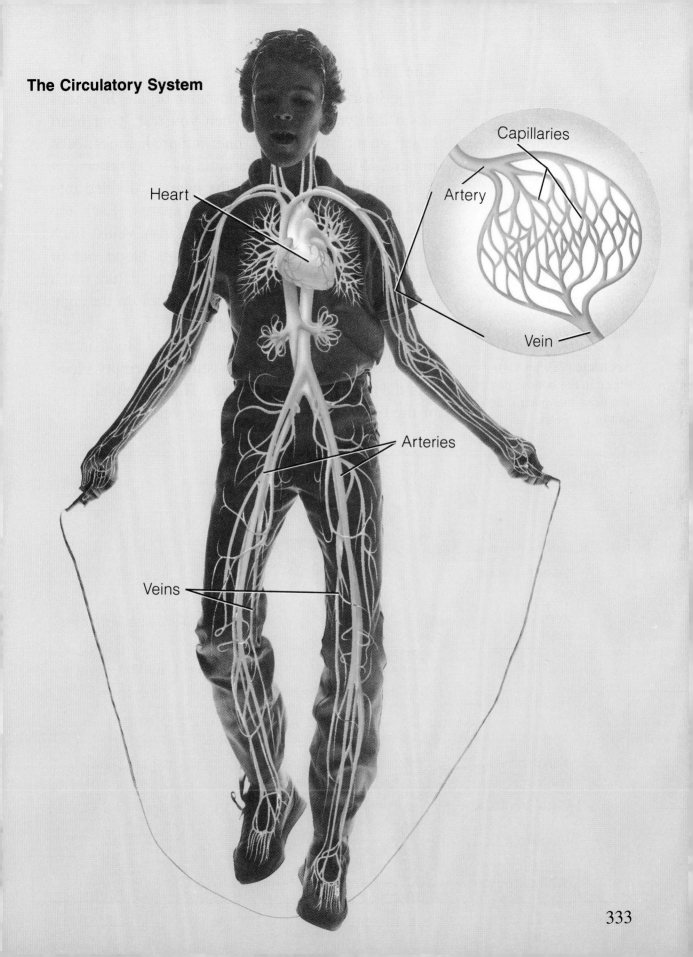

The Circulatory System

Heart

Capillaries

Artery

Vein

Arteries

Veins

Scientists are learning to build better artificial hearts. Some people with diseased hearts are kept alive with an artificial heart for a short time until a human heart is available.

atrium (ā′trē əm), a space in the top part of the heart that receives blood from the veins.

ventricle (ven′trə kəl), a space in the bottom part of the heart that pumps blood out of the heart.

The Heart

The heart is a hollow, muscular organ. It pumps blood into your arteries. When you rest, your heart beats about seventy to one hundred times each minute. When you move around, it beats faster.

The hollow space inside the heart is divided into two top spaces and two bottom spaces. Each top space—or **atrium**—receives blood from veins. Each bottom space—or **ventricle**—pumps blood out of the heart through arteries. Notice in the picture that a wall of muscle separates the two spaces on the right from the two spaces on the left.

Use your finger to trace the path of blood in the picture of the heart. Find the veins that empty blood into the right atrium of the heart. Blood from all parts of the body flows into these large veins.

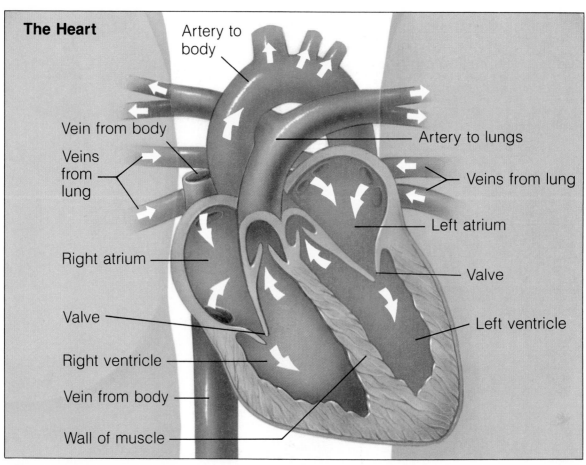

The Heart

Artery to body

Vein from body

Veins from lung

Right atrium

Valve

Right ventricle

Vein from body

Wall of muscle

Artery to lungs

Veins from lung

Left atrium

Valve

Left ventricle

Blood flows from the right atrium into the right ventricle. When the heart beats, the right ventricle pumps blood through an artery. The blood is pushed into other arteries and to capillaries in the lungs. Here the blood picks up oxygen from the lungs.

Now find the veins that return blood from the lungs to the heart. Blood returning from the lungs flows into the left atrium. Next, the blood goes to the left ventricle. When the heart beats, the blood in the left ventricle is pumped into arteries that carry the blood to all parts of the body.

Blood moves through the heart in one direction. Valves between each atrium and ventricle keep blood from flowing backwards. Find these valves in the drawing. Valves between the ventricles and the arteries also keep the blood from flowing backwards.

Lesson Review

1. List the three kinds of cells or cell parts in blood and give one job of each.
2. In which kind of blood vessel does oxygen move through the vessel wall?
3. List the four spaces of the heart in the order that blood passes through them.
4. **Challenge!** Almost every cell in your body is close to a capillary. How does this help each cell?

Study on your own, pages 400–401.

Use magazines, encyclopedias, or other books to find out about some health problems of the circulatory system. You could read about anemia, high blood pressure, or other problems. Pick one of these health problems and write a paragraph about it. Your paragraph could tell about what the problem is and what causes it.

FIND OUT ON YOUR OWN

ACTIVITY

Measuring Your Pulse

Purpose
Observe pulse rates of different students before and after exercise.

Gather These Materials
• pencil • paper • watch or clock with second hand

Follow This Procedure
1. Use a chart like the one shown to record your observations.
2. Find your pulse as shown in the picture. Press your index and middle fingers against your wrist near the base of your thumb. Move your fingers slightly and press until you feel your pulse.
3. Sit very still for 2 minutes. Have your partner time for 1 minute while you count your pulse. Record your results in your chart.
4. Do jumping jacks for 1 minute. Make sure that you have enough room to do these exercises without bumping into other people or into objects. *CAUTION: If you have a health problem, do not do jumping jacks without your doctor's permission.* Then count your pulse for 1 minute while your partner times you. Record your results.
5. Have your partner do steps 2, 3, and 4.
6. Record the results of other students in your class.

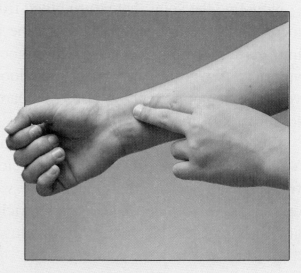

Record Your Results

	Your pulse	Other students' pulses
Resting rate		
Exercise rate		

State Your Conclusion
1. How does exercise change the pulse rate?
2. Compare the resting and exercise rates of the students in your class. How much do different students' rates vary?

Use What You Learned
When during your day do you think your pulse rate is the lowest? When do you think it is the highest?

Saving Lives with New Ideas

Plasma, the watery part of blood, might not seem to be very important. After all, the blood cells are in charge of carrying oxygen and fighting germs. However, in the 1930s, the scientist in the picture made a discovery. Dr. Charles Drew discovered that plasma alone can save lives.

A person who loses a large amount of blood needs help immediately. Doctors can give the person extra blood from another person. The blood runs through a tube into the person's vein. This process, called a transfusion, replaces the blood that is lost.

Early in Dr. Drew's career, doctors had to find a person to give blood when a transfusion was needed. Blood was not stored at the hospital. Dr. Drew knew that blood would spoil in a week, even if kept in a refrigerator. If no blood was available, the patient might die. Dr. Drew wanted to find a way to store blood for emergencies.

He decided to test a new idea. Dr. Drew separated the blood cells from the plasma and used only the plasma in a transfusion. For injuries, plasma worked even better than whole blood. Since plasma did not need to be kept cold, it could be stored for a long time. Then it was ready whenever it was needed.

Dr. Drew's discovery came just in time to save many lives during World War II. He directed a program to send plasma overseas for wounded soldiers. His work as a doctor, a researcher, and a teacher helped people see just how important plasma can be.

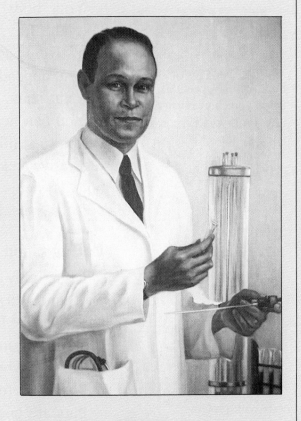

What Do You Think?
1. Think of situations in which it would be helpful to have stored plasma for transfusions.
2. For transfusions, how does plasma differ from whole blood?

How Can You Help Keep Your Body Systems Healthy?

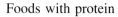

You will learn
- what kinds of nutrients your body needs.
- how regular exercise helps your body systems.
- how drugs can harm the body systems.

Foods with protein

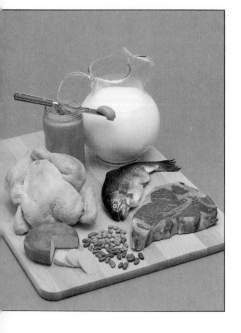

Your body systems work together to keep your body healthy. Every body system depends on the digestive system to break down foods. Every body system depends on the circulatory system for oxygen and nutrients.

You can help keep your circulatory and digestive systems healthy by eating good foods, exercising regularly, and avoiding harmful drugs. Because your body systems work together, you help your whole body stay healthy by helping these two systems.

Eating Good Foods

Your body needs six kinds of nutrients to work well and stay healthy. Proteins are one kind of nutrient. The body needs proteins to build new cells. Proteins are important for healthy muscles and skin. Milk, egg whites, meat, and beans have proteins in them. What foods with proteins are in the picture?

Fats are another kind of nutrient the body needs. Fats give the body energy. The body also uses fats to make some parts of cells and certain chemicals your body needs. Milk and meats have fats in them. Vegetable oils are fats.

Even though the body needs fats, too much can harm the circulatory and digestive systems. Some people get too much fat in the foods they eat. Fatty deposits can stick to the walls of their arteries. The arteries can become clogged. Too much fat also can make a person overweight. Weighing too much makes the circulatory system work harder.

Carbohydrates are another kind of nutrient. The body should get most of the energy it needs from carbohydrates. Sugars and starches are two kinds of carbohydrates. Fruits and fruit juices have sugars. Breads, cereals, rice, and potatoes have starches.

Some carbohydrate foods also have fiber. One way to help keep your digestive system healthy is to eat foods that have fiber in them. Fiber helps foods move through the digestive system. Fresh vegetables and whole grain cereals and breads have fiber in them.

Vitamins and minerals are two kinds of nutrients that you need in small amounts. They help your body work properly. For example, vitamin A helps keep your eyes healthy. Calcium is a mineral that keeps your teeth and bones strong. Your body uses the mineral iron to make red blood cells. Milk, fruits, and vegetables have vitamins and minerals. What foods with vitamins and minerals in them do you know in the picture?

Water is also a nutrient your body needs to work properly. Water makes up much of your body. Most foods have water in them. Many fruits and vegetables are mostly water. You also need to drink water every day to take the place of water your body uses and loses. Drinking fruit juices and milk are other good ways to get water.

Eating many different foods helps you get all the different nutrients your body needs. Each food you eat has different nutrients in different amounts.

Foods with vitamins and minerals

Exercising Regularly

If you can play actively for an hour without getting tired, you are probably getting the exercise you need. Like the students in the picture, you can have fun while you exercise. Exercise helps keep your whole body healthy and strong.

Exercise helps your circulatory system. When you exercise hard, your heart beats faster. You are exercising your heart muscle and making it stronger. As your heart becomes stronger, it can pump more blood with each beat. You can work or play longer without becoming tired.

Exercise also helps your arteries. Scientists have found that exercise can help keep your arteries from being clogged by fats.

Regular exercise helps you sleep better. Then you get the rest your body needs.

Exercise helps keep you healthy.

340

Avoiding Harmful Drugs

Most people know that smoking cigarettes harms the body. Smoking causes lung diseases, such as lung cancer. Smoking also harms the circulatory system. Chemicals in the smoke move through the lungs and the walls of the capillaries into the blood. These chemicals make the heart work harder. People who smoke are more likely to have a heart attack than people who do not smoke.

Almost any drug can harm the body. For example, alcohol can harm the lining of the stomach. Cocaine can keep the heart from working properly. Once a person starts smoking or using harmful drugs, quitting can be hard. The best way to help keep your body healthy is to never start to smoke or use harmful drugs. Like the picture shows, just say no to drugs.

Saying no to drugs helps keep you healthy.

Lesson Review

1. What are the six kinds of nutrients that your body needs to work well and stay healthy?
2. How does regular exercise help the circulatory system?
3. How can smoking cigarettes harm the circulatory system?
4. **Challenge!** If a person's body needed to make new bone cells to fix a broken bone, which two kinds of nutrients might be needed the most? Explain your answers.

Study on your own, pages 400–401.

Different foods have different kinds of fats. Look in an encyclopedia or other book to find out the difference between saturated fats and unsaturated fats. Which kind of fat harms health the most? What foods have each kind of fat?

FIND OUT ON YOUR OWN

Using Clocks and Bar Graphs

Problem: How long does the digestive process take?

Part A. Using Clocks to Collect Information

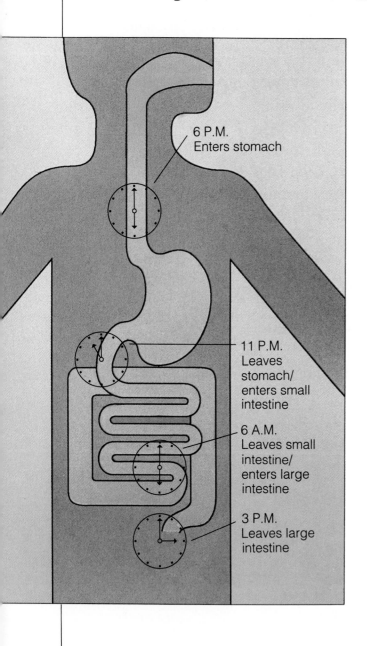

6 P.M.
Enters stomach

11 P.M.
Leaves
stomach/
enters small
intestine

6 A.M.
Leaves small
intestine/
enters large
intestine

3 P.M.
Leaves large
intestine

1. Find the four clocks in the diagram. Then trace with your finger the path food takes in the body. Find the stomach, the small intestine, and the large intestine. Where does food enter the body?

2. A day has 24 hours. The dial on a clock has divisions for only 12 hours. The clock's hands rotate twice around the 12 divisions every day. The first 12 hours, from midnight to noon, are the morning cycle, called A.M. The second 12 hours, from noon to midnight, are the evening cycle, called P.M. Look at the clocks on the drawing of the digestive system. What time did digestion begin? Was it in the morning or evening cycle?

3. Look at the clocks to learn how long food stops in each of the parts of the digestive system. Look at the first clock. When did food enter the stomach? Look at the second clock. When did the food leave? How long was the food in the stomach?

4. When did the food enter the small intestine? How long did it stay? How long did it stay in the large intestine?

Part B. Using a Bar Graph to Organize and Interpret Information

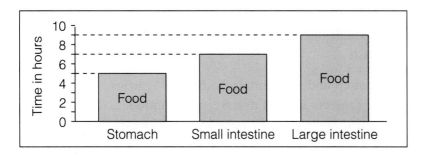

5. The bar graph organizes the information collected from the clocks. Each bar represents one of the main parts of the digestive system. The scale at the left of the graph shows the hours. To find how long food stayed in the stomach, place your finger at the top of the bar labeled Stomach. Then move your finger across the graph to the scale of hours at the left. How long did food stay in the stomach?

6. How long did food stay in the small intestine? in the large intestine? In which part of the digestive system did food stay the longest time? the shortest time?

7. How long did food stay in the digestive system?

Part C. Using Clocks and Bar Graphs to Solve a Problem

Problem: What happens to the digestive process when a person eats food that is spoiled?

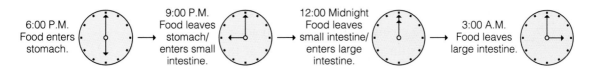

8. The four clocks in this diagram record the time food takes to pass through the digestive system if a person has eaten spoiled food. Make a bar graph similar to the one in Part B to organize your information.

9. Look at your graph. How long did food remain in the stomach? the small intestine? the large intestine?

10. How do these lengths of time compare to the lengths of time food normally stays in the stomach?

343

Chapter 13 Review

☑ Chapter Main Ideas

Lesson 1 • The digestive system breaks food down into forms that the body can use. • An enzyme in saliva begins digestion. • Digestion continues in the stomach and small intestine. • The large intestine removes water from liquid waste.

Lesson 2 • Blood carries oxygen and nutrients to body cells, carries wastes away from body cells, protects against disease, and controls bleeding. • Arteries, capillaries, and veins are three kinds of blood vessels. • The heart pumps blood through the body.

Lesson 3 • Eating a variety of good foods gives your body the nutrients it needs. • Regular exercise makes your heart stronger. • Avoiding harmful drugs helps prevent harm to your body systems.

☑ Reviewing Science Words

artery	large intestine	saliva
atrium	nutrient	small intestine
capillary	plasma	vein
digestion	platelet	ventricle
enzyme	red blood cell	white blood cell
esophagus		

Copy each sentence. Fill in the blank with the correct word or words from the list.

1. A _____ is a blood vessel that has the thinnest wall.
2. Blood from the body enters the right _____ of the heart.
3. The breaking down of food into forms the body can use is _____ .
4. A _____ pumps blood out of the heart.
5. The tube that takes food to the stomach is the _____ .
6. An _____ in saliva changes starches to sugars.
7. Most water passes through the thin lining of the _____ in the digestive system.
8. A blood vessel that carries blood away from the heart is an _____ .
9. The liquid in the mouth that begins digestion is _____ .
10. A _____ is a material your body uses from food.
11. Most digestion takes place in the _____ .
12. _____ is the watery part of blood in which blood cells float.

13. A ▨ carries oxygen.
14. A ▨ fights germs.
15. A tiny part of a cell that helps stop bleeding is a ▨ .
16. A blood vessel that carries blood back to the heart is a ▨ .

☑ Reviewing What You Learned

Write the letter of the best answer.

1. Undigested food is stored in the
   (a) stomach.   (b) esophagus.   (c) large intestine.   (d) small intestine.
2. Blood is pumped from the left ventricle to the
   (a) body.   (b) lungs.   (c) right atrium.   (d) left atrium.
3. Which nutrient does the body need in small amounts?
   (a) proteins   (b) carbohydrates   (c) vitamins   (d) water
4. Which system of the body changes food?
   (a) circulatory   (b) digestive   (c) energy   (d) blood
5. The circulatory system is harmed by
   (a) exercise.   (b) proteins.   (c) minerals.   (d) smoking.
6. Which blood vessels are so small that blood cells travel through them in
   single file?
   (a) arteries   (b) capillaries   (c) veins   (d) ventricles

☑ Interpreting What You Learned

Write a short answer for each question or statement.

1. List the parts of the digestive system in the order that food passes
   through them.
2. Name the two kinds of blood cells and what each does.
3. Describe how exercise helps your circulatory system.
4. What do the three kinds of blood vessels have in common?
5. What is fiber and how does it help the digestive system?

☑ Extending Your Thinking

Write a paragraph to answer each question.

1. Why can oxygen move out of the blood through capillary walls but
   not through artery walls?
2. How might a drug that keeps the muscles in the esophagus and
   stomach from working properly harm a person?

• For further review, use Study Guide pages 400–401.

Chapter 14

Your Brain
and Your Sense Organs

As the boy below plays the piano, the piano keys feel cold
and smooth. He can feel the keys move as his fingers push
on them. The boy can hear how well he is playing.

346

Introducing the Chapter

Your senses and your brain work together. They give you information about the world around you. How your brain explains this information depends on your experiences. The activity below shows how your experiences can change what your brain tells you. In this chapter, you will learn about your brain and sense organs. You also will learn how you can take care of your sense organs.

Observing Warm and Cold

You will need three pans. Pour ice water into one pan. Pour water that is room temperature into the second pan. Pour warmer water into the third pan. Label the pans.

Put your left hand in the ice water and your right hand in the warm water. Notice how the water feels to each hand. Keep your hands in the water for about thirty seconds.

Now move both hands into the room-temperature water. Notice how the water feels to each hand.

Talk About It
1. How did the room-temperature water feel to your left hand? How did it feel to your right hand?
2. What made the water feel different to each hand?

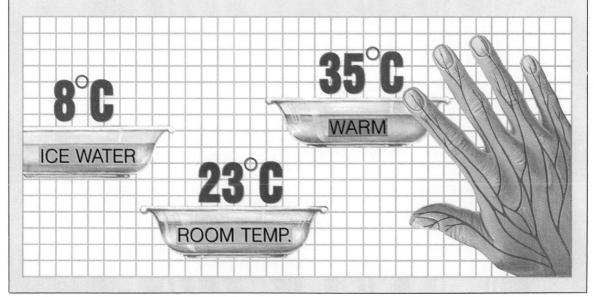

1 How Does Your Brain Get Information?

LESSON GOALS

You will learn
- what information each sense organ gathers.
- how information gets from sense organs to the brain.

Sense organs help you enjoy food.

Sit quietly for a moment. After you read this paragraph, close your eyes. What can you hear? What can you smell? What sounds are other people making? Now think about what you can feel. How does the air in the room feel? How do your clothes feel? How does your chair feel?

Often you do not notice many of the sights, sounds, and smells around you. If you stop and think, what you see, hear, taste, smell, and touch tells you much about your surroundings. Your senses gather information all the time. They send this information to your brain. If you are busy with other things, you might not notice what your senses tell you.

Your Sense Organs

You notice your surroundings with your **sense organs.** Your eyes, ears, nose, tongue, and skin are sense organs. Each sense organ has special **nerve cells.** These nerve cells gather information from your surroundings. What information might the boy's sense organs gather as he eats the orange?

The nerve cells in different sense organs gather different information. Nerve cells in the eyes gather information about light. Nerve cells in the ears gather information about sound. The skin has different kinds of nerve cells. They gather information about pressure, touch, pain, heat, and cold. What do nerve cells in the tongue and nose gather?

Nerve cells have a special shape. Find the tiny branches—or **nerve endings**—in the picture of the nerve cell. Some of these tiny branches end in your sense organs. The nerve endings that end in your sense organs gather information. Find the longer branch on the other side of the nerve cell. This branch carries the information to the next nerve cell.

sense organ (səns ôr′gən), a body part that has special nerve cells that collect information about the surroundings.

nerve cell (nėrv sel), a cell that carries information to and from different parts of the body.

nerve ending, a tiny branch of a nerve cell.

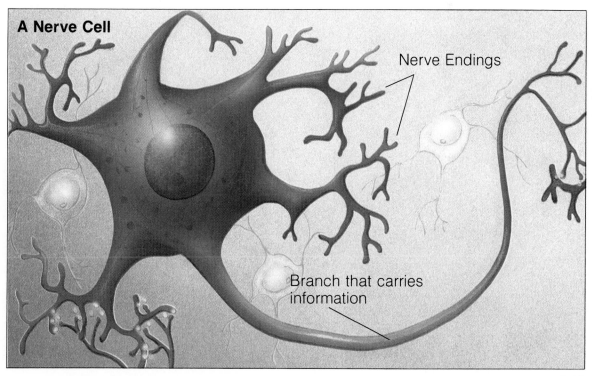

A Nerve Cell

Nerve Endings

Branch that carries information

Your Brain and Spinal Cord

Your brain is made up of millions of nerve cells. The information gathered by nerve cells in your sense organs travels along nerves to the brain. A nerve is a bundle of nerve cells.

Your brain changes the messages it receives so you can understand them. In your brain, messages from your tongue become tastes. Messages from your ears become sounds.

Messages from most parts of your body travel through the **spinal cord.** The spinal cord is a bundle of nerves that connects your brain with nerves in your body. The bones of your backbone protect your spinal cord. The nerves in the spinal cord carry the information to and from your brain. Use your finger to trace the path of information from the boy's hand to his brain.

The spinal cord carries information to the brain.

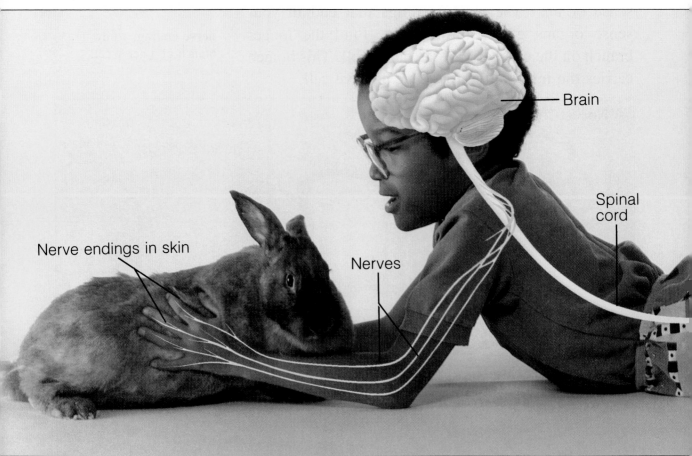

Brain

Spinal cord

Nerves

Nerve endings in skin

Your brain decides how important the messages from your sense organs are. Your brain uses the messages and your experiences to get your attention when needed. For example, imagine you are playing in a park near a busy street. As cars drive by, you might not hear them. If you are crossing the street like the girl in the picture is doing, you do pay attention to the sounds of cars.

Messages from sense organs help keep you safe.

Lesson Review

1. What information does each sense organ gather?
2. How does the information from your sense organs get to your brain?
3. **Challenge!** Sometimes, you might decide not to pay attention to what your senses tell you. How could not paying attention be harmful?

Study on your own, pages 402–403.

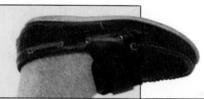

Take a sheet of paper. Put these headings at the top: Sight, Hearing, Taste, Touch, Smell. For fifteen minutes record everything you notice in your surroundings. List the things in the correct column. Which sense did you use the most? Which sense did you use the least? Record everything you notice for another fifteen minutes in different surroundings. You could try in the lunchroom or on the playground. Which sense did you use the most this time? Which sense did you use the least?

**FIND OUT
ON YOUR OWN**

2 How Do Your Eyes Work?

LESSON GOALS

You will learn
- the path that light takes through the eye.
- how you can take care of your eyes.

pupil (pyü′pəl), a hole in the eye where light enters.

iris (ī′ris), the colored part of the eye that changes the size of the pupil.

retina (ret′n ə), a layer of nerve cells in the back of the eye.

Look around you. What do you see? Most people get most of the information about their world with their sense of sight. What are some of the ways you use your eyes? How would your life be different if you could not see?

The Path of Light

When you look in a mirror, you see only a small part of your eyes. The drawing of the eye on the next page shows you the parts that are inside your eyes. The front of the eye has a clear covering. This covering protects the eye and bends light.

The pupil and iris are two parts of the eye that you can see. The **pupil** is a hole that lets light inside the eye. The **iris** is a ring of muscle that changes the size of the pupil. The pupil gets smaller in bright light and larger in dim light. These changes in size let the right amount of light into the eye. Find the pupil and iris in the picture below and on the next page. What do they look like when you look in a mirror?

A clear lens is behind the pupil. The lens bends light that enters the eye. The inside of the eye is filled with a jellylike material. This material helps the eye keep its round shape. Find the retina inside the eye at the back. The **retina** is a thin layer of special nerve cells. These cells gather messages about light. A nerve carries these messages to the brain.

The pupil and iris

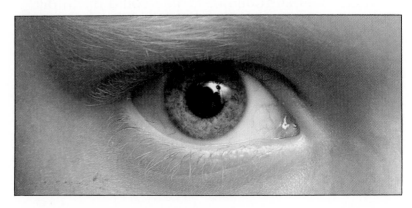

352

You see most things because light reflects off them. For example, light from the sun or a light bulb reflects off a dog. Some of this light travels to your eyes. Once light gets to your eyes, it passes through the clear covering, the pupil, the lens, and the jellylike center. Parts of the eye bend the light along the way. The lens bends the light so that it makes a clear picture on the retina. Nerve cells in the retina gather information about the light. They send a message along a nerve to the brain. The brain changes the message so you understand it. You know that you are looking at a dog. Use your finger to trace the path of light through the eye in the drawing below.

What do you notice about the picture on the retina in the drawing on the right? It is upside down. However, you do not see things around you upside down. Your brain changes the picture to right side up. When something really is upside down, how does it appear on your retina?

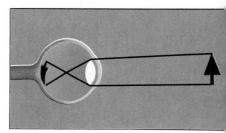

A picture on the retina

The Eye

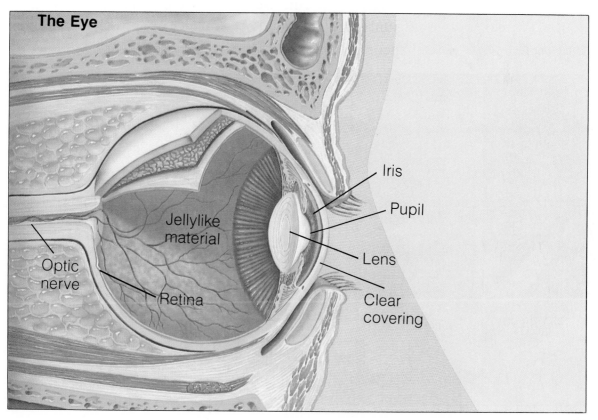

Iris

Pupil

Lens

Clear covering

Jellylike material

Optic nerve

Retina

353

Taking Care of Your Eyes

Your body protects your eyes in several ways. The bones in your skull help protect your eyes from harm. You blink your eyelids when something comes close to your eyes. Blinking and your eyelashes help keep dust and other things out of your eyes. Tears help wash away things that do get in your eyes.

You can help protect your eyes. Keep sharp things away from your eyes. Pencils and other sharp things can hurt an eye if they hit it. Protect your eyes from things that could fly or splash into them. Many cleaners used around homes can harm the eyes. Sometimes people wear goggles to protect their eyes.

If something does get in your eyes, do not rub them. Rubbing can scratch or poke the covering of your eye. Have an adult help you right away. If something splashes in your eye, have an adult help you wash it out right away.

Good sunglasses can help protect your eyes from bright sunlight. Sunglasses are very helpful when sunlight is reflected off of water or snow. How are the people below protecting their eyes?

Protecting the eyes

If you have trouble with your eyes, have a checkup with an eye doctor like the girl in the picture is doing. The doctor can find out if anything is wrong with your eyes. If something is wrong, the doctor can order glasses for you. If you have glasses, wear them as the doctor told you to. Also, have your eyes and glasses checked when the doctor told you to. Glasses that worked last year may not be right for you now. Taking care of your eyes can help you see all the wonderful sights in the world.

An eye checkup

Lesson Review

1. What part of the eye contains the nerve cells that gather information about light?
2. What should you do if you get sand in your eye?
3. **Challenge!** You have been playing in bright sunlight. You go into a dark room. What happens to the pupils of your eyes?

Study on your own, pages 402–403.

Some people are color-blind. They cannot see certain colors the way most people see them. Find out what colors look like to color-blind people. Are most color-blind people males or females? Write a short paragraph on what you find out.

FIND OUT ON YOUR OWN

3 How Do Your Ears Work?

LESSON GOALS

You will learn
- the path sound takes through the ear.
- ways you can take care of your ears.

Sounds give you information. Sirens tell you of danger. A bell can tell you when it is time for school to start. Spoken words tell you what another person is saying. The sound of a person laughing can tell you someone is happy. The sound of crying tells you someone is sad or hurt.

Sounds also make life more interesting. Music or a friend's voice can make you feel happy. Imagine you are listening to the boy in the picture. What sounds would you hear? You hear sounds because of the way your ears and brain work together.

The Path of Sound

Sounds that you hear start as sound waves in the air. You make sound waves when you talk. Radios and televisions also give off sound waves. The part of your ear that you can see works like a funnel. It catches the sound waves in the air and moves them into the part of your ear inside your head.

The drawing shows the parts of the ear inside your head. Find each part as you read about how sound waves travel through the ear. The sound waves enter the ear through the **ear canal.** The part of your ear outside your head and your ear canal make up your **outer ear.** Find the ear canal in the picture. What is at the end of the ear canal?

The **eardrum** is a thin skin that covers the end of the ear canal. Sound waves make the eardrum vibrate or move quickly back and forth. These vibrations then move through tiny bones of the **middle ear.**

From the middle ear, the vibrations move to the **inner ear.** The vibrations move through the fluid that fills the inner ear. These vibrations cause tiny hairs in the inner ear to move. These tiny hairs are connected to nerve cells that send messages about the vibrations. A nerve carries the messages to the brain. The brain changes the messages and tells you what you hear.

Look at the drawing of the ear again. Use your finger to trace the path of sound through the ear.

ear canal (kə nal′), tunnel that sound travels through to the eardrum.

outer ear, the part of the ear outside of the head and the ear canal.

eardrum, the thin skin that covers the end of the ear canal.

middle ear, the three tiny bones that carry sound waves from the eardrum to the inner ear.

inner ear, the fluid-filled part of the ear that sends messages to the brain.

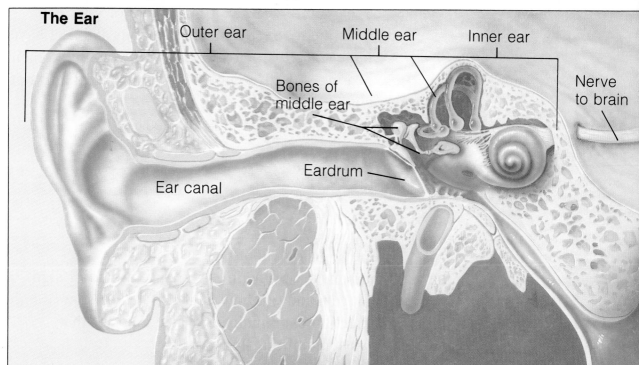

The Ear

Outer ear · Middle ear · Inner ear · Bones of middle ear · Nerve to brain · Eardrum · Ear canal

Some people have a permanent hearing loss. Many of these people can hear with the help of a hearing aid. These devices are so small that they can fit inside the ear.

Protecting the ears

Taking Care of Your Ears

The bones of your skull help protect your ears from harm. You also can protect your ears. Never put things into your ear canal. They can harm the eardrum or carry germs into the ear.

Sudden loud sounds can harm your hearing. Being around loud sounds for a long time can also harm hearing. The person in the picture works around loud sounds. How is the person protecting her hearing? Loud music is another loud sound that can harm your ears. How can you protect your ears from loud sounds such as music?

Tell an adult if you have trouble hearing or if your ears hurt. Either could be a sign of an infection in the middle ear. This kind of infection is the most common cause of hearing loss in children. A doctor can treat ear infections to stop harm to the ears.

Lesson Review

1. What part of the ear has nerve cells that send messages to the brain?
2. What are three ways to take care of your ears?
3. **Challenge!** Such animals as rabbits and deer have large ears that move. How do you think their hearing would compare to yours? Explain your answer.

Study on your own, pages 402–403.

FIND OUT ON YOUR OWN

People who cannot hear use other ways to communicate. Sometimes they use a kind of sign language. Find out how deaf people use sign language to communicate. Make a poster that shows some of the signs.

Helping People Hear

Many people cannot hear as well as they would like to. Some people are born with poor hearing. Others become deaf or hard of hearing. Some illnesses, such as mumps or measles, can cause hearing loss by damaging the auditory nerve. Then, sound messages cannot reach the brain.

Hearing can also be lost when sound waves cannot move easily through the outer and middle ear. A broken eardrum can be one cause. In some people, the small bones in the middle ear get harder. Then, the bones do not vibrate very well, making hearing difficult.

Gwenyth Vaughn helps people with hearing problems. She knows that hearing aids can help many people. However, she also knows that hearing aids do not solve all listening problems. Suppose a hard of hearing person is trying to listen to someone talking. Loud sounds made by cars, footsteps, or machines can get in the way. Dr. Vaughn decided to use a different kind of listening device.

The picture shows Dr. Vaughn driving a car. She speaks into a microphone clipped to her collar. A signal travels from the microphone through a wire to a device in the other woman's hand. This device makes the sound louder. A wire carries the sound to the woman's ear. She can listen to her friend, even in a noisy car.

Other listening devices help people listen to television, to voices on the telephone, or to a speaker at a large meeting. With Dr. Vaughn's help, people who are hard of hearing can again hear the enjoyable sounds around them, not just the noise.

What Do You Think?
1. Explain how sound gets from Dr. Vaughn to the listener in the picture.
2. How would the listening device you read about need to be changed to help people listen to television or the telephone?

4 How Do Your Tongue and Nose Work?

You will learn
• where the nerve endings for smell are located in the nose.
• where nerve endings for different tastes are located on the tongue.

Your nose and tongue give you information about what is around you. Sometimes these sense organs can help protect you. The smell of smoke can warn you of a fire. Some spoiled food smells and tastes bad. Mostly, your tongue and nose help you enjoy tastes and smells around you. Which of the objects below have smells and tastes that you like? What are some of your favorite smells and tastes?

Your tongue and nose work together to help you enjoy food. Each of these sense organs sends information about food to the brain. The brain puts this information together and tells you the flavor of the food. When you have a cold, your sense of smell does not work well. Then your brain does not get much information about food from your nose. Food does not have as much flavor as it usually does.

Imagine these smells and tastes.

Nerve Endings in the Nose

When you breathe in through your nose, the air moves into a space. Find this space in the drawing of the nose. Now find the nerve cells that line the top of this space. These are the nerve cells for your sense of smell. Each nerve cell has nerve endings that are like tiny hairs. When a smell enters your nose, these special nerve endings gather information about the smell. They send a message to your brain. Then your brain tells you what you smell.

Look at the drawing of the nose again. Use your finger to trace the path of a smell from the flower to the nerve endings.

Many people use natural gas in their homes for heating and cooking. This gas is safe to use but is dangerous if it leaks out of the pipes into a home. Natural gas has no smell. Chemicals with strong smells are added to natural gas. If the gas leaks into a home, people can smell the chemicals and call for help.

The Nose

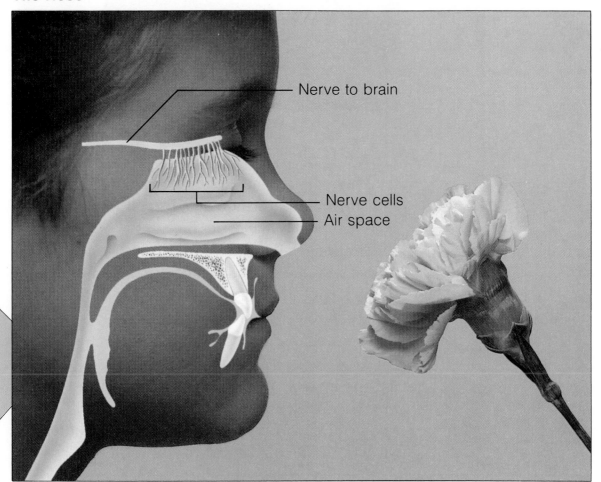

Nerve to brain

Nerve cells

Air space

Taste Buds on the Tongue

taste bud, an organ in the tongue that collects information about taste.

Your sense of taste comes from tiny **taste buds** on your tongue. Taste buds have nerve endings that gather information about different tastes. Your tongue's taste buds gather information about only four tastes—sweet, sour, salty, and bitter. All the different flavors you know are combinations of these four tastes and how things smell.

Each kind of taste bud is found on a different part of the tongue. When you eat an orange, messages from the taste buds for sweet travel to your brain. The picture on the left shows where each kind of taste bud is. Each of the bumps in the picture below is made of about 10,000 taste buds.

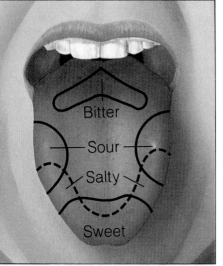

The four kinds of taste buds

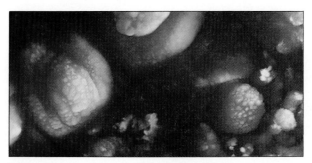

The tongue enlarged eight times

Lesson Review

1. Where in the nose are the nerve endings for gathering information about smell found?
2. What are the four tastes?
3. **Challenge!** Pretend you have just tasted a food that does not remind you of any other food. Since the tongue only has four kinds of taste buds, how would you explain this new flavor?

Study on your own, pages 402–403.

FIND OUT ON YOUR OWN

Look up *nose* in an encyclopedia. Find out why your sense of smell does not work well when you have a cold. Write a sentence that tells what you find out.

Mapping Your Tongue

ACTIVITY

Purpose
Locate and *map* different taste buds on the tongue.

Gather These Materials
• 3 cotton swabs • 3 small paper cups
• salt solution • sweet solution • sour solution • 1 paper drinking cup
• drinking water

Follow This Procedure
1. Use a table like the one shown to record your observations.
2. Dip a cotton swab in a small cup of sweet solution for 30 seconds.
3. Ask your partner to stick out his or her tongue. Using the sweet cotton swab, touch the different areas of the tongue shown in the table. *CAUTION: Do not dip the cotton swab in the solution again. Do not use the swab on anyone else.* In your table, put an X on the tongue labeled sweet every place your partner tasted sweet.
4. Have your partner take a sip of clean water to rinse his or her mouth.
5. Repeat steps 2 through 4 using a clean cotton swab and the sour solution. Record your results.
6. Repeat steps 2 through 4 using a clean cotton swab and the salty solution. Record your results.

Record Your Results

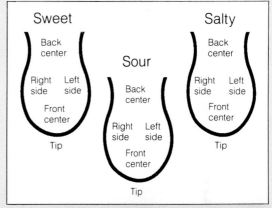

State Your Conclusion
1. Where are the taste buds for sweet, sour, and salty found?
2. How could you find out where the taste buds for bitter are located?

Use What You Learned
If you were to eat a food that was both sweet and sour, which taste might you notice first? Explain your answer.

363

5 How Does Your Skin Gather Information?

LESSON GOALS

You will learn
- the different kinds of nerve endings that are in the skin.
- how you can take care of your skin.

epidermis (ep/ə dėr/mis), the outer layer of skin.

dermis (dėr/mis), the inner layer of the skin where most nerve endings are found.

Your skin is a covering for your body. It is a part of your appearance. Skin also is a sense organ. What kinds of information about the world does your skin give you?

Nerve Endings in the Skin

Your skin is made up of two layers. The **epidermis** is the outer layer that you see. The surface of the epidermis is made of dead skin cells. These cells wear off. New cells take their place. The **dermis** is the layer of skin below the epidermis. This layer grows new cells for the epidermis. Blood vessels and most nerve endings are in the dermis.

Your skin has many nerve endings in it. These nerve endings gather different kinds of information. Find the nerve endings in the drawing of skin. Some nerve endings gather information only about cold. Other nerve endings gather just information about heat, touch, pressure, or pain.

The Skin

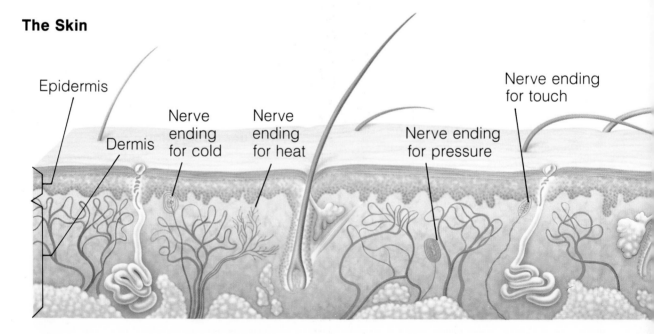

Epidermis

Dermis

Nerve ending for cold

Nerve ending for heat

Nerve ending for pressure

Nerve ending for touch

When something hot touches your skin, your nerve endings for heat send a message to the brain. Your brain tells you that you are touching something hot. If you touch something that is too hot, your nerve endings for pain send a message. How could this message help keep you safe?

Sometimes you might notice only one kind of information from your skin. You might feel heat or cold. Most times, you notice several kinds of information at once. Think about holding a glass of cold milk. You can feel the pressure of your hand holding the glass. You can feel the cold. What other information might you notice? The different nerve endings in your skin work together to tell you about the glass of milk. What information might you notice by touching an animal like the one in the picture?

The skin covering different parts of your body has different numbers of nerve endings. Your face and hands have many nerve endings. Your back and legs have fewer nerve endings. Would you get more information from touching something with your hands or with your legs?

Other parts of your body, such as your muscles, also have nerve endings for pain. Sometimes, pain helps warn you that you are sick or that you should rest.

Blood vessels

Nerve ending for pain

Washing removes dirt and germs.

Taking Care of Your Skin

Washing your skin with soap and water removes dirt, extra oil, sweat, and some dead skin cells. Your skin will look clean and smell good. Washing also removes germs that could make you sick. If you get a cut or scrape, wash it with soap and water to remove dirt and germs. The student in the picture is washing his hands before eating lunch. Washing your hands before eating prevents passing germs from your hands to your food and into your body.

Avoid sunburn and other harm to the skin from the sun. Use creams that block out some sunlight when you stay in the sun for a long time. Avoid other burns by being careful around hot water, hot objects, and fires. Even water from a faucet can be hot enough to cause burns.

Exercise, eating good foods, and getting enough sleep help keep your skin healthy. When your skin is healthy, you look your best.

Lesson Review

1. What are the five kinds of nerve endings that are in your skin?
2. What are two ways you can take care of your skin?
3. **Challenge!** What might happen if your nerve endings for pain did not work?

Study on your own, pages 402–403.

FIND OUT ON YOUR OWN

Look up *nail* and *skin* in an encyclopedia. Find out what kind of nails and skin different animals have. Write a paragraph describing different animals' skin and nails.

Identifying the Closeness of Nerve Endings

Purpose
Compare the closeness of nerve endings in different parts of your body.

Gather These Materials
• 2 file cards • scissors • ruler • stapler

Follow This Procedure
1. Use a table like the one shown to record your observations.
2. Cut a file card in half. Put the two pieces together. Slide one piece down and to the left until you have 2 points that are 1/2 cm apart. Staple the pieces in this position.
3. Very gently touch the back of your partner's neck using either the card with 1 or 2 points. Be careful that your partner does not turn around.
4. Ask your partner if he or she felt one or two points. Record your results in your chart by putting a / mark in the correct column.
5. Repeat steps 3 and 4 until you have tried each card 5 times.
6. Repeat this procedure on the wrist, palm of the hand, and fingertips.

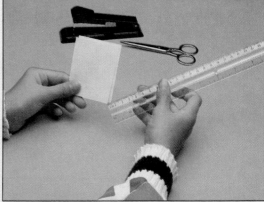

Record Your Results

	Felt 1 point with 1 point card		Felt 2 points with 2 point card	
	Yes	No	Yes	No
Neck				
Wrist				
Palm				
Finger				

State Your Conclusion
1. Are the nerve endings closer together where you can feel just 1 point or where you can feel 2 points?
2. Which part or parts of the body you tested have nerve endings that are the closest together? Explain your answer.

Use What You Learned
Based on where you found nerve endings closest together, what is the advantage of having nerve endings closer together?

Skills for Solving Problems

Using Timers and Line Graphs

Problem: At what rate does the sound of thunder travel?

Part A. Using a Timer to Collect Information

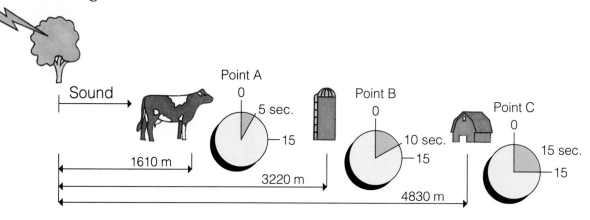

1. Timers record seconds, minutes, and hours. Some also record days, months, and years. Moving hands show the passage of time on a timer's dial. The timers shown record seconds. How many seconds are in a minute?

2. The diagram shows lightning hitting a tree. Light travels so fast we see the lightning almost as soon as it takes place. Sound travels more slowly. Lightning and thunder take place at the same time, but they travel to our eyes and ears at different rates. Point A is 1,610 m from where lightning struck the tree. How long does the timer show the sound of thunder took to reach Point A?

3. How far from the tree is Point B? Point C? How long did the sound of thunder take to reach Point B? Point C?

Part B. Using a Line Graph to Organize and Interpret Information

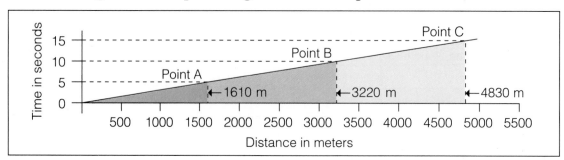

4. The line graph contains the information you collected in Part A about how sound travels. What units does the line at the bottom of the graph show? What does the line at the left of the graph show?

5. Put your finger on the line at the bottom of the graph at the place that represents the distance to Point A. Move your finger up the line until it is as high as the unit that matches the time on the timer at Point A. How many seconds did the sound of thunder take to travel to Point A? to Point B? to Point C? How far does sound travel every five seconds?

Part C. Using a Timer and a Line Graph to Solve a Problem

Problem: How long does the sound of a baseball bat hitting a ball take to travel every 100 meters?

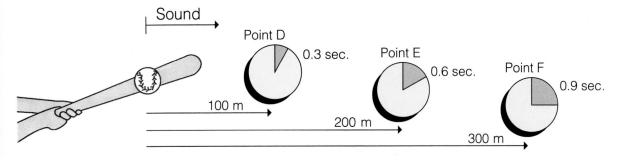

6. Use the picture to collect the information you need to solve the problem. At Point D, Point E, and Point F a person watches a batter hit a baseball and hears the crack of the bat. Make a line graph similar to the one shown in Part B to organize your information.

7. Look at your graph. How long does the sound take to travel from the time the bat hits the ball until you hear the crack of the bat when you are at Point D? at Point E? at Point F? How long does sound take to travel every 100 meters?

8. How long would the sound take to reach you if you were 400 m away from the batter?

Chapter 14 Review

☑ Chapter Main Ideas

Lesson 1 • Your sense organs are your eyes, ears, nose, tongue, and skin. • Nerve endings in your sense organs gather information and send it along nerves to the brain.

Lesson 2 • Different parts of the eye bend light to make a picture on the retina. • Do not rub your eyes.

Lesson 3 • The outer ear funnels sound waves into the ear. • Nerve cells in the inner ear gather information about sounds and send it to the brain. • Protect your ears from loud sounds.

Lesson 4 • Nerve endings in the nose gather information about smells. • Taste buds have nerve endings for salty, sour, sweet, and bitter.

Lesson 5 • The skin has nerve endings that gather information about touch, pressure, heat, cold, and pain. • Avoid sunburn.

☑ Reviewing Science Words

dermis	iris	pupil
ear canal	middle ear	retina
eardrum	nerve cell	sense organ
epidermis	nerve ending	spinal cord
inner ear	outer ear	taste bud

Copy each sentence. Fill in the blank with the correct word or words from the list.

1. A tiny branch of a nerve cell is a _____ .
2. Messages from most parts of the body travel through the _____ .
3. Light enters the eye through the _____ .
4. Messages about sound are sent to the brain from the _____ .
5. A cell that carries information is a _____ .
6. The tunnel that carries sound to the eardrum is the _____ .
7. Most nerve endings in the skin are in the _____ .
8. An eye is a _____ .
9. The _____ changes the size of the pupil.
10. A _____ gathers information about taste.
11. The three tiny bones that carry sound waves are in the _____ .
12. The ear canal is part of the _____ .
13. The layer of skin that you can see is the _____ .
14. The thin skin at the end of the ear canal is the _____ .
15. The _____ is a layer of nerve cells in the back of the eye.

☑ Reviewing What You Learned

Write the letter of the best answer.

1. Which part of your eye can you see?
   (a) retina   (b) lens   (c) iris   (d) nerve
2. Which part of your ear vibrates first?
   (a) nerve   (b) eardrum   (c) inner ear   (d) tiny bones
3. Which sense organ works with your tongue to help you taste food?
   (a) eyes   (b) ears   (c) skin   (d) nose
4. Besides the ear, which sense organ has nerve endings that are like tiny hairs?
   (a) nose   (b) eyes   (c) skin   (d) tongue
5. Which part of your eye bends light to make a clear picture on the retina?
   (a) lens   (b) iris   (c) nerve   (d) pupil
6. The dermis and epidermis are parts of the
   (a) eyes.   (b) ears.   (c) nose.   (d) skin.
7. A bundle of nerves protected by the backbone is the
   (a) brain.   (b) sense organ.   (c) spinal cord.   (d) nerve ending.
8. Which sense organ can be damaged by loud sounds?
   (a) eyes   (b) ears   (c) skin   (d) nose

☑ Interpreting What You Learned

Write a short answer for each question or statement.

1. List the following parts of the eye in the order that light reaches them: retina, pupil, jellylike material, clear covering, lens.
2. List the following parts of the ear in the order that sound travels through them: inner ear, ear canal, middle ear, eardrum.
3. How are all your sense organs alike?
4. Explain how the skin can gather more than one kind of information.
5. Since you have only four tastes, how can food have so many different flavors?
6. How are all your sense organs different from each other?

☑ Extending Your Thinking

Write a paragraph to answer each question.

1. People who have lost their sight find that they hear more sounds than they did before. Why might they think they hear more sounds?
2. A camera works something like an eye. Which part of the eye is like the film in a camera? Explain your answer.

• For further review, use Study Guide pages 402–403.

Careers

Have you ever visited someone in a hospital? Or have you ever been a patient in a hospital? If so, you probably saw hospital workers dressed in various kinds of uniforms. People work in many different jobs in a hospital. These people are all working to help other people become well again.

A **serology technologist** helps make medicines to treat diseases. Many of these medicines come from plants or animals. This technologist also finds out how much of a medicine the patient should take.

Blood bank technologists collect, test, and store blood. After collecting blood from a person, the technologist finds out the type of that blood. He or she also tests the blood for disease. Patients who need blood depend on blood bank technologists, like the woman below, to make sure the blood is safe. Serology technologists and blood bank technologists go to college for four years.

Cardiologists are physicians who specialize in treating heart problems. Cardiologists might perform surgery to fix a damaged heart. To become a cardiologist, you must go to medical school after college. Then you must work with experienced cardiologists for several years before you can treat patients on your own.

A **dietician** helps plan meals for patients in a hospital. Some patients need special diets. Dieticians choose foods for meals to fit those special diets. They also plan healthy meals for other patients. Dieticians, like the ones below, might work in nursing homes, schools, and some restaurants. Sometimes they do research on how the body uses food or how foods affect the body. A dietician goes to college for at least four years.

Audiologists work in hospitals, clinics, and schools. They test the hearing of people to find out what problems they might have. Then they help treat people who have hearing problems. They might fit a person with a hearing aid. They also work with doctors to plan other treatments. An audiologist goes to college for four years or more.

The Telephone

To travel by plane to the other side of the earth would take many hours. Yet you can send a message to the other side of the earth by telephone in less than one second!

In some ways, the telephone works the same way your ear works. In your ear, a vibrating membrane—your eardrum—causes a signal to be sent to your brain. In the telephone, a different kind of vibrating membrane cause an electrical signal to travel to another telephone where a friend is listening. The picture shows how the telephone works.

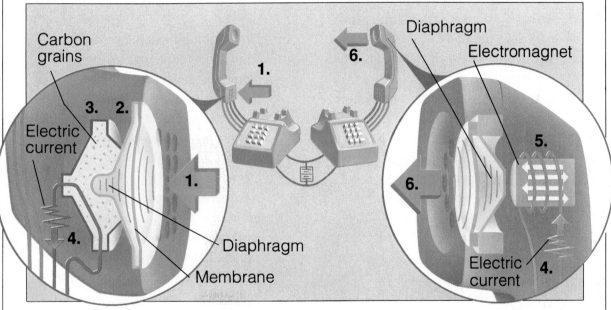

Carbon grains

Electric current

3. 2.

1.

4.

1.

6.

Diaphragm

Electromagnet

5.

6.

Electric current

4.

Diaphragm

Membrane

1 When you speak, your voice is carried by sound waves. The sound waves enter the mouthpiece on the telephone. They cause a membrane to start vibrating.

2 The vibrating membrane passes its motion to a plastic cone called a diaphragm. The diaphragm vibrates along with the membrane.

3 Beneath the diaphragm is a layer of tiny grains of carbon. The carbon grains look like fine black sand.

The thickness of the carbon layer changes as the diaphragm vibrates. When the diaphragm pushes down, the layer gets thin. When the diaphragm pulls up, the layer gets thick.

4 An electric current runs through the carbon layer. When the layer is thick, little current gets through. When the layer is thin, more electricity gets through. The changing electric current travels along telephone wires

and enters a telephone at the receiving end.

5 The earpiece of the telephone contains an electromagnet. The electricity in the electromagnet creates magnetism which makes a metal diaphragm vibrate.

6 This vibrating diaphragm creates sound waves just like those that started the conversation. You hear the words the other person spoke into the mouthpiece.

Unit 4 Review

Complete the Sentence

Fill in the blank with the correct word or words from the list.

atrium	platelet
dermis	pupil
digestion	retina
epidermis	sense organ
middle ear	spinal cord
nutrients	vein

1. The ▨▨ connects the brain with nerves in the body.
2. A tiny part of a cell that helps stop bleeding is a ▨▨ .
3. Light enters the eye through a hole called the ▨▨ .
4. The changing of food into a form the body can use is called ▨▨ .
5. A ▨▨ collects information about the surroundings, such as sight, sound, or taste.
6. Body cells use ▨▨ for growth, repair, and energy.
7. A layer of nerve cells called the ▨▨ is in the back of the eye.
8. Blood is carried from a capillary through a ▨▨ on its way back to the heart.
9. The three tiny bones of the ▨▨ carry sound waves.
10. Blood flows from veins to an ▨▨ in the top part of the heart.
11. Most of the skin's nerve endings are in the layer of skin called the ▨▨ .
12. A layer of skin called the ▨▨ has a surface made up of dead skin cells.

Short Answer

Write a short answer for each question or statement.

1. Tell the order in which these body parts are used during digestion: esophagus, large intestine, mouth, small intestine, stomach.
2. Name three types of blood cells, and tell what each type of cell does in the body.
3. How is blood in arteries different from blood in veins?
4. Name the six types of nutrients that the body needs.
5. People who smoke usually have less oxygen in their blood than people who do not smoke. Explain why.
6. Describe the path that information travels from a sense organ to the brain.
7. How is the retina like film in a camera?
8. How does sound reach the nerve endings in the inner ear?
9. Why do people have trouble tasting foods when their noses are stuffy because of a cold?
10. Tell the five kinds of information that nerve endings in the skin send to the brain.

Essay

Write a paragraph for each question or statement.

1. Explain why the heart must beat faster during hard exercise.
2. What sense organs would a robot need to answer a door when the doorbell rings?

Unit Projects and Books

Science Projects

1. You can find your average resting heart rate by taking your pulse. Sit in a chair and relax for two minutes. Then take your pulse as described on page 336. Record your pulse. Take your pulse two more times. Then add the three numbers together. Divide by three. This number is your average resting heart rate. If you do not have any health problems, find out how long your heart takes to return to this resting rate after exercise.

2. Many foods have fat in them. You can easily test for fats by putting the food on paper cut from a brown grocery bag. If a grease spot appears, then the food has fat in it. Use a brown grocery bag to test the following foods for fat: margarine, slice of apple, piece of cookie, peanut butter, and slice of potato. Which of the foods have fat in them?

3. Fiber is not a nutrient, but it is an important part of your diet. Fiber might help prevent cancer of the intestines. Fiber also helps undigested food move easily through the large intestine. Look at packages of cereal. Find out which cereals have fiber in them. Make a list of high-fiber cereals.

4. Foods usually have one of four different kinds of taste. They can be sweet, sour, salty, or bitter. Make a list of some foods. Then classify each food as sweet, sour, salty, or bitter.

Science and Society

Truth in Advertising The health teacher and her students are discussing truthful advertising. One student asks about the new slogan for The Better Burger Stand. The slogan says, ''Fast food is good food. You will get most of the nutrients you need, and the price will be less.'' ''That is not the whole story,'' the health teacher says. ''You might get some nutritious food at The Better Burger Stand. Other food might not be so good. You will probably eat more fats, sugars, and salt than you should.'' In what ways is the advertising truthful. In what ways could the advertising be misleading?

Books About Science

What Happens to a Hamburger by Paul Showers. T. Y. Crowell, 1985. Discover how food changes as it travels through your digestive system.

Uncle Bob Talks with My Digestive System by Bob Devine. David C. Cook, 1985. Learn more about how your digestive system works.

The Heart by John Gaskin. Watts, 1985. Find out all about your heart.

Drug Use and Drug Abuse by Geraldine Woods. Watts, 1986. Learn how drugs can affect your body.

The Senses by John Gaskin. Watts, 1985. Learn about your senses and how they help you.

Independent Study Guide

Use the *Independent Study Guide* to Review the lessons in each chapter.

Chapter 1   Study Guide

On a separate sheet of paper, write the word or words that best complete the sentence or answer the question.

LESSON 1

pages 12–15

1. What do scientists do when they classify plants?
2. What two groups are plants that make seeds divided into?
3. The ⬚ of a plant covers and protects its seeds.
4. Conifers make their seeds in ⬚.
5. Most ⬚ have needlelike leaves.
6. Ferns and mosses make ⬚ to reproduce.

LESSON 2

pages 16–18

1. Name the parts of the flower in the picture.

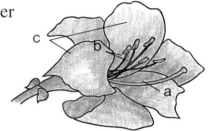

2. What do sepals do for a flower?
3. The ⬚ protect the part of the flower that makes seeds.
4. What must happen for an egg from the pistil to grow into a seed?
5. Some trees, like the ⬚, have flowers without petals.
6. Give four examples of plants that have two kinds of flowers on the same plant.
7. What is one way in which a cottonwood tree is different from many other plants?

LESSON 3

pages 20–24

1. Butterflies use ⬚ from flowers as food.
2. Describe what happens as a butterfly gathers nectar from a flower.
3. Pollination is the movement of ⬚ from stamens to pistils.
4. What helps attract birds and butterflies to a plant?

5. How do moths find flowers at night?

6. Corn plants and grasses depend on ___ for pollination.

7. What kind of plant might not have petals?

8. After pollination, each pollen grain grows a thin ___ from the tip to the bottom of the pistil.

9. The bottom part of the pistil is the ___.

10. What is fertilization?

11. Each ovule contains an ___.

12. List the parts of a seed.

13. A corn seed has ___ seed leaf.

14. What is a dicot seed?

15. What does a dicot seed's seed leaf do?

16. As a seed develops, the ___ swells and forms the fruit.

17. Peanuts and peas are ___ fruits.

LESSON 4

pages 26–30

1. The fruit helps ___ a plant's seeds.

2. What are two ways animals help scatter fruit and their seeds?

3. Fruits that are too heavy to float in the air can often be scattered by ___.

4. Explain how the seeds of the plants in the pictures below are scattered.

5. Describe the way a seed germinates.

6. If a seed is hard and dry, it probably is ___.

7. The stem of a ___ seed pushes upward through the soil, carrying the seed coat with it.

8. The seed coat of a growing ___ seed remains in the soil.

9. The stem that grows from a corn seed forms a ___.

Chapter 2   Study Guide

On a separate sheet of paper write the word or words that best complete the sentence or answer the question.

LESSON 1

pages 38–45

1. What kind of animals live together in groups called prides?
2. What word describes a group of fish?
3. In what two ways are fish protected by moving in a group?
4. What word describes a group of baboons?
5. As baboons search for food, the largest animal moves in the ___ of the troop.
6. What animal becomes the head of a troop of baboons?
7. Where in a troop of baboons would you find the mother baboons with babies and the young baboons?
8. What do the female members of a troop of baboons do?
9. How does a baboon communicate that it is not the strongest?
10. A baboon that is ___ will keep its teeth together and pull its lips back.
11. What would you find in the different rooms under an ant hill?
12. What are ant cows?
13. What are two ways in which ants communicate?
14. How many queen bees does a bee hive have?
15. How are the animals in the pictures below communicating?

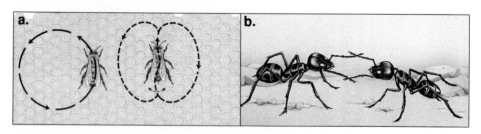

16. Birds that live near cows and eat insects off them live with the cows in a way known as ___ .
17. A parasite lives on the ___ animal.

LESSON 2

pages 46–50

1. The changes that animals go through during their lives make up their ▨ .
2. What does a mother sea turtle do after she lays her eggs?
3. After hatching, what is the first thing sea turtles must do for themselves?
4. Why do not all the young sea turtles survive?
5. A ▨ goes through many changes before it becomes an adult frog.
6. What does a mother butterfly do after she lays her eggs?
7. List four kinds of animals that need care when they are young.
8. How are newborn baby bears fed?
9. How do mother kangaroos protect their young?
10. How does a baby opossum move around?
11. What are two reasons some animals need their parents to keep them warm?
12. How do parent birds keep their babies warm?
13. What do parent birds do for their young before they hatch?

LESSON 3

pages 52–55

1. Flying away when someone goes near it is an example of a bird's ▨ .
2. What are instincts?
3. How do sea turtles know how to crawl to the ocean?
4. What instinct do baby herring gulls show?
5. What is a reflex?
6. Blinking is a reflex that helps ▨ your eyes.
7. What reflex helps you to see better in a dark room?
8. The wind is a ▨ that causes you to blink your eyes.
9. The opening of your pupils is a ▨ to the dark room.
10. Combing your hair is a ▨ behavior.
11. Animals can be taught tricks by ▨ their responses.
12. What do porpoise trainers use to reward the porpoises for a correct response to a stimulus?
13. What kinds of behaviors are not easily changed?
14. How do bluejays learn not to eat monarch butterflies?

Chapter 3   Study Guide

On a separate sheet of paper, write the word or words that best complete the sentence or answer the question.

LESSON 1

pages 64–67

1. Where do plants get their energy?
2. What gives plants their green color?
3. What two things do plants need to use the trapped energy?
4. ▨ in the roots carry water and chemicals from the roots to the leaves of a plant.
5. What are two waste products of photosynthesis?
6. How do a plant's waste products leave the plant?
7. ▨ makes plants different from most other living things.
8. A strawberry plant is a ▨ because it makes sugar.

LESSON 2

pages 68–70

1. Why must animals eat food?
2. Because a frog eats other living things, it is a ▨.
3. What eats only plants?
4. What are three examples of herbivores?
5. What eats only other animals?
6. What are three examples of carnivores?
7. What eats both plants and animals?
8. What kind of a consumer is a racoon?
9. What kind of consumer eats the food shown in each of the following pictures?

LESSON 3

pages 72–74

1. All the plants, animals, and other living things that live together in one place make up a ▨.
2. What do members of a community share?

3. Look at the living things in the pictures below. Put the letters of the pictures in the order that the living things come in a food chain.

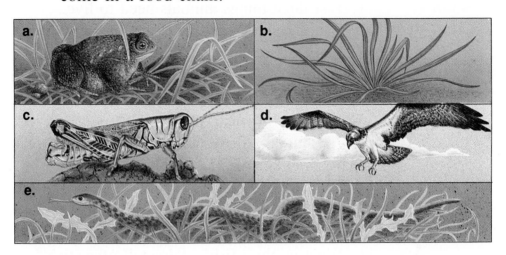

a.
b.
c.
d.
e.

4. A snake is a ▨ because it hunts and kills other animals for food.
5. What are prey?
6. When an animal dies, the ▨ get energy from the animal's remains.
7. What are two examples of decomposers?
8. ▨ take in the material that decomposers put back into the soil.
9. ▨ are producers that live in the ocean.
10. Algae come ▨ in the ocean food chain.

LESSON 4

pages 76–80

1. Why do most animals belong to more than one food chain?
2. All the members of the food chains in a community also belong to the ▨ .
3. What happens when the number of producers in a community gets larger?
4. How can weather make changes in the food web?
5. What happens to the herbivores in a community if most of the producers are killed?
6. By cutting down trees, people change the ▨ .
7. Water ▨ can harm animals living in a stream.

381

Chapter 4 Study Guide

On a separate sheet of paper write the word or words that best complete the sentence or answer the question.

LESSON 1

pages 88–91

1. List three things animals need to live.
2. Plants need ▨, water, and space to grow.
3. Plants use energy from ▨ to make sugar.
4. How do living things in the desert meet their need for water?
5. How do fish meet their need for oxygen?
6. An animal's body parts and the parts of plants are ▨.
7. What is behavior?
8. Gills are adaptations for living in ▨.
9. Structures that help desert plants save water are ▨.
10. What adaptation helps sharks to catch and eat other fish?
11. What might a fish's color tell other fish?
12. What adaptation helps protect the puffer fish from predators?
13. What is an adaptation that helps plants get the most energy from sunlight?

LESSON 2

pages 92–97

1. What adaptation helps hawks find food on the ground?
2. What adaptation helps spiders trap food?
3. Why are a woodpecker's beak and a hummingbird's beak different from one another?
4. The ▨ has a beak adapted for catching fish.
5. What adaptations help anteaters get food?
6. Why do rabbits have large ears?
7. How are katydids protected from being eaten by birds?
8. What is protective coloration?
9. In what way do flounders show protective coloration?
10. What color does a snowshoe rabbit's fur change for winter?
11. Porcupines have sharp ▨ that help protect them.
12. Puffing itself up is an adapted ▨ that protects a toad from being eaten by a snake.

13. Look at the animals in the pictures. What adaptations help each animal protect itself?
14. What behavior helps monarch butterflies survive the winter?
15. What is migration?
16. Why do hibernating animals not need to eat?

LESSON 3

pages 100–104

1. What adaptation do pitcher plants have that help them get nitrogen?
2. How are the roots of desert plants adapted for getting water?
3. A cactus plant stores water in its ▒▒.
4. Desert plants have ▒▒ on their leaves and stems to keep water from escaping.
5. The spines on a cactus are a type of ▒▒.
6. Plants living in cold places all year long are called ▒▒ plants.
7. Compare the roots of alpine plants and desert plants.
8. What adaptations do alpine plants have that help keep water from escaping?
9. How are alpine plants adapted to survive the cold winds?
10. Losing their leaves in the fall helps keep some trees from losing ▒▒ during the winter.
11. An annual is a plant that lives for ▒▒ year.
12. Why do annuals appear each spring?
13. What is a perennial?
14. What part of the tulip plant lives for many years?
15. What part of the potato plant will sprout in the spring?
16. How are climbers adapted for getting sunlight?

Chapter 5   Study Guide

On a separate sheet of paper, write the word or words that best complete the sentence or answer the question.

LESSON 1

pages 118–120

1. The air, objects, and you are all made of _____.
2. What is volume?
3. Does a lion or a house cat have more mass?
4. The white color of milk is a _____ of milk.
5. Liquid, solid, and gas are three _____ of matter.
6. How do liquids and solids differ?
7. A _____ does not have a shape or a volume of its own.
8. How can matter be changed from one state to another?
9. What happens if you freeze liquids?
10. What happens if you boil liquids?
11. Water _____ is the gas that escapes from boiling water.
12. The states of matter are _____ properties of matter.

LESSON 2

pages 122–127

1. What is an atom?
2. Scientists know of _____ different elements.
3. _____ is an element that you need from the air you breathe.
4. Atoms of the element _____ make bones and teeth strong.
5. The smallest bit of a compound is a _____.
6. How many hydrogen atoms are in every molecule of water?
7. The properties of a compound are _____ the properties of the elements in it.
8. What are three physical properties of carbon?
9. What is a molecule of each of these things made of?

10. The air you breathe is a _____ of gases.
11. What are two elements in the air you breathe?

12. What are two compounds in the air you breathe?
13. The air over a desert has ▓ water vapor than the air over a warm forest.
14. Soil is a ▓ of sand, clay, and plant matter.
15. One substance dissolving into another substance forms a ▓.
16. Some soft drinks are a solution of a ▓ in a liquid.

LESSON 3

pages 128–131

1. ▓ measures the distance between two points.
2. Every ▓ includes a number and a unit.
3. What unit of measurement would you use to measure your classroom?
4. There are 100 ▓ in a meter.
5. There are ▓ millimeters in a meter.
6. What is a kilometer?
7. How could you find the volume of a room?
8. A ▓ is a cube 1 meter long, 1 meter wide, and 1 meter high.
9. Liters and milliliters are used to measure ▓.
10. What else is the same size as a milliliter?
11. When using a graduated cylinder, you read the volume of water at the ▓ part.

LESSON 4

pages 134–137

1. An object with a mass of one kilogram has a mass ▓ times greater than an object with a mass of 1 gram.
2. You can use a tool called a ▓ to measure mass.
3. What is density?
4. Water has a ▓ density than oil does.
5. Oil has ▓ matter in it than the same volume of alcohol does.
6. Water has a ▓ density than alcohol does.
7. Density is another ▓ of matter that you can measure.
8. A unit for density uses a unit for measuring mass and a unit for measuring ▓.
9. An object has ▓ density if it has the same amount of matter in a much smaller volume.

Chapter 6   Study Guide

On a separate sheet of paper, write the word or words that best complete the sentence or answer the question.

LESSON 1

pages 144–146

1. What is a force?
2. What are four ways in which force can be used?
3. Objects fall when you drop them because of ___.
4. The ___ in a car measures the car's speed.
5. A car moving at a speed of 30 kilometers an hour will take ___ hours to go 90 kilometers.
6. What two things did Isaac Newton realize about moving objects?
7. If you push an object and it keeps moving after you have let go of it, you are seeing an example of ___.
8. What is friction?
9. The friction between smooth surfaces is ___ than the friction between rough surfaces.

LESSON 2

pages 148–151

1. Moving your chair across the room is an example of ___.
2. The more ___ that is used, the more work is done.
3. If you are climbing a hill with a friend, what are two ways that you can do more work than your friend?
4. What is energy used for?
5. Where do you get the energy to do work?
6. Cars get energy from ___.
7. A ball rolling down a hill has ___ energy.
8. A roller-skater at the top of a hill has ___ energy.
9. When you wind the rubber band on a model airplane, you are storing ___ energy.
10. Chemical energy is a kind of ___ energy.
11. What kind of energy do cars use to move?
12. Energy cannot be made or destroyed, but it can be ___.
13. A television changes ___ energy into light, sound, and heat energy.

1. What is one characteristic of a machine?
2. How many parts does a simple machine usually have?
3. A lever is held up on a point called the ▨▨.
4. What does a fulcrum of a lever do?
5. What kind of machine is a ramp?
6. What are inclined planes used for?
7. What are wedges used for?
8. Give three examples of wedges.
9. ▨▨ always wastes some of the energy put into a machine.
10. What does a machine's efficiency compare?
11. ▨▨ efficiency means you get a lot of work done for the amount of energy you use.
12. ▨▨ efficiency means you get a small amount of work done for the amount of energy you use.
13. A lever's efficiency is ▨▨.
14. When is the efficiency of an inclined plane high?
15. A ▨▨ is an inclined plane wrapped around a rod.
16. A doorknob is a ▨▨.
17. Look at the wheelbarrow in the picture below. What two simple machines are part of the wheelbarrow?

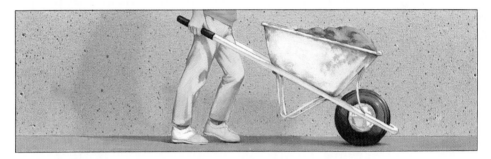

18. What is a pulley?
19. What simple machines make up a hedge clipper?
20. When you turn the handle of a pencil sharpener, the ▨▨ moves the gears.
21. The gears of the pencil sharpener move ▨▨ which cut the wood away.
22. What is a complex machine?
23. What lowers the efficiency of many complex machines?

Chapter 7 Study Guide

On a separate sheet of paper, write the word or words that best complete the sentence or answer the question.

LESSON 1

pages 166–171

1. An electron has a ▨ electric charge.
2. A proton has a ▨ electric charge.
3. Atoms have ▨ electron for every proton.
4. What usually happens to the positive and negative charges in an atom?
5. An object has a negative electric charge when it has ▨ electrons than protons.
6. Two objects with ▨ charges attract each other.
7. What happens when two objects with negative charges are placed next to each other?
8. What are sparks?
9. What makes electric current?
10. What is a material that is a good conductor?
11. What are four materials that are good insulators?
12. Good conductors have ▨ resistance.
13. Good insulators have ▨ resistance.
14. Electric current flows when it follows a ▨ circuit.
15. A light bulb will not light up when the circuit is ▨.
16. Look at the two kinds of circuits in the pictures below. Name both kinds of circuits.

a.   b.

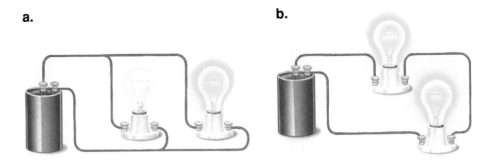

17. Which of the circuits is used for the lights and appliances in your home?

18. Explain why the other circuit in the pictures is not used in homes or businesses.

19. What can happen if electricity travels through a person's body?

20. What is the danger in plugging too many electrical objects into the same outlet?

21. What object keeps too much current from flowing through a circuit?

LESSON 2

pages 172–174

1. What do magnets attract?
2. A ▨ is something that pulls or pushes.
3. What is magnetism?
4. What are the two poles of a magnet called?
5. What happens when the south poles of two magnets are placed near one another?
6. What is a magnetic field?
7. How do people use the earth's magnetic field?
8. What does the magnet in a compass always point to?

LESSON 3

pages 176–179

1. What do generators use energy for?
2. What sources of energy do generators use to make electricity?
3. What does the piece of iron at the center of an electromagnet do for the magnet?
4. One electromagnet has ten loops of wire. Another electromagnet is the same size but has fifty loops of wire. Which is stronger? Explain your answer.
5. Pushing the button on a doorbell causes current to flow because it ▨ a circuit.
6. In what form does sound travel through telephone wire?
7. What causes the metal disk in a telephone to vibrate?

Chapter 8   Study Guide

On a separate sheet of paper, write the word or words that best complete the sentence or answer the question.

LESSON 1

pages 188–189

1. What form of energy can you see?
2. What are the colors that make up white light?
3. Give one way in which each color of the visible spectrum is different from the other colors.
4. The color ▨ has the most energy of the colors of the visible spectrum.
5. Which color light has the least energy?
6. What allows you to see most objects?
7. Where does light from the moon come from?

LESSON 2

pages 190–195

1. How does light travel?
2. Light rays can pass through ▨ objects.
3. Give three examples of objects you can see through.
4. What happens to light when it passes through a translucent material?
5. You cannot see through a wall because it is made of an ▨ material.
6. Why can light not go around objects?
7. When opaque objects block light, they make ▨.
8. What two things happen when light hits an object?
9. Look at the pictures below. Tell what happens to light as it reaches each of the objects.

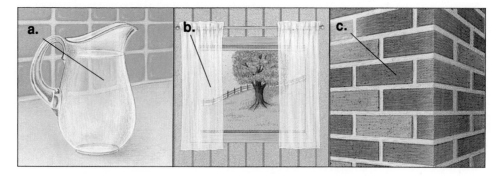

10. The color of an object is the color it ▨.
11. An object that absorbs every color but blue will appear ▨.

390

12. Why do black objects look black?
13. A piece of red glass ▦ only red light.
14. Why does a piece of clear glass have no color?
15. What kind of surfaces form good reflected images?
16. When light hits a ▦ surface, the rays reflect in many different directions.
17. ▦ mirrors reflect images that are actual size.
18. The images reflected in a ▦ mirror might be larger, smaller, or upside down.
19. How are curved mirrors used in stores?
20. When light changes speed, it changes ▦.
21. Light travels ▦ through air than through water.
22. Light ▦ when it moves from the air into a lens.
23. Describe a lens.
24. Each of your eyes has a ▦ lens.

LESSON 3
pages 198–200

1. Waves get ▦ as they move away from their source.
2. What is wavelength a measurement of?
3. Different ▦ of light have different wavelengths.
4. How are microwaves different from light waves?
5. What happens when something vibrates?
6. Light waves move like waves in the ocean, but sound waves move like waves through a ▦.
7. The ▦ of a sound wave is the distance between two parts of the wave that are squeezed together.
8. People ▦ hear sound at all the wavelengths.
9. Light waves travel ▦ through empty space.
10. What happens to the speed of light as it passes through matter?
11. Why must sound waves have matter to travel through?
12. Sound waves travel more ▦ through air than through water.
13. Light waves travel more ▦ than sound waves.
14. Name three ways in which light waves and sound waves are similar.

Chapter 9 Study Guide

On a separate sheet of paper, write the word or words that best complete the sentence or answer the question.

LESSON 1

pages 214–217

1. The light energy from the sun heats the solids and liquids on the earth's surface, but not the _____.
2. Sunlight hits the earth at different _____.
3. In which of the following pictures would the air temperature be the highest? Explain your answer.

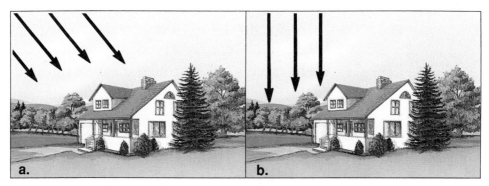

a.   b.

4. Sunlight heats the earth's surface most around _____.
5. Sunlight is most direct during _____.
6. During a summer day, the air above a lake will be _____ than the air above land.
7. What does it mean if the liquid in a thermometer moves down the tube?

LESSON 2

pages 218–222

1. A sudden change in _____ in an airplane makes your ears pop.
2. As you move higher above the surface of the earth, the air gets _____.
3. What happens to air pressure as you move higher above the earth's surface?
4. What happens to air molecules that move higher above the earth's surface?
5. How does a rise in air temperature change the air pressure?
6. Cool air sinks because it is _____ than warm air.
7. Air moving from a high pressure area to a low pressure area is _____.

8. Knowing what the air pressure is in different places helps people ___ the weather.
9. When air pressure is high, mercury in a barometer moves ___ the tube.
10. What is a wind vane?
11. What does an anemometer do?

LESSON 3

pages 224–227

1. What is needed for clouds to form?
2. What happens to water vapor as warm air rises?
3. When air cools, the water vapor ___ .
4. White fluffy clouds that you see in fair weather are ___ clouds.
5. What are cirrus clouds made of?
6. Clouds that form in layers that spread across the sky are ___ clouds.
7. What are snow, sleet, rain, and hail?
8. Where does snow form?
9. Warm air can hold ___ water vapor than cold air can.
10. What is fog?
11. What is the humidity if the air has half of the water vapor that it can hold?
12. What does a hygrometer measure?
13. What does a rain gauge measure?

LESSON 4

pages 228–233

1. ___ sends radio waves into the air, which bounce off of any precipitation.
2. An ___ is a large amount of air that has the same temperature and humidity.
3. What often happens when there is a cold front?
4. What often happens when a warm air mass slides up over a cold air mass?
5. In what direction do most air masses and fronts move in much of the United States?
6. High-pressure areas often have ___ weather.
7. What kind of weather do low-pressure areas often have?
8. What six things do meteorologists try to predict?

Chapter 10   Study Guide

On a separate sheet of paper, write the word or words that best complete the sentence or answer the question.

LESSON 1

pages 242–245

1. Plateaus and plains are two kinds of ▒ .
2. Mountains are often found in groups, or ▒ .
3. What is the earth's crust made of?
4. The mantle of the earth is about ▒ kilometers thick.
5. What makes up the two layers of the earth's core?
6. What do scientists think the continents were like millions of years ago?
7. The ▒ that make up the earth's crust move over the melted rock in the earth's mantle.
8. The earth's plates move about ▒ centimeters each year.
9. When melted rock from under the earth's plates move up to the top, a ▒ forms.
10. When the earth's plates move past each other, an ▒ can take place.

LESSON 2

pages 246–250

1. The melted rock that is deep inside the earth is called ▒ .
2. What is lava?
3. What bursts out of a volcano when it erupts?
4. What is the shape of a volcano that erupts explosively?
5. What is the shape of a volcano that formed from quiet eruptions?
6. In what two ways can volcanoes help people?
7. Where do faults form?
8. What is the length of the San Andreas Fault?
9. A ▒ measures the movement of the ground during an earthquake.
10. The stronger the earthquake, the higher a number an earthquake is given on the ▒ scale.
11. If an earthquake measures a 7 on the Richter scale, it is ▒ times stronger than an earthquake that measures a 6 on the scale.
12. Sometimes, the ▒ changes shape before an earthquake.

LESSON 3

pages 252–256

1. Water, wind, and ▨ can break rocks apart.
2. How does the wind weather rock?
3. When melted snow carries rocks and soil into lakes and streams, ▨ occurs.
4. What is sediment?
5. What is a delta made from?
6. How do glaciers change the earth's surface?
7. What is a dune?
8. In some places, erosion helps add ▨ to the soil.
9. How does planting grass between strips of crops help stop erosion?

LESSON 4

pages 258–262

1. Gold and diamonds are ▨ .
2. A mineral's color is one of its physical ▨ .
3. What is one of the ways you can identify the mineral pyrite?
4. What is the hardness of the hardest mineral?
5. Most of the earth's crust is made of ▨ .
6. Name an igneous rock that forms above ground.
7. What is shale made from?
8. Where are fossils often found?
9. Great heat and pressure inside the earth can change ▨ into marble.
10. What kind of rock is marble?
11. What kind of rocks form in each of the areas marked in the pictures below?

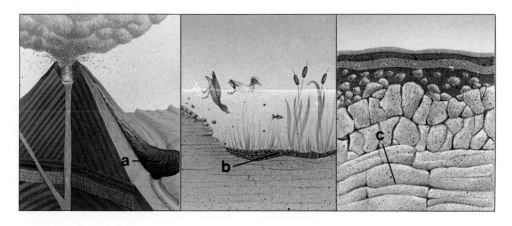

Chapter 11 Study Guide

On a separate sheet of paper, write the word or words that best complete the sentence or answer the question.

LESSON 1

pages 270–273

1. The largest ocean is the ▓ Ocean.
2. The Pacific Ocean averages more than ▓ meters deep.
3. Why are the four main oceans considered part of one large world ocean?
4. Fish and other seafood are ▓ from the ocean.
5. Name an ocean plant that is used as food.
6. What are four kinds of metals that can be found in the ocean?
7. Why do people not take many metals from the ocean?
8. About a ▓ of the petroleum used comes from wells under the ocean.
9. What are three products made from petroleum?
10. People ▓ the ocean by dumping wastes into it.
11. Where do some waste chemicals that pollute the ocean come from?
12. Sometimes oil ▓ from tankers pollute the ocean.
13. Some cities ▓ their waste to clean it.

LESSON 2

pages 274–278

1. In what two ways do currents differ from the ocean water around them?
2. What happens if a ship sails against a current?
3. What causes currents at the surface of the ocean?
4. Currents that flow from the ▓ move cold water.
5. Currents that flow from the ▓ move warm water.
6. Pictures taken from satellites show the ▓ of water on the earth.
7. What makes the winter weather in Great Britain warmer than it is in Canada?
8. Most places along the ocean have tides ▓ a day.
9. The ▓ pull on the earth causes high and low tides.
10. What causes waves?
11. The wave height of most ocean waves is about ▓ meters.

12. Storm waves can rise as high as ▦ meters.
13. The distance between the crest of one wave and the crest of the next wave is the ▦.
14. The wave on the surface of the ocean moves ▦, but the water does not.
15. The ▦ on a beach can wear away parts of the shore.

LESSON 3

pages 280–283

1. Why do sound waves return to the surface of the ocean?
2. Name each of the ocean features marked in the picture below.

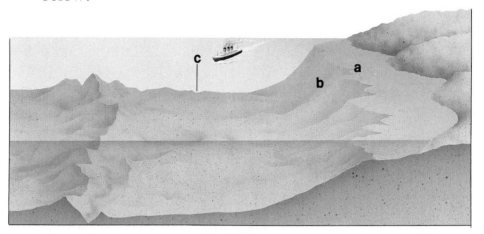

3. ▦ under the ocean can build underwater mountains.
4. When mountains rise above the level of the sea, ▦ are formed.
5. How did scientists first learn about the earth's plates?
6. When the earth's plates move apart, ▦ from inside the earth can move up between the plates.
7. Give an example of a place where the ocean bottom is getting wider.
8. Trenches are the ▦ places in the ocean floor.
9. Trenches form where two ▦ come together.
10. What do oceanographers do?
11. What do oceanographers use to get information from places more than 4 kilometers below the surface of the ocean?
12. What do samples from the ocean bottom show?

Chapter 12 Study Guide

On a separate sheet of paper, write the word or words that best complete the sentence or answer the question.

LESSON 1

pages 292–294

1. A part of the earth is always facing the sun as the earth spins on its ▨ .
2. The part of the earth that faces away from the sun has ▨ .
3. The earth makes one ▨ every twenty-four hours.
4. What is the earth's orbit?
5. The earth makes one revolution around the sun in about ▨ days.
6. ▨ is the force that keeps the earth from moving straight ahead into space.
7. The earth's axis is not straight up and down, it is ▨ .
8. What would happen to the seasons of the year if the earth moved around the sun the way you see in the picture below?

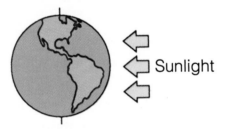

Sunlight

LESSON 2

pages 296–298

1. Moonlight is sunlight ▨ from the moon.
2. An object that revolves around another object is a ▨ .
3. How much of the moon is lit by sunlight?
4. The different shapes of the moon are its ▨ .
5. What phase of the moon appears as a full circle?
6. When the dark side of the moon faces the earth, it is called a ▨ .
7. The changes from a full moon and back to another full moon take about ▨ days.
8. During a ▨ , the moon makes a small shadow on the earth.

LESSON 3

pages 300–307

1. Where does a star's light come from?
2. Where does the light from planets come from?
3. People have known for about ▨ years that planets are satellites of the sun.
4. The planet closest to the sun is ▨ .
5. Which two planets are closest to Earth?
6. Jupiter takes ▨ time to orbit the sun than Earth does.
7. What shape is Earth's orbit?
8. Pluto's orbit sometimes crosses ▨ orbit.
9. When will Neptune be closer to the sun than Pluto?
10. Neptune revolves around the sun once every ▨ years.
11. What is the planet Saturn made of?
12. ▨ might be made of frozen material.
13. Mercury is covered with large holes called ▨ .
14. Jupiter is the ▨ planet.
15. Earth is about the same size as ▨ .
16. What makes Venus a hot planet?
17. Why is the sky around Mars pink?
18. Mars has a giant canyon and giant ▨ .
19. The temperature on Mars is usually ▨ than on Earth.
20. What planet has 16 moons and bands of colorful clouds?
21. What is the Giant Red Spot on Jupiter?
22. Saturn has a moon that is bigger than the planet ▨ .
23. Uranus is about ▨ times bigger than Earth.
24. Which planet is about the same size as Earth's moon?

LESSON 4

pages 308–310

1. The largest ▨ is about the same size across as Texas.
2. Where are most of the asteroids?
3. What causes a rock to burn as it passes through the earth's air?
4. Any part of a ▨ that reaches the earth is a meteorite.
5. The orbits of ▨ are much longer and flatter than the orbits of planets.
6. When a comet moves closer to the sun, some of its ice turns into a ▨ .
7. How long can a comet's tail be?

Chapter 13   Study Guide

On a separate sheet of paper, write the word or words that best complete the sentence or answer the question.

LESSON 1

pages 324–328

1. What happens to food during digestion?
2. What helps break down food in the digestive system?
3. Your ▨ makes food wet and easy to swallow.
4. How does food move from the back of your mouth into your stomach?
5. What do the cells in the lining of the stomach do?
6. The stomach squeezes food that has been broken down into a liquid into the ▨ .
7. What kind of foods cannot be digested by the small intestine?
8. Most digested food reaches the large intestine in ▨ form.
9. Name the parts of the digestive system in the picture below and tell what each part does.

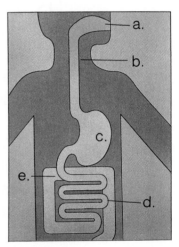

LESSON 2

pages 330–335

1. What are three parts of your circulatory system?
2. What can you feel when you place your fingertips on your wrist?
3. What does your circulatory system carry to your body cells?
4. Blood is mostly made of blood cells and ▨ .
5. What gives blood its color?
6. How do white blood cells protect the body from sickness?
7. Platelets make blood ▨ .
8. An artery carries blood ▨ the heart.

9. The smallest arteries of the body are ▓ .
10. What three things move in and out of the blood through the capillary walls?
11. The walls of veins have ▓ muscle than artery walls.
12. What structures keep blood from flowing backwards through a vein?
13. Blood carried in the arteries has ▓ oxygen than does the blood carried in the veins.
14. The atriums of the heart receive blood from ▓ .
15. The ventricles of the heart pump blood through the ▓ .

LESSON 3

pages 338–341

1. The body needs ▓ to build new cells.
2. What four different foods have proteins in them?
3. In what three ways does your body use fats?
4. What three foods have fats?
5. Eating too much fat can harm the arteries of the ▓ system.
6. How can being overweight harm a person?
7. Sugars and starches are two kinds of ▓ .
8. Breads and potatoes have starches, but fruits have ▓ .
9. The ▓ in carbohydrates can help keep the digestive system healthy.
10. How does eating fresh vegetables and whole grain cereals help the digestive system?
11. Eating foods with ▓ can help keep your eyes healthy.
12. Calcium is a mineral that strengthens your ▓ and teeth.
13. Why do you need to eat foods that are high in iron?
14. The nutrient that makes up much of your body is ▓ .
15. What two body organs can be harmed by smoking cigarettes?
16. Smoking causes diseases, such as ▓ .
17. People who smoke increase their chances of having a ▓ .
18. ▓ is a drug that can harm the lining of the stomach.
19. What can cocaine do to the body?
20. What is the best way to avoid the damage from drug abuse?

Chapter 14 Study Guide

On a separate sheet of paper, write the word or words that best complete the sentence or answer the question.

LESSON 1

pages 348–351

1. How do you get information from your surroundings?
2. Nerve cells in your eyes gather information about ▨ .
3. What information do nerve cells in the skin gather?
4. What two things do nerve endings do?
5. Your brain is made up of ▨ of nerve cells.
6. What do nerves do?
7. Your ▨ is the sense organ that picks up information about taste.
8. The ▨ is a bundle of nerves that connects the brain with nerves of the body.
9. How is the spinal cord protected?
10. Your brain uses the messages from sense organs and your ▨ to get your attention when necessary.

LESSON 2

pages 352–355

1. What is the iris of the eye?
2. The pupil gets ▨ in bright light.
3. How does your pupil's change in size help you?
4. The lens ▨ light that enters the eye.
5. Name the parts of the eye in the picture below.

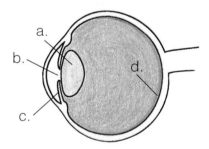

6. What allows you to see things?
7. The ▨ changes messages from the retina so you can understand them.
8. A picture on the retina is in an ▨ position.
9. What four things help protect your eyes?
10. People who use strong chemicals that could splash into their eyes often wear ▨ to protect their eyes.

LESSON 3

pages 356–358

1. Sounds that you hear start as ▨ in the air.
2. What makes up the outer ear?
3. Vibrations from the ▨ move through tiny bones of the middle ear.
4. Vibrations move through fluid, causing tiny hairs in the ▨ to move.
5. The tiny hairs are connected to ▨ that send messages to the brain.
6. What are two ways in which putting things in your ears can harm them?
7. Having trouble hearing can be a sign of an ▨ in the middle ear.

LESSON 4

pages 360–362

1. What are two ways that your sense of smell can protect you?
2. Why are you unable to taste food very well when you have a cold?
3. What part of your nose gathers information about smell?
4. What four tastes do taste buds recognize?
5. Where are the taste buds for sweet located?
6. How can you taste so many different flavors?

LESSON 5

pages 364–366

1. The skin is made up of ▨ layers.
2. The surface of the ▨ is made up of dead skin cells.
3. Where do new cells of the epidermis come from?
4. What body structures are in the dermis of the skin?
5. What two messages would your brain receive if you were to touch the handle of a boiling pot of water.
6. Your face and hands have ▨ nerve endings.
7. Washing your skin removes ▨ that could make you sick.
8. What should you do if you get a cut or a scrape?
9. How can you protect your skin from harm?
10. How can you help keep your skin healthy?

Glossary

Pronunciation Key

The pronunciation of each word is shown just after the word, in this way: **ab bre vi ate** (əbrē′vē āt). The letters and signs used are pronounced as in the words below. The mark ′ is placed after a syllable with primary or heavy accent, as in the example above. The mark ′ after a syllable shows a secondary or lighter accent, as in **ab bre vi a tion** (əbrē′vē ā′shən).

a	hat, cap	**j**	jam, enjoy	**u**	cup, butter		
ā	age, face	**k**	kind, seek	**ù**	full, put		
ä	father, far	**l**	land, coal	**ü**	rule, move		
		m	me, am				
b	bad, rob	**n**	no, in	**v**	very, save		
ch	child, much	**ng**	long, bring	**w**	will, woman		
d	did, red			**y**	young, yet		
		o	hot, rock	**z**	zero, breeze		
e	let, best	**ō**	open, go	**zh**	measure, seizure		
ē	equal, be	**ȯ**	order, all				
ėr	term, learn	**oi**	oil, voice	**ə**	represents:		
		ou	house, out		**a**	in about	
f	fat, if				**e**	in taken	
g	go, bag	**p**	paper, cup		**i**	in pencil	
h	he, how	**r**	run, try		**o**	in lemon	
		s	say, yes		**u**	in circus	
i	it, pin	**sh**	she, rush				
ī	ice, five	**t**	tell, it				
		th	thin, both				
		ᴛʜ	then, smooth				

A

absorb (ab sôrb′), to take in.

adaptation (ad′ap tā′shən), a structure or behavior that helps a living thing live in its surroundings.

adapted (ə dapt′ed), made fit to live under certain conditions.

air mass, a large amount of air with the same temperature and humidity.

air pressure, the amount that air presses or pushes on anything.

algae (al′jē), a group of producers that live in water.

anemometer (an′ə mom′ə tər), a tool that measures wind speed.

annual (an′yü əl), a plant that lives only one year.

artery (är′tər ē), a blood vessel that carries blood away from the heart.

asteroid (as′tə roid′), a rocky object orbiting the sun between the planets.

atom (at′əm), the smallest whole bit of an element.

atrium (ā′trē əm), a space in the top part of the heart that receives blood from veins.

axis (ak′sis), an imaginary line through a spinning object.

B

barometer (bə rom/ə tər), a tool that measures air pressure.

behavior (bi hā/vyər), the way a living thing acts.

C

capillary (kap/ə ler/ē), a tiny blood vessel with thin walls through which oxygen, nutrients, and wastes pass.

carbon dioxide (kär/bən dī ok/sīd), a gas in air.

carnivore (kär/nə vôr), a consumer that eats only other consumers.

cell (sel), the smallest living part of an organism.

centimeter (sen/tə mē/tər), 1/100 of a meter.

chemical (kem/ə kəl) **energy,** energy from chemical changes.

chlorophyll (klôr/ə fil), a green material in plants that traps energy from sunlight and colors plants.

cirrus (sir/əs) **clouds,** high, feathery clouds made of tiny pieces of ice.

classify (klas/ə fī), to sort into groups based on similarities and differences.

colony (kol/ə nē), a kind of animal group in which each member has a different job.

comet (kom/it), a frozen chunk of ice and dust that orbits the sun.

compass (kum/pəs), a small magnet that can turn freely.

complex (kəm/pleks) **machine,** a machine made of many simple and compound machines.

compound (kom/pound), a substance formed when atoms of two or more elements join together.

compound machine, a machine made of two or more simple machines.

concave lens (kon kāv/ lenz), a lens that is thinner in the middle than at the edges.

condense (kən dens/), to change from a gas to a liquid state.

conductor (kən duk/tər), a material through which electric current passes easily.

conifer (kon/ə fər), a plant that makes seeds inside cones.

consumer (kən sü/mər), a living thing that depends on producers for food.

continental (kon/tə nen/tl) **shelf,** the shallow part of the ocean floor close to the edge of a continent.

continental slope, the land from the continental shelf to the ocean basin.

convex lens (kon veks/ lenz), a lens that is thicker in the middle than at the edges.

core (kôr), center part of the earth.

crest (krest), highest point of a wave.

crust (krust), top layer of the earth.

cubic (kyü/bik) **meter,** a unit for measuring volume.

cumulus (kyü/myə ləs) **clouds,** clouds that look like cotton puffs.

current (kėr′ənt), a river of water that flows through the ocean.

D

decomposer (dē′kəm pō′zər), a consumer that puts materials from dead plants and animals back into soil, air, and water.

delta (del′tə), land that is formed by sediments where a river empties into a lake or ocean.

density (den′sə tē), how much mass is in a certain volume of matter.

dermis (dėr′mis), the inner layer of skin where most nerve endings are.

dicot (dī′kot) **seed,** a seed with two seed leaves containing stored food.

digestion (də jes′chən), the breaking down of food into forms the body can use.

dormant (dôr′mənt), a resting state of a seed.

dune (dün), pile of sand formed by the wind.

E

ear canal (kə nal′), tunnel that sound travels through to the eardrum.

eardrum, the thin skin that covers the end of the ear canal.

earthquake (ėrth′kwāk′), a shaking or sliding of the earth's crust.

efficiency (ə fish′ən sē), the amount of work a machine does compared to the amount of energy put into using the machine.

egg, a material that will grow into a seed when combined with a sperm.

electromagnet (i lek′trō mag′nit), a magnet made when electric current flows through a wire.

electron (i lek′tron), a tiny bit of an atom that has a negative charge.

element (el′ə mənt), matter that has only one kind of atom.

ellipse (i lips′), the shape of a circle that has been flattened a little.

embryo (em′brē ō), tiny part of a seed that can grow into a plant.

energy (en′ər jē), ability to do work.

enzyme (en′zīm), a digestive chemical that changes food.

epidermis (ep′ə dėr′mis), the outer layer of skin.

erosion (i rō′zhən), the moving of weathered rocks and soil by wind, water, or ice.

esophagus (ē sof′ə gəs), the tube that carries food and fluids from the mouth to the stomach.

evaporate (i vap′ə rāt′), to change from a liquid state to a gas.

evergreen, a plant that stays green all year, including firs and pines.

F

fault (fôlt), a crack in the earth's crust along which rocks move.

fertilization (fėr′tl ə zā′shən), the combination of material from pollen with an egg to form a seed.

fog, a cloud that forms near the ground.

food chain, the path energy and materials take in a community.

food web, the flow of energy and materials through connected food chains.

force (fors), a push or a pull.

forecast (fôr′kast′), a prediction of what the weather will be like.

fossil (fos′əl), a trace of a plant or animal that is often found in sedimentary rock.

friction (frik′shən), a force that slows moving objects.

front, the line where two air masses meet.

fulcrum (ful′krəm), point on which a lever is supported and turns.

G

gas, a state of matter that does not have a shape or volume of its own.

gear (gir), a wheel with jagged edges like teeth.

generator (jen′ə rā′tər), a machine that uses an energy source and a magnet to make electricity.

germinate (jér′mə nāt), begin to sprout or grow.

glacier (glā′shər), a large mass of ice that moves.

graduated cylinder (graj′ü āt ed sil′ən dər), a piece of equipment used for measuring the volume of liquids.

gram (gram), 1/1000 of a kilogram.

gravity (grav′ə tē), a force that pulls any two objects together, such as you and the earth.

H

herbivore (hėr′bə vôr), a consumer that eats only producers.

hibernate (hī′bər nāt), to spend the winter in a state in which the body greatly slows down.

high-pressure area, an area where cool air sinks and pushes down on the earth with more pressure.

host (hōst), an animal that is harmed by a parasite.

humidity (hyü mid′ə tē), the amount of water vapor in the air.

hygrometer (hī grom′ə tər), a tool that measures humidity.

I

igneous (ig′nē əs) **rock,** rock that forms from magma.

image (im′ij), a copy or likeness.

inclined (in klīnd′) **plane,** a simple machine that is a flat surface with one end higher than the other.

inertia (in ėr′shə), the tendency of a moving object to stay in motion or a resting object to stay still.

inner ear, the fluid-filled part of the ear that sends messages to the brain.

instinct (in′stingkt), a behavior that an animal has at birth and does not need to learn.

insulator (in′sə lā′tər), a material through which electric current does not pass easily.

iris (ī′ris), colored part of the eye that changes the pupil's size.

K

kilogram (kil′ə gram), a unit for measuring mass; 1,000 grams

kilometer (kə lom′ə tər), 1,000 meters; a unit for measuring length.

kinetic (ki net′ik) **energy,** energy of motion.

L

landform, a shape of the land, such as a mountain, plain, or plateau.

large intestine, the last organ of the digestive system, which removes water and stores the waste material.

lava (lä′və), hot, melted rock that flows from a volcano.

length (lengkth), a measure of the distance between two points.

lever (lev′ər), a simple machine made of a bar that is held up on a point called a fulcrum.

life cycle (sī′kəl), the stages in the life of a plant or animal.

liter (lē′tər), a unit for measuring volume.

low-pressure area, an area where warm air rises and pushes down on the earth with less pressure.

lunar eclipse (lü′nər i klips′), the darkening of the moon as it passes through the earth's shadow.

M

magma (mag′ma), hot, melted rock deep inside the earth.

magnet (mag′nit), an object that pulls iron and steel things to it.

magnetic field, the space around a magnet where magnetism acts.

magnetism (mag′nə tiz′əm), the force around a magnet.

mantle (man′tl), Earth's middle layer.

mass (mas), the amount of material that an object has in it.

matter (mat′ər), substance of which all objects are made.

mechanical (mə kan′ə kəl) **energy,** the energy an object gets from its motion.

metamorphic (met′ə môr′fik) **rock,** a rock that forms when igneous or sedimentary rock is changed by heat and pressure.

meteor (mē′tē ər), a piece of rock or dust from space burning up in the earth's air.

meteorite (mē′tē ə rīt′), a rock from space that has passed through the air and landed on the ground.

meteorologist (mē′tē ə rol′ə jist), a person who studies weather.

meter (mē′tər), a unit for measuring length.

middle ear, the three tiny bones that carry sound waves from the eardrum to the inner ear.

migration (mī grā′shən), movement from one place to another when the seasons change.

milligram (mil′ə gram), 1/1000 of a gram.

milliliter (mil′ə lē′tər), 1/1000 of a liter.

millimeter (mil′ə mē′tər), 1/1000 of a meter.

mineral (min′ər əl), (1) nonliving solid matter from the earth; (2) a nutrient the body needs in small amounts to work properly.

mixture (miks′chər), two or more substances that are placed together but can be easily separated.

molecule (mol′ə kyül), two or more atoms held together in a special way.

monocot (mon′ə kot) **seed,** a seed that has one seed leaf and stored food outside the seed leaf.

N

National Weather Service, a government agency that collects information about weather from all over the United States.

nerve cell (nėrv sel), a cell that carries information to and from different parts of the body.

nerve ending, a tiny branch of a nerve cell.

nitrogen (nī′trə jən), a mineral that plants need to grow.

nodule (noj′ül), lump of metals found on the ocean floor.

nutrient (nü′trē ənt), a material your body gets from food to use for energy, growth, and repair.

O

ocean basin, the deep ocean floor.

oceanographer (ō′shə nog′rə fər), scientist who studies the oceans.

omnivore (om′nə vôr), a consumer that eats producers and consumers.

opaque (ō pāk′), does not allow light to pass through.

orbit (ôr′bit), the path of an object around another object.

outer ear, the part of the ear outside of the head and the ear canal.

ovary (ō′vər ē), bottom part of the pistil in which seeds form.

ovule (ō′vyül), the inner part of an ovary that contains an egg.

oxygen (ok′sə jən), a gas in the air that most living things need to live.

P

parallel (par′ə ləl) **circuit,** a circuit that connects several objects in a way that the current for each object has its own path.

parasite (par′ə sīt), an animal that is helped by living with another animal that it harms.

perennial (pə ren′ē əl), a plant that can live two years or more.

petroleum (pə trō′lē əm), liquid fuel made from living things that lived millions of years ago.

photosynthesis (fō′tō sin′thə sis), the way in which green plants trap the sun's energy and use it to change carbon dioxide and water into sugars.

pistil (pis′tl), part of a flower that makes eggs that grow into seeds.

plain (plān), a flat area of land.

planet (plan′it), a large body of matter revolving around the sun.

plasma (plaz′mə), the watery part of blood that carries nutrients, wastes, and blood cells.

plate, a large section of rock that makes up part of the earth's crust.

plateau (pla tō′), a flat area of land higher than the surrounding area.

platelet (plāt′lit), a tiny part of a cell that helps stop bleeding.

pole (pōl), a place on a magnet where the magnetism is strongest.

pollen (pol′ən), tiny grains that make seeds when combined with a flower's eggs.

pollination (pol′li na′tion), the movement of pollen from a stamen to a pistil.

pollution (pə lü′shən), addition of harmful substances to a community.

potential (pə ten′shəl) **energy,** stored energy.

precipitation (pri sip′ə tā′shən), moisture that falls to the ground from clouds.

predator (pred′ə tər), a consumer that hunts and eats animals.

prey (prā), the animal that predators hunt and eat.

pride, a group of lions.

producer (prə dü′sər), a living thing that can use sunlight to make sugars.

protective coloration (prə tek′tiv kul′ə rā′shən), colors or patterns on an animal that help keep the animal from being seen by predators.

proton (prō′ton), a tiny bit of an atom that has a positive charge.

pulley (pùl′ē), a simple machine made of a wheel and a rope.

pupil (pyü′pəl), a hole in the eye where light enters.

R

rain gauge (gāj), a tool that measures precipitation.

ray, a narrow beam of light that travels in a straight line from a light source.

red blood cell, the kind of cell that carries oxygen from the lungs to the rest of the body.

reflect (ri flekt′), to bounce back.

reflex (rē′fleks), a simple, automatic behavior.

reproduce (rē′prə düs′), to make more of the same kind.

resistance (ri zis′təns), how well electricity flows through a material.

resource (ri sôrs′), material that people use.

response (ri spons′), a behavior caused by a stimulus.

retina (ret′n ə), a layer of nerve cells in the back of the eye.

revolution (rev′ə lü′shən), the movement of one object around another object.

ridge (rij), a chain of underwater mountains.

rotation (rō tā′shən), one full spin of an object around an axis.

S

saliva (sə lī′və), the fluid in the mouth that makes chewed food wet and begins digestion.

satellite (sat′l īt), an object that revolves around another object.

school, a group of one kind of fish that move together.

screw (skrü), a simple machine used to hold objects together.

sediment (sed′ə mənt), tiny bits of rocks, shells, and other materials.

sedimentary (sed′ə men′tər ē) **rock,** rock made of sediments that have been pressed together.

seed leaf, leaflike part in a seed.

sense organ (səns ôr′gən), a body part that has special nerve cells that collect information about the surroundings.

sepal (sē′pəl), one of the leaflike parts that protect a flower bud and that is usually green.

series (sir′ēz) **circuit,** a circuit that connects several objects one after the other so that the current flows in a single path.

simple machine, a machine made of only one or two parts.

small intestine (in tes′tən), the organ of the digestive system in which most digestion takes place.

sodium chloride (sō′dē əm klôr′īd), table salt.

solar eclipse (sō′lər i klips′), the blocking of sunlight by the moon as the moon passes between the sun and the earth.

solar system, the sun, the nine planets and their moons, and other objects that orbit the sun.

solution (sə lü′shən), a mixture in which one substance spreads evenly throughout another substance.

sperm (spėrm), a material in pollen that fertilizes an egg.

spinal cord (spī′nl kôrd), a bundle of nerves that connects the brain and the nerves in the body.

spore (spôr), a tiny cell that can grow into a new plant.

stamen (stā′mən), part of a flower that makes pollen.

state of matter, the form that matter has—solid, liquid, or gas.

stimulus (stim′yə ləs), the cause of a behavior.

stomach (stum′ək), an organ of the digestive system that is like a sack that receives food.

stratus (strā′təs) **clouds,** clouds that form in sheets or layers and spread out over the sky.

symbiosis (sim′bē ō′sis), a special way in which two different kinds of animals live together.

system (sis′təm), a group of organs that work together to do a job.

T

taste bud, an organ in the tongue that collects information about taste.

tide (tīd), the rise and fall of the surface level of the ocean.

translucent (tran slü/snt), allows light to pass through but scatters it so that whatever is behind cannot be clearly seen.

transmit (tran smit/), to pass through.

transparent (tran sper/ənt), allows light to pass through so that whatever is behind can be seen.

tremor (trem/ər), a weak earthquake.

trench (trench), a deep, narrow valley in the ocean floor.

troop (trüp), a kind of group in which animals live.

trough (trôf), the lowest point of a wave.

V

valve (valv), a part of a vein and the heart that acts as a one-way door to keep blood flowing in the right direction.

vein (vān), (1) a blood vessel that carries blood back to the heart; (2) a pipelike part in a plant that carries water and chemicals from the roots to the leaves.

ventricle (ven/trə kəl), a space in the bottom part of the heart that pumps blood out of the heart.

vibrate (vī/brāt), to move quickly back and forth.

visible spectrum (viz/ə bəl spek/trəm), light energy that can be seen and can be broken into the colors of light in the rainbow.

vitamin (vī/tə mən), a nutrient the body needs in small amounts to work properly.

volume (vol/yəm), the amount of space that matter takes up.

W

water vapor (wô/ter vā/pər), water in the form of a gas.

wave height, distance between the crest and the trough.

wavelength (wāv/lengkth/), the distance from a point on a wave to the same point on the next wave.

weathering (weΤΗ/ər ing), the breaking and wearing away of rocks.

wedge (wej), a simple machine used to cut or split an object.

wheel and axle (hwēl and ak/səl), a simple machine that has a center rod attached to a wheel.

white blood cell, the kind of cell that fights germs.

wind, air that is moving from an area of high pressure to an area of low pressure.

wind vane (vān), a tool that shows wind direction.

work, the result of a force moving an object.

Index

A **bold-faced** number indicates a page with a picture about the topic.

A

Adaptation, **88-97, 100-104**
Air mass, **230-231,** 232
Air pressure, **218-220**
Algae, **74**
Anemometer, **222**
Animals
  adaptations of, 88, **89-90, 92-97**
  behaviors of, **52-55**
  food of, **68-70**
  groups of, **38-43**
  and symbiosis, **44-45**
  and young, **46-50**
Annual plant, **102**
Archibald, George, 81
Artery, 332, **333**
Asteroid, **308**
Atom, 122-123
Atrium, **334**
Axis, **292**

B

Barometer, **220**
Behavior, 52-55
Birdseye, Clarence, 25
Blood, **330-331**
Brain, 348, **349-351**

C

Capillary, **332**
Carbon dioxide, 65
Careers
  aerospace engineer, 316
  animal nutritionist, 110
  audiologist, 372
  blood bank technologist, 372
  cardiologist, 316
  dietician, 372
  dispensing optician, 206
  electrical engineer, 206
  geology technician, 316
  landscape architect, 110
  mechanic, 206
  mechanical engineer, 206
  oceanographer, 316
  park management technician, 110
  photographer, 206
  serology technologist, 372
  U.S. Coast Guard member, 316
  zoo designer, 110
  zookeeper, 110
  zoo veterinarian, 110
Carnivore, **69,** 70, 74
Centimeter, 129
Chang-Diaz, Franklin, 311
Chemical energy, 151
Chlorophyll, **64**
Chu, Paul, 181
Circulatory system, **330-335, 338-341**
Clouds, **224-226**
Colony, of insects, **41-43**
Comet, **310**
Compass, **174**
Complex machine, **159**
Compound, **124-125**
Compound machine, **158**
Concave lens, **195**
Conductor, **168**
Conifers, **13**
Consumer, **68-70,** 73, 74
Continental shelf, **281**
Continental slope, **281**
Convex lens, **195**

Core, of earth, **243**
Crest, of wave, 277
Crust, of earth, **243**
Cubic meter, 130
Current, ocean, **274-275**

D

Decomposer, 73, 74
Delta, **254**
Density, 134, **136-137**
Dermis, **364**
Dicot seed, **23**
Digestive system, **324-328, 338-341**
Drew, Charles, 337
Dune, **255**

E

Ear canal, **357**
Eardrum, **357**
Ears, **356-358**
Earth
  movement of, **292-294**
  nature of, **242-245**
  See also Landforms
Earthquakes, **248-250**
Efficiency, 155
Einstein, Albert, 197
Electric charge, 166, **167**
Electric current, **168-170**
Electricity, 166, **167-170,** 171
  and magnetism, **176-179**
Electromagnet, **177-179**
Electron, 166-167
Element, **123**
Ellipse, 301
Embryo, **23**
Energy, 149, **150-151**

Enzyme, 324, 325, 326
Epidermis, **364**
Erosion, **254-256**
Esophagus, **325**
Evergreen plant, **102**
Eyes, **352-355**

F

Fault, **248,** 249
Fertilization, **22**
Flowers, **16-18**
Food, **338-339**
Food chain, **72-74**
Food web, 76, **77-80**
Force, 144
Forecast, 231
Forecasting weather, *Science and Technology*, 235
Friction, 145, 146, 155
Front, **230-231,** 232
Fruit, **24**
Fruit, storing, *Science and Technology*, 25

G

Generator, 176
Glacier, **255**
Goodall, Jane, 99
Graduated cylinder, **131**
Gram, 134
Gravity, 144

H

Health, **338-341**
Heart, **334,** 335
Herbivore, 69, 70, 74
Hibernation, 97

High-pressure area, 219, 232
Host, 44
Humidity, 226-227
Hygrometer, 227

I

Igneous rock, **260**
Inclined plane, **155**
Inertia, 145-146
Inner ear, **357**
Instinct, 52
Insulator, **168**
Iris, **352-353**

K

Kilogram, 134
Kilometer, 129
Kinetic energy, 150

L

Landforms, **242**
  and rocks, **258-262**
  and volcanoes, earthquakes,
    246-250
  and weathering, **252-256**
Large intestine, **326, 327, 328**
Lasers, *Science and Technology*, 197
Length, 128, **129**
Lever, **154**
Light
  and eyes, **352-353**
  how it travels, **190-195**
  nature of, **188-189**
  and sound, **198-200**
Liter, 130
Low-pressure area, 218, 232
Lunar eclipse, **297**

M

Machines, **154-159**
Magnet, **172-173, 176, 177**
Magnetic field, **173**
Magnetism, **172-173**
  and electricity, **176-179**
Maiman, Theodore, 197
Mantle, of earth, **243**
Mass, **118, 134-135**
Matter
  measuring length, volume, 128,
    129-131
  measuring mass, density, **134-137**
  nature of, **122-127**
  states of, **118-120**
McNally, Karen, 263
Mechanical energy, 151
Metamorphic rock, **262**
Meteor, 309
Meteorite, 309
Meteorologist, **228-231,** 232, 235
Meter, 129
Meter, *Science and Technology*, 133
Middle ear, **357**
Migration, 96
Milligram, 134
Milliliter, 130-131
Millimeter, 129
Mineral, **258-259**
Mixture, **126-127**
Molecule, **124-125**
Monocot seed, **23**
Moon, **296-298**
Motion, 145

N

National Weather Service, 229
Nerve cell, **349,** 350

Nerve ending, **349**
Nitrogen, 100
Nodule, 272
Nose, 360, **361**
Nutrient, 324, 338-339

O

Ocean basin, **281**
Ocean exploration, *Science and Technology,* 285
Oceanographer, 283
Oceans, **270-273**
　bottom of, **280-283**
　food chain in, **74**
　movements of, **274-278**
Omnivore, **70**
Orbit, **293**
Outer ear, **357**
Ovary, **22,** 24
Ovule, **22**

P

Parallel circuit, **170**
Parasite, 44
Perennial plant, **103**
Peress, Joseph (Pop), 285
Petroleum, 272
Photosynthesis, **65-66**
Pistil, **17,** 18, 22
Planets, **300-307**
Plants
　adaptations of, 88, 89, **91, 100-104**
　classifying, **12-15**
　energy of, **64-66**
　flower parts, **16-18**
　fruits, **20,** 24
　seeds, **20-23, 26-30**
Plasma, **331**

Plate, of earth, **244-245**
Platelets, 331
Polaroid, 207
Pole, in magnet, **172-173**
Pollen, 17, 22
Pollination, **20-21**
Pollution, 79-80, 272-273
Potential energy, 150
Precipitation, 225-226, **226**
Predator, **73**
Prey, **73,** 74
Pride, of lions, **38**
Producer, **66,** 74
Protective coloration, **94-95**
Proton, 166
Pulley, 156, **157**
Pupil, **353-353**

R

Rain gauge, **227**
Ray, 190
Red blood cells, **331**
Reflex, 53
Resistance, 168
Resource, 271, **272**
Response, 53
Retina, 352, **353**
Revolution, **293**
Ridge, ocean, **281**
Robots, *Science and Technology,* 153
Rocks, **258-262**
Rotation, 292

S

Saliva, **325**
Satellite, 297
School, of animals, **38**

Screw, **156**
Sediment, **254**
Sedimentary rock, **261**
Seeds, **13**, 18, **23**, **24**, **26-30**
Sense organs, **349-351,**
  352-355, 356-358, 360-362,
  364-366
Series circuit, **170**
Simple machine, **154-155**
Skin, **364-366**
Small intestine, 326, **327**
Sodium chloride, 271
Solar eclipse, **298**
Solar system
  and other objects, **308-310**
  and planets, **300-307**
Solution, **127**
Sound, **198-200, 356-358**
Spinal cord, **350-351**
Spore, **14,** 15
Stamen, **17,** 18
Stimulus, 53
Superconductors, *Science and*
  Technology, 181
Symbiosis, **44-45**

T

Taste bud, **362**
Telephone, 273
Temperature, **214-217, 218,**
  224-227
Tide, ocean, **276**
Tongue, 360, **362**
Tracking, 111
Trench, ocean, **281**
Troop, of animals, **39-40**
Trough, of wave, 277

V

Vaughn, Gwenyth, 359
Vein, 332, **333**
Ventricle, **334**
Visible spectrum, **188**
Volcano, **246-247**
Volume, 118, **130-131**

W

Water erosion, **252-253**
Wave, ocean, **277**
Wave height, **277**
Wavelength, 198
Weather
  and air pressure, wind, **218-222**
  and clouds, precipitation, **224-225**
  how it works, 317
  predicting, **228-232**
  and temperature, **214-217, 218-222,**
    224-225
Weathering, **252-256**
Wedge, **155**
Wheel and axle, **156**
White blood cells, **331**
Willard, Mary Joan, 57
Wind, 221-222, **255**
Wind vane, **221**
Work, 148-149

Acknowledgments

Unless otherwise acknowledged, all photos are the property of Scott, Foresman and Company. If more than one photo appears on a page, abbreviations are as follows: (l) left, (r) right, (t) top, (b) bottom, (c) center, (ins) insert.

Page iv-v (left to right):
Scott, Foresman and Company
R. Hamilton Smith
Dwight R. Kuhn
M.P. Kahl/DRK Photo

Page vi-vii (left to right):
Hans Pfletschinger/Peter Arnold, Inc.

Page viii-ix (left to right):
David R. Frazier Photolibrary
John Bowden/Discover Magazine (Family Media)
Harald Sund
Georg Gerster/Photo Researchers
Marty Snyderman

Page x-xi (left to right):
Lennart Nilsson/Bonnier Fakta
Scott, Foresman and Company
Centre National de Recherches Iconographiques

Page xii(l): Tom Smylie
Page xii(r): Breck Kent/Earth Scenes
Page 1(t): E.R. Degginger/Bruce Coleman Inc.
Page 1(c): UPI/Bettmann Newsphotos
Page 1(b): Terry G. Murphy/ANIMALS ANIMALS
Page 4(l): The Bettmann Archive
Page 4(r): The Bettmann Archive
Page 5(tl): Courtesy Quasar Corporation
Page 5(tr): Pete Saloutos/The Stock Market
Page 5(b): Courtesy Quasar Corporation
Page 6(l): Stan Osolinski/FPG
Page 6(tr): The Granger Collection, New York
Page 6(b): NASA
Page 7: NASA
Page 8: Wyman P. Meinzer Jr.
Page 10: D. Wilder
Page 12: Walter Chandoha
Page 13(tl): Sandved and Coleman Photography
Page 13(tc): Robert E. Lyons/Color Advantage
Page 13(bl): Ruth Dixon
Page 13(bc): Don and Pat Valenti
Page 14(tl): Don and Pat Valenti
Page 14(tr): Dan Suzio
Page 14(bl): Dwight R. Kuhn
Page 14(br): Dan Suzio
Page 18(all): William E. Ferguson Photography
Page 20-21: David Muench
Page 21(tl): Don and Pat Valenti
Page 21(tr): William E. Ferguson Photography
Page 22-23: Mary E. Goljenboom/Ferret
Page 25: Craig Sherburne/West Stock
Page 26(l): Dwight R. Kuhn
Page 26(r): David M. Stone
Page 27(l): Doug Wechsler
Page 27(r): Breck P. Kent/Earth Scenes
Page 36: Stephen J. Krasemann/DRK Photo
Page 38(l): Alex Kerstitch/Sea of Cortez Enterprises
Page 38(r): Jen & Des Bartlett/Bruce Coleman Inc.
Page 39: Anthro-Photo
Page 40(l): M.P. Kahl/DRK Photo
Page 40(r): Dieter Blum/Peter Arnold, Inc.
Page 42: Hans Pfletschinger/Peter Arnold, Inc.
Page 44(l): Frans Lanting
Page 44(c): Frans Lanting
Page 44(r): Carl Roessler
Page 46(all): Frans Lanting
Page 47(t): Wolfgang Kaehler
Page 47(b): Frans Lanting
Page 48(t): Hans Reinhard/Bruce Coleman Inc.
Page 48(b): Lynn M. Stone
Page 49(t): Dwight R. Kuhn
Page 49(bl): Jen & Des Bartlett/Bruce Coleman Inc.
Page 49(br): Frans Lanting
Page 50: Don and Pat Valenti
Page 52: Frans Lanting

Page 53(l): Charles Palek/ANIMALS ANIMALS
Page 53(tr): M.A. Chappell/ANIMALS ANIMALS
Page 53(br): Lynn M. Stone/ANIMALS ANIMALS
Page 54: Baliotti/ANIMALS ANIMALS
Page 55: Stephen J. Kraseman/DRK Photo
Page 57(all): Jose Azel/Contact Press Images
Page 62: Jim Brandenburg/Bruce Coleman Inc.
Page 67: Everett C. Johnson
Page 68: Don and Pat Valenti
Page 69: Brandenburg Pictures
Page 74(c): Carl Roessler
Page 74(b): Manfred Kage/Peter Arnold, Inc.
Page 78(l): Arthus-Bertrand/Peter Arnold, Inc.
Page 78(r): G. Ziesler/Peter Arnold, Inc.
Page 79: Brandenburg Pictures
Page 80(l): Eric Kroll/Taurus Photos, Inc.
Page 80(r): Alfred Owczarzak/Taurus Photos, Inc.
Page 81: Kyoko Archibald/International Crane Foundation
Page 86: Dwight R. Kuhn
Page 88: Carl Roessler
Page 88(ins)(t): Alex Kerstitch/Sea of Cortez Enterprises
Page 88(ins)(b): Carl Roessler
Page 89: Marty Snyderman
Page 89(ins): Carl Roessler
Page 90(t): Howard Hall
Page 90(bl): Zig Leszczynski/ANIMALS ANIMALS
Page 90(br): Zig Leszczynski/ANIMALS ANIMALS
Page 91(t): Lynn M. Stone
Page 91(b): Gregory G. Dimijian/Photo Researchers
Page 92(l): Brandenburg Pictures
Page 92(r): J. Serrao
Page 93(l): Lynn M. Stone
Page 93(c): C.C. Lockwood/Cactus Clyde Productions
Page 93(r): Tom Bledsoe/DRK Photo
Page 94(l): Doug Wechsler
Page 94(r): Zig Leszczynski/ANIMALS ANIMALS
Page 95(l): Bill Ivy
Page 95(c): R. Hamilton Smith
Page 95(r): C.C. Lockwood/Cactus Clyde Productions
Page 96(all): Peter Menzel
Page 97: T. Wiewandt
Page 99(l): Penelope Breese/Gamma-Liaison
Page 99(r): Penelope Breese/Gamma-Liaison
Page 100: Dwight R. Kuhn
Page 101(both): Don and Pat Valenti
Page 102: R. Hamilton Smith
Page 102(ins): Walter Chandoha
Page 103(l): Mary E. Goljenboom/Ferret
Page 104(l): Sandved and Coleman Photography
Page 104(c): Sandved and Coleman Photography
Page 104(r): Wolfgang Kaehler
Page 114: Alan Schwartz
Page 116: Peter Menzel
Page 118: Walter Chandoha
Page 122(all): The Art Institute of Chicago. All Rights Reserved. Helen Birch Bartlett Memorial Collection
Page 133: International Bureau of Weights and Measures
Page 142: David R. Frazier Photolibrary
Page 144: Don and Pat Valenti
Page 145(t): Courtesy Ford Motor Company
Page 145(b): Michael A. Candee
Page 150: Roger Ressmeyer
Page 151(t): Nancy Sefton
Page 153: Vic DeLucia/NYT Pictures
Page 157(l): Greg Pease
Page 159: Cy Furlan
Page 164: American Museum of Science and Energy, Oak Ridge, Tennessee
Page 181: Dan Ford Connolly/Picture Group
Page 186: Hans Pfletschinger/Peter Arnold, Inc.
Page 188: Runk/Schoenberger/Grant Heilman Photography
Page 193(r): Coco McCoy/Rainbow

Using Metric

Metric Measures   Customary Measures

LENGTH

10 millimeters (mm) = 1 centimeter (cm)
100 centimeters   = 1 meter (m)
1000 meters   = 1 kilometer (km)

12 inches (in.) = 1 foot (ft.)
3 feet   = 1 yard (yd.)
5280 feet   = 1 mile (mi.)

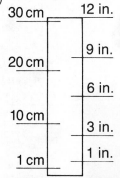

MASS (WEIGHT)

1000 milligrams (mg) = 1 gram (g)
1000 grams   = 1 kilogram (kg)
1000 kilograms   = 1 metric ton (t)

16 ounces (oz.) = 1 pound (lb.)
2000 pounds   = 1 ton (t.)

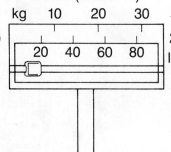

VOLUME

1000 milliliters (mL) = 1 liter (l)
1000 liters   = 1 kiloliter (kl)

8 fluid ounces (fl. oz.) = 1 cup (c.)
2 cups   = 1 pint (pt.)
2 pints   = 1 quart (qt.)
4 quarts   = 1 gallon (gal.)

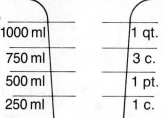

TEMPERATURE

CELSIUS   FAHRENHEIT

Water boils 100° — 212° Water boils

Body temperature 37° — 98.6° Body temperature

Water freezes 0° — 32° Water freezes